MAURICE DAVIN
(1842 - 1927)

First President of the GAA

Séamus Ó Riain

GEOGRAPHY PUBLICATIONS

Published in Ireland by
Geography Publications,
Templeogue, Dublin 6W

ISBN 0 906602 25 4

Cover design by Christy Nolan
Typesetting by Phototype-Set Ltd., Dublin
Printed by Colour Books, Dublin

Maurice Davin (*The Irish Athletic Record*, Dublin, 1906, p. 4, courtesy of Dr Noel K.

Contents

Acknowledgements

During many years while preparing this biography I have received great assistance from a number of people who deserve my grateful thanks and acknowledgments. My greatest debt is due to Pat Walsh, of Deerpark, Carrick-on-Suir, grandson of Pat Davin and grandnephew of Maurice Davin. He and his wife, Sheila, have extended to me the hospitality of their ancestral home on my numerous visits there, and they have made available to me the private papers of Maurice Davin, including his note-books, photographs and a large collection of newspaper cuttings put together over his long life. Pat has also been generous with his own clear recollections of traditions handed down in the family from previous generations and he has introduced me to some old 'residenters' and to people who had spent long years in the employment of the Davin family and their reminiscences were valuable in filling in the background in farming, boating, fishing and the hauling trade on the river. Deserving of special mention are Mick and Paddy Callaghan, Jack Torpey, Tucker Parle, Hugh Ryan and Tom Higgins, all of them now deceased except Mick Callaghan.

I am indebted to John M. Davin, great-grandnephew of Maurice Davin for his co-operation in supplying additional family details and valuable assistance in facilitating the publication of this book. I extend a sincere word of thanks to the following who loaned me some rare photographs: John O'Grady, Thurles and Michael Frawley, Emly, for photographs of the American Invasion teams; Mick Hickey, former Waterford All-Ireland hurler, for identifying members of the teams; Liam O'Donoghoe, Thurles, for the photograph of the first Central Council in 1888, and John Hassett, Cashel for giving me access to the volumes of the *Cashel Sentinel* in his possession.

I am also grateful to Sean Quinn of Nenagh who loaned me a bound volume of the *Shamrock* and to Gerard Quirke, Carrick-on-Suir who kindly let me have a copy of the minutes of the Carrick-on-Suir Amateur, Athletic, Cricket and Football club for the years 1879 to 1883.

I owe a particular debt for the encouragement and assistance received over many years from Marcus de Búrca, Liam P. Ó Caithnia, Dom Mark Tierney and Tomas P. O'Neill, historians, whose standard works in related fields of study have been an inspiration to me. Pat Davin's *Recollections of a Veteran Irish Athlete* has proved to be a valuable source of information which I am pleased to acknowledge.

My thanks are due to Alf Mac Lochlainn for his invaluable help in tracing Joseph P. O'Ryan's life in Canada; and to Professor C. B.

Roester, of the University of Regina in Canada for his permission to use material for the Davin family tree. My thanks to Carmel Murphy, calligrapher, Nenagh, for her expert presentation of the tree.

I have a kind word of thanks for the former Taoiseach, Jack Lynch, who first told me about the presentation to W. E. Gladstone.

The staff of the National Library were courteous and helpful in responding to my numerous calls and I am especially obliged to Kevin Brown for his interest and advice. The staffs of the Public Record Office and the State Paper Office, when in Dublin Castle, were always ready to locate manuscript material that I needed, and the newspaper section of the British Library was prompt in answering my requests for copies.

I have a word of thanks for the County Librarian and his staff in the County Library in Thurles and its branches in Roscrea and Carrick-on-Suir. My thanks also to Gerry Slevin, editor of *The Guardian,* Nenagh, who always welcomed me to his office and gave me access to the newspaper files. I feel indebted to the following friends who supplied helpful information: Willie Corbett, Drombane; T. K. O'Dwyer, Turtulla, Thurles; Eddie O'Donnell, Mallow and Nenagh; Seamus Leahy, Clonmel; Donal and Nancy Murphy, Nenagh and Michael O'Meara, Clonmel.

Willie Nolan of Geography Publications has been a tower of strength to me; he spared neither time nor energy in preparing this volume for publication, and I owe him special thanks for the valuable suggestions he made at the editing stage. Thanks to Teresa Nolan for putting the typescript on disc.

I wish to acknowledge financial assistance from both the Central Council of the GAA and the Munster Council of the GAA towards the cost of publication.

Finally my wife Mary has been patient and understanding when most of the house has been taken over for notes and papers for a long time and she had refrained from disturbing this 'order in chaos' although her housekeeping instinct would urge her to tidy them away. Our family has helped in many ways and they have earned my formal word of thanks: Orla Uí Riain for typing the original manuscript, Michael Culloty for assisting Monica and the boys, Jack, Séamus and Eugene, with proof-reading and the preparation of the index.

Whatever defects are found within these pages are my responsibility. This book is my tribute to the memory of a man I have learned to appreciate and admire.

Abbreviations

AAA	Amateur Athletic Association (England).
AACFC	Amateur Athletic Cricket and Football Club (Carrick-on-Suir).
AAU	Amateur Athletic Union (America).
CE	*Cork Examiner.*
DAAC	Dublin Amateur Athletic Club.
DHC	Dublin Hurling Club.
EAAA	English Amateur Athletic Association.
IAAA	Irish Amateur Athletic Association.
ICAC	Irish Champion Athletic Club.
INAC	Irish National Athletic Club.
INL	Irish National League.
IRB	Irish Republican Brotherhood.
NA	National Archives.
NAA	National Athletic Association (America).
NACA	National Athletic and Cycling Association.
NLI	National Library of Ireland.
RIC	Royal Irish Constabulary.
SPIL	Society for the Preservation of the Irish Language.
SPO, CBS	State Paper Office, Crime Branch Special.
TV	*Tipperary Vindicator.*
UI	*United Ireland.*

Chapter 1

The Davins of Carrick-on-Suir

'I know of no finer prospect than the valley of the Suir presents as it opens upon one from the heights above Carrick.' Thus wrote H.D. Inglis in *A Journey through Ireland* when he visited the country about 1830. He went on to comment on the broad navigable river laden with commerce and the most fertile land stretching away from its banks. Carrick-on-Suir had a population of 10,000, but a number of its shops and houses had a deserted appearance and some of its inhabitants were living in extreme poverty. The town had suffered a severe recession over a few decades and this resulted in high unemployment.[1]

Forty years earlier Arthur Young had ranked Carrick-on-Suir as one of the greatest manufacturing towns in Ireland, especially skilled in making woollens and rateens which gave employment to three or four hundred people. The surrounding countryside was prosperous, producing an abundance of potatoes for human and animal consumption, milk and butter for the local population as well as for export, and grain for milling and as forage for horses.[2] These contrasting accounts reflect the economic history of the town where periods of relative prosperity were followed by years of hardship and unemployment. Today the river Suir flows wide and tranquilly, with only an odd boat disturbing its waters, where a little over a century ago it was a busy waterway with barges and a variety of river-craft bearing merchandise to and from Clonmel.

In the first quarter of the nineteenth century the only public means of transport from Carrick to Waterford was by the river. Bianconi who lived in Carrick for a short period and carried on his business in a little shop opposite the castle, experienced the difficulties of travelling by boat down to Waterford with his wares; he considered an alternative route by road, and in 1825 he began carrying passengers on his cars from Clonmel to Waterford.[3]

When the Clonmel to Waterford railway line was constructed in the 1850s the trade on the river gradually declined, although it continued, considerably reduced, up to the 1920s. In turn road transport has to a large extent superseded the railway, and now articulated trucks, tankers, lorries, passenger vehicles and farm machinery make an almost continuous flow of traffic on the roads of Carrick.

To the north of the river fertile lands stretch to the foothills of Sliabh na mBan. Today, as in the past, the farms here engage in dairying, raising dry stock and producing corn crops and grass. But there is a major difference in the way the farms are held. The occupiers now own their holdings, but in the last century they were tenants on large estates, paying rents to landlords such as the Marquess of Ormond.

On one of those farms, Deerpark, approximately a mile west of Carrick-on-Suir, Maurice Davin was born, on 29 June 1842, the eldest of five surviving children of John Davin and his wife Bridget Walsh. He was baptised on 3 July, with William Maher and Frances Keating as sponsors.[4] The Davins had lived in Carrick for many generations, but their remote origin was in County Fermanagh where their ancestors were chieftains in ancient times.

The name O Devine is chiefly found in county Tyrone and county Fermanagh and up to the fifteenth century the chiefs of the sept were lords of Tír Chinnéidigh (Kennedy) in Fermanagh. According to John O'Donovan, the Irish form is O Daimhin and the Tipperary Davins are probably a branch of the O Devines, an offshoot of the Maguires. The Four Masters record one O Devine as ecclesiastical successor (comharba) in Derry in 1066 and a number of others of the name as chiefs of Tír Chinnéidigh.[5]

The circumstances which led to the migration of some of the Davin sept from Fermanagh to Tipperary are not clear. Family tradition holds that they came south with the army of Aodh Dubh Ó Néill in the mid-seventeenth century and assisted in the defence of Clonmel against Cromwell in May 1650. Two regiments of the army of Eoghan Rua Ó Néill came to the assistance of Aodh Dubh, and some of the men brought their families with them; it is believed that there were Davins among them although there is no clear evidence to support this claim. However, it is known that there were Davins in Clonmel at the end of the seventeenth century, giving credence to the family tradition. In the early eighteenth century when priests faced penalties of transportation, or worse, under the Penal Laws, anyone who helped to conceal them was also liable to be punished by the law. In 1712, amongst a few suspected of giving shelter to priests in Clonmel was a merchant named Michael Davin. He was also one of six prominent Catholics in the town who objected to the mayor levying certain monies on Catholics for the purpose of renewing a lease and rent on land for the military barracks.[6]

Michael Davin displayed strength of character and the courage of his convictions in taking a stand against the injustice of the law as administered then, when it would have been more prudent for him to steer a safe course on the side of the law. Pride of ancestry and high moral principles were distinguishing features of the Davins of Carrick.

The indications are that the Davins engaged in trade and commerce and that some of them moved east along the south bank of the river to the Churchtown and Carrickbeg areas. The graveyard in Churchtown, a few miles west of Carrickbeg, is the burial place of the Davins. A religious establishment was founded there in the sixth century by St Aidan and a number of recumbent headstones have interesting inscriptions, some dating from the sixteenth century. The inscription on one of the stones reads:

> Here lieth the body of Mary Pierce alias Daven who departed this life Feb. the 2nd 1779 aged 52 years. Also her husband Morace Daven who departed this life Oct 6th 1782 aged 69 years.[7]

This Morace Daven (Maurice Davin) carried on a business as corn merchant in Carrickbeg and was probably the first of the Davins to settle there. He was born in 1713 and it could be reasonably inferred that he was a near relative, if not a son, of Michael Daven who was a merchant in Clonmel in 1712.

Maurice married Mary Pierce, daughter of Parson Pierce of Churchtown, and it is from this family that the Davins of Deerpark trace their descent.[8] Their son Denis, born in 1751, and a younger son Maurice, continued their father's business and extended it to include the transportation of merchandise on the river. Their operations flourished and like many enterprising traders they looked for an opportunity to establish themselves on the land. Denis acquired the lease of a holding on the Ormond Estate in Deerpark on the north bank of the river and he was the first of the Davins to settle there.

Denis's eldest son John died in 1802, aged twenty-three, and when Denis died in 1826 at the age of seventy-five the property passed to another son Maurice, who had married Bridget O'Brien in 1811. Their son John, born in 1814, married Bridget Walsh, the daughter of Tom Walsh, a prominent building contractor in the town. Amongst the buildings which he constructed were the Friary in Carrickbeg, completed in 1822, the Union House (Workhouse), and a portion of the quay near the old bridge. He was given the contract to erect the military barracks in Fermoy, indicating his status as a builder. Bridget inherited her father's business acumen which she in turn passed on to her own family.[9]

When the first child of John and Bridget was born in their comfortable home in Deerpark there could be little discussion regarding what the new arrival would be called since generations of Davin boys had been named Maurice. The other surviving children of the couple were Denis, born in September 1846, Tom born in June 1851, Pat born in June 1857 and Bridget born in 1859.

Farming in Deerpark
The Davins proved to be excellent farmers, concentrating on intensive cultivation of the land. Pierce Davin, probably an uncle of John, and named after his grandmother Mary Pierce, held eighteen statute acres in Deerpark in 1834, where he cultivated seven and a quarter acres with potatoes, three and a half acres with wheat, six and a half acres with oats and the remainder (threequarters of an acre) devoted to an orchard.[10] John Davin's business was increased as extra acres were added to the holding and a system of mixed farming was pursued, based on dairying, along with grain and potato growing. The traditional haulage business on the river was extended and all this activity called for constant and efficient management. Although the Davins did not have to endure the worst effects of landlordism, there was a stiff rent of £82.13s.6d due annually to the Marquess of Ormond and a poor rate on top of that. Contemporary evidence[11] from the *Devon Commission Report* makes it clear that the Marquess was considered to be a good landlord who took a sympathetic interest in the welfare of his tenants. While he was reluctant to grant leases and allowed possession only from year to year for the most part, yet, if a tenant built a house or made improvements to one, the landlord allowed him slates and timber for the work and an allowance was also made if he drained the land. Most of the holdings ranged from five or six to twenty acres, and if properly worked and fertilised with farmyard manure and lime it would yield ten barrels of wheat to an acre and eighty to one hundred barrels of potatoes. When Ormond purchased part of the estate of William Ponsonby of Kilcooley Abbey, the tenants on that estate rejoiced that they had a new landlord, giving testimony to the high regard they had for Ormond.

The effective running of the farm from day to day was ensured by the dedication of a small staff of workers who were looked upon as part of the family. Jack Quann, the herd, was one of the old-style 'cow doctors' who saw to the milking, kept a sharp eye on all the stock during the day and supplied the necessary remedies for the common ailments that affect cattle. When old age forced him to retire, he was succeeded by Bill Rockett who was an equally skilled herd and a knowledgeable herb man who would not disclose the secrets of his bovine cures. He gathered the herbs he needed, mixed them with some other ingredients and administered the magic bottle to the sick animal which usually made a rapid recovery. Mick Thompson began working on the farm as a youth in 1830 and later on progressed to being a hauler, driving a team of horses which towed the barges to Clonmel. He was a faithful servant to the family and devoted most of his life to them until he died in 1889.[12]

At harvest time a dozen or so seasonal workers came every year from the foothills of the Comeragh Mountains to reap the corn crops. It was slow laborious work with sickles, but they were expert reapers and when they had finished on the Davin farm they moved on to the neighbours, so that they had many weeks' work before returning home. When the scythe took over, the work of ten people with sickles could be done by one man and the labour was not so toilsome. These reapers were all native Irish-speakers and some of them spoke no English. They had comfortable sleeping quarters in the big loft over the stables and when the day's labour was over the young Davins liked to join them in the loft, listening to their conversations, story-telling and singing and picking up the Irish language. Some of the reapers' women-folk came with them to glean and bind the corn and prepare the meals, and in the evening they sat knitting and spinning.

When the time for potato harvesting arrived, groups of pickers and diggers came from Sean-Phobal in Waterford, knowing that they were sure of some work from the farmers for a few months at a fixed rate of pay. This was their traditional labour and they returned year after year to the same places. They were experts in the use of the flail and when the potato digging was over they spent their days threshing the corn in the barn. They too were native Irish-speakers.[13]

River traders

The other arm of the Davin economy was the river trade which was of long standing, having been initiated by Denis senior in the previous century. Succeeding generations maintained and developed the enterprise. In the early years small craft called noddies were hauled along the southern or Waterford bank of the river by teams of men working in relays bearing merchandise from Carrick to Clonmel. The first team pulled the noddy as far as Ballydine, the second took it forward to Kilsheelan and the third completed the journey to Clonmel.[14] A towing path was constructed on the northern bank which made it possible for teams of horses to do the hauling. Goods were conveyed from Waterford in 'lighters', boats capable of carrying up to sixty tons. The usual cargo was coal, iron, timber and feeding stuffs. Sweeps of oars propelled the lighter with the tide to Carrick where the cargo was transferred to smaller craft called 'yawls'. These boats were constructed by Kehoes of Carrickbeg who had earned a high reputation as boat builders. They used Oregon pine which was robust and durable enough to withstand the pressures of the strong river currents and the heavy merchandise they had to carry.

Four and sometimes six horses formed a team to pull the yawl. At least two teams were needed and took alternate trips so that each team got a rest period. Big bony horses were chosen and specially schooled for the work. The strongest and most reliable animal was given the lead position and the other horses were positioned in line behind him. They were hitched with strong ropes to a forked post of oak set in the deck of the yawl. While all the horses had halters, only the leading one had a bit in its mouth. A fold of hay was fixed to the halter on the river side to act as a blinker so that the horse would not shy from the water. Two men took charge of the yawl and four others attended to the horses, guiding them along the tow path as they hauled the boat against the current. Haul marks were cut in places along the way and if the water rose above this height, as it would whenever the river was in flood after heavy rain, the horses had to be stopped because they could not contend with such a force of water. The skipper worked the tiller which had a yard arm attached to it to provide greater leverage in guiding the yawl.

Work started at six in the morning when the cargo was transferred from the lighter to the yawl, which could hold from twenty to thirty tons. The hauling commenced at nine o'clock and it took five and a half hours to make the twelve miles to Clonmel. The horses were stabled and fed and the cargo unloaded on to the dock. The yawl was poled (propelled) back with the current (i.e. without the use of horses), taking two and a half hours to reach Carrick in the evening before seven, with a cargo of pigs, dairy produce, poultry and grain. When the horses were rested they were trotted back by road to Carrick. It was a long day and strenuous work for men and beasts. The horses were treated well, fed on gruel, oats and yellow meal (i.e. maize) and stabled comfortably. The haulers were specialists who were devoted to their work and to the Davin family, to whom they gave a life-time of service. They were emotionally attached to the river and the life thereon. The depth of this feeling is illustrated in the last wish of a hauler: 'Bury me in Churchtown where I can hear the creak of the yawlman's tiller and the crack of the hauler's whip.' Churchtown cemetery, situated beside the river on the Waterford side, is the family burial ground of the Davins. The arrival of steam tugs on the river and the increase in the transport of goods by rail brought a decline in the hauling trade which the Davins abandoned in the early years of this century.

Family tradition

The influence of family traditions played an important role in forming the character and outlook of the youthful Maurice. The Davins were extremely proud of their reputation as strong, athletic men and the extraordinary feats of their ancestors were handed down as examples of manly achievements to be admired and emulated. No less than six of Maurice Davin's ancestors were remarkable in their day for their strength and agility, foremost among them being his great grandfather Denis and his son Maurice. Both were men of great strength and stature and in their day were invincible at anything demanding strength of arm and fleetness of foot.[15] Denis earned a high reputation as a pugilist, mainly on account of his victory over a black boxer in Waterford. Responding to a challenge, he swam the twelve miles of the Suir from Clonmel to Carrick and claimed the wager.

Denis's brother Tom emigrated to Newfoundland when a young man, as a consequence, it is said, of having broken an opponent's jaw in a boxing bout. He gained popularity among the numerous Irish in the new country as a champion of the ring and they raised a memorial to him in St. Johns to celebrate his exploits.

Denis's son John was noted as a skilful hurler. The supreme test of a hurler in those days was to be able to strike a *sliotar* into the air, and to connect with it as it dropped, striking it up again, and to continue doing this several times while holding one's position in a seven-foot circle. The *sliotar* was larger and heavier than the one used today but the width of the hurley *bas* at that time was scarcely three inches. John died aged twenty-three.

John's brother Billy was an exceptional jumper with a powerful spring. It was said that he could leap over two horses standing side by side. His more serious activities brought about his death at the hands of the notorious Hessians in 1798.[16]

Although the sporting traditions of the family had a strong influence in forming Maurice Davin's character, the political events of Ninety-Eight had a lasting effect in shaping his national outlook. The afore-mentioned Jack Quann, one of the oldest employees on the Deerpark farm, was an eye witness to some of the atrocities perpetrated on the populace in the stirring days of 1798 and these he recounted in detail to Maurice and his brothers. Likewise Billy Cahill had tales to tell of public executions which he witnessed when he was a young man.[17]

There is no direct evidence of the numerical strength of the United Irishmen in Carrick, but information was passed to the sheriff about their activities and the extent to which they had infiltrated the town's military garrison. This led to a reign of terror by Judkin Fitzgerald with his force of Hessians and the North Cork Militia who took over the town, flogging and killing indiscriminately. Three men Lawlor, Healy and Brien were accused of raiding for arms, and publicly hanged on the bridge.[18] It is recorded that one of the Davins from Carrickbeg and another boatman named Reilly, suspected of being members of the United Irishmen, were publicly executed on the Fair Green. Could Davin in this case have been John's brother Billy who was a noted jumper?[19]

During the 1798 Rising in Wexford, regiment after regiment of government forces passed through Carrick on their way to put down the insurgents and going the same way were groups of young men from the town area to assist in the Rising.[20] Those assembling at Sliabh na mBan found themselves leaderless due probably to the wholesale arrests in the spring and early summer of 1798. Their sad fate is recorded in the popular lament 'Sliabh na mBan':

> Níor tháinig ár Major i dtúis an lae chughainn
> 'S ní rabhmar fein ann i gcóir ná i gceart![21]

Taken by surprise, without a leader and ill-prepared, they were in no shape to withstand a superior force. The events of that time left bitter memories which were passed on to a younger generation.

At the time of Maurice Davin's birth (1842), the Young Ireland movement was gathering strength and *The Nation* newspaper was being avidly read and raised hopes for a new dawn in Ireland's fortunes. When the leaders decided to resort to arms, the triangle formed by Callan, Killenaule and Carrick-on-Suir was the centre of activity.[22] Several clubs were formed in the district headed by influential people in the town of Carrick and the surrounding countryside. As many as 3,000 were ready to take the field, but they were poorly armed with only 300 guns. The remainder had to depend on pikes and improvised weapons.

John O'Mahony of Ballydine assured Smith O'Brien and John Dillon that the country between Carrick and Clonmel was ready to strike the first blow. Thomas Francis Meagher was given a tumultuous reception when he addressed a huge gathering in the town. O'Mahony was in favour of making a stand in Carrick and Dillon was willing to take the chance, but two prominent local leaders, Fr Byrne and Dr O'Ryan, were adament that an attempt to hold the town would be drowned in blood since the poorly armed insurgents would be no match for a fully equipped force. O'Brien agreed, although later on he regretted the decision. No one was more disappointed than O'Mahony who believed that if the town had been seized at least three counties would have risen within forty-eight hours. Carrick had failed to take the initiative and the insurgents fell back on the villages of Mullinahone and Ballingarry.[23]

At this time Maurice Davin was six years old and while he would have witnessed some of the commotion and excitement, his notions of what was afoot would be very limited. But in the following years when the accounts of the events of Forty-Eight were debated and sifted in the homes of Carrick, he arrived at a clear perception of where he stood in relation to the important issues at the core of the Young Ireland movement. Growing up during the famine years of the late forties, Maurice would have witnessed the terrible poverty and misery which the workers of the town and its neighbourhood had to endure. Their experiences left a lasting impression on him and his feeling for the poor can be traced back to what he heard of the famine years. On 6 April 1846 a riot took place in Carrick-on-Suir. A mob marched through the town, demanding work. Troops were called out. The rioters, however, quietened down on being given some temporary employment to enable them to buy food.[24] Some relief works were put into effect, walls were built, swamp lands at the Green were reclaimed, but they were not sufficient to meet the urgent needs of the hungry people. They thronged in their hundreds to the Workhouse for food. The Society of Friends doled out free soup in a kitchen in Oven Lane. Many died from hunger and fever. Many more emigrated; the population of the town dropped from 8,369 in 1841 to 5,059 in 1851. Tenant farmers such as the Davins were to some extent cushioned against the extreme famine conditions. Like everyone else their potato crop was destroyed by blight, yet they had corn and dairy products as well as being in the way of getting fish from the river, so the family and their employees were not at risk. However, they were not free from the depressing effects of the famine years on agriculture and trade and it took some years for them to recover.

Maurice Davin was growing up a strong and healthy boy, interested in all the activity around him and becoming familiar with local customs and manners. During this period of informal education he was developing a deep attachment to the soil and the life on the farm and becoming familiar with the ways of animals and crops. He also spent a lot of time on the river enjoying the mysteries of the water and the variety of craft on it. Land and river were to become two abiding interests throughout Davin's life.

Education
Information about Maurice Davin's early formal schooling is vague but it is possible that he received private tuition or that he attended one of the 'pay schools' to get a foundation in the three Rs before moving on to further study. The people of Carrick were keenly aware of the value of education for their children and according to a report in 1827 there

were fourteen 'pay schools' operating in the town. The classes as a rule were held in the homes of the teachers which might be a miserable garret, a cabin, a kitchen or more often a good room in a dwelling house. The numbers attending the schools varied from fifteen to fifty pupils and the 'pay' ranged from two shillings and two pence per quarter, to twenty-two and ninepence, depending on the reputation of the teacher and the quality of the accommodation he provided. Michael Wallace, for example, who held classes in a room in his dwelling house in New Lane, charged the highest fees to his forty pupils, while John Duggan charged a lower rate to his fifteen scholars in a miserable garret in Greystone Street.[25] The Christian Brothers had a free school at Mount St Nicholas, the Presentation nuns had another on the Green and the Kildare Place Society operated one in St John's Road.

Wherever Maurice acquired his elementary education he was ready to attend the O'Shea Academy in his early teens to pursue further study. This school in Castle Street was attended by Catholic and Protestant students of both sexes, who wished to follow an academic career and whose parents could afford to pay the fees. It attracted some students from miles away who boarded in the house from Monday to Friday, had their meals prepared there and received comfortable accommodation. The schoolmaster, William O'Shea, was a tall, handsome man, showing a slight limp when he walked. He was neat and well-groomed in appearance and very correct in his manners. He was a conscientious teacher, anxious to promote the education of his students, but he also saw to their moral development and ensured that they attended to their religious duties. He was assisted in the general running of the school by his wife, their daughter Sarah and an old woman, Aunt Peggy. All the family were considered to be kind and gentle in their treatment of the students who received the benefit of a very good example from the staff.[26]

Some reports on the school say that the course of study included classics, mathematics and English literature; but on the other hand a claim was made that the curriculum was rather narrow in its scope. O'Shea was thought to be a strong nationalist with leanings towards the Fenian philosophy. This impression accorded with the general view of schoolmasters at that time. He was a regular subscriber to The Irish People which came under a governmental ban for promoting revolutionary doctrines. One of the students would be sent to collect a copy of the paper from a house at the top of Cook Lane occupied by a well-known Fenian. There was an air of conspiracy about this operation and before the paper would be delivered to the messenger he had to give a secret sign to show that he was bona fide. On one occasion when the military were searching houses in the town for arms or incriminating evidence, the master was seen to be burning some papers. It was important for him to conceal his Fenian sympathies because if they were exposed he would be liable to imprisonment, and certainly his Academy would suffer.

It is not possible to establish how long Maurice spent in O'Shea's school and how far he progressed in his studies, but his life offers abundant proof that he was a well-educated man. According to his brother Pat he was studious and well-read and always anxious to add to his store of knowledge.[27]

While still at school and giving a helping hand at home Maurice Davin had other interests and talents which he developed during his leisure time. He attended Irish dancing classes and proved to be an apt learner. Although of sturdy and muscular build, he was light on his feet and possessed a well-balanced and co-ordinated physique. Clubs and halls for entertainment were rare at that time and cross-roads dancing was frowned on by the police and the clergy, so house dances were very popular. Hardly a Sunday night passed without a party in one of the homes, especially during the winter months. The dancing was held on the stone-floored kitchen or in the barn and all the neighbours were welcome. Maurice was a popular guest and a leading spirit at such events. He was full of gaiety and energy and was an expert dancer whether it was steps or sets that were called for. It is said that he scarcely ever left the floor during the night.[28]

Coupled with dancing talent he had a keen ear for music and it was probably due to his mother's influence that he went for lessons to Mr Daly, a music teacher of high reputation who taught classes in the town. His chosen instrument was the violin and as in all activities that held his interest he aimed for perfection through concentration and regular practice. He became a competent performer of dance music and Irish airs and as he progressed he acquired a Perry violin.[29]

The instrument became a constant companion for Maurice all through his life and he entertained visitors to his home with renderings of Irish airs such as An Chuileann, Cill Cais and Sliabh na mBan. That he was an exceptionally keen student of the violin is indicated by the large volume of music exercises in his library.

When Maurice was eighteen the untimely death of his father in 1859 brought about a profound change in the affairs of the family. For one thing it marked the end of Maurice's formal education. It is not known whether it had been intended that he should proceed to further study to acquire a professional qualification, or that as the eldest son he was destined to remain at home to eventually take charge of the business. There is no doubt about his intellectual ability and his studious approach to learning which would have ensured his success in whatever course he chose to follow if circumstances had been different. What we have of his writings on behalf of the Gaelic Athletic Association offer evidence of his fluency and clarity of expression and his ability to sum up the points at issue in concise and forceful language.

His father's death left his mother to assume charge of the management of the farm and the river trade as well as looking after her young family. Bridget was an infant, Pat was then two, Tom was eight and Denis thirteen. Her main reliance was placed on her eldest son Maurice. At eighteen years of age he was called on to take his father's place and to share the responsibilities of the household in co-operation with his mother.

References

1. Inglis, H.D., *Ireland in 1834: A Journey through Ireland during the Spring, Summer and Autumn of 1834* . . . 2 vols London, 1840.
2. Young, A., *A Tour in Ireland 1776-1779*. London, 1780.
3. O'C. Bianconi, M. and Watson, S.J., *Bianconi, King of the Irish roads*, Dublin, 1962.
4. Carrick-on-Suir Parish register in N.L.I.
5. MacLysaght, E., *Irish Family Names*, Dublin, 1964.
6. Burke, Canon., *History of Clonmel*, Waterford, 1912, pp 138-143.
7. Connolly, E., *Survey of Inscriptions at Churchtown Cemetery* Copy held by Pat Walsh.
8. Koester, C.B., Thesis on Nicholas Flood Davin for University of Regina, Canada. An undated manuscript was taken down by C.B. Koester, from the late Mrs F. Davin, Mallow in the early 1970s when he was preparing a thesis on the life of the Canadian politician, Nicholas Flood Davin. Mr Pat Walsh and Mr John Davin added further details.
9. An interview with Pat Walsh, 1984.
10. Tithe Applotment Books, N.A., Dublin.
11. *Devon Commission Reports,* vol. iii. Evidence (Iffa and Offa), pp 400-416.
12. Davin, P., *Recollections of a Veteran Irish Athlete*, Dublin, 1939, pp 74-75.
13. Ibid., pp 77-79.
14. Information on hauling trade from Paddy and Mick Callaghan, Jack Torpey and Pat Walsh in 1984.
15. Maher, J., *Chief of the Comeraghs*, Mullinahone, 1957, pp 257-258.
16. Healy, J.J., Papers in N.L.I.
17. Davin, P. op. cit., p. 73.
18. Power, P.C., *Carrick-on-Suir and its people*. Anna Livia, 1976, pp 90-91.
19. Healy, J.J., Papers in N.L.I. Diary of a Carrick man. *Waterford and South-East Archaeological Journal*, 1787-1809.
20. Ibid.
21. Mac Dómhnaill, T. and Ó Meadhra, P. *The spirit of Tipperary,* Nenagh, 1938, p. 132.
22. Comerford, R.V., *C.J. Kickham,* Dublin, 1979, p. 21.
23. Duffy, C.G., *Four Years of Irish History 1845-1849: a sequel to "Young Ireland"*, New York, 1882, pp 648-653.

24. Woodham Smith, C., *The Great Hunger*, London, 1962, p. 80.
25. *Commission of Education Second Report, 1826-7*, vol. ii. N.L.I.
26. MacDonald, Rev. W., *Reminiscences of a Maynooth professor*, edited by D. Gwynn, Cape, 1925, pp 19-21.
27. Davin P., op. cit., pp 39-40.
28. Information from Pat Walsh.
29. *National Museum Bulletin*, Part iii, July, 1911.

Chapter 2

Davin, the young, successful athlete

Since no organised sports association existed in the country, the rural community depended on their own ability and inclination to arrange pastimes. In the summer months the Sunday gatherings were held in a field in the locality made available by the goodwill of the owner. Young and old assembled there to enjoy the rural amusements such as Kickham has described in *Knocknagow*. Throwing the sledge or heavy weight, wrestling contests and standing jumps for length and height entertained the crowd and a hurling or football match was a central feature of the day's sport. The tradition of hurling was strong in the Carrick district. A little over forty years before Maurice Davin's birth, Edward Mandeville of Ballydine had published a poem describing a hurling match. The following verse describes the scene as the teams enter the arena:

> The lusty youths advance in equal rows,
> Each parent's breast with blushing transport glows,
> Silk kerchieves bind their close compacted hairs,
> Each strong-nerved hand a polished hurley bears.

The description of the play could apply to the game today:

> The steady back their bossy weapons rear,
> And twirl them nimbly in th' intrenchant air,
> Men above men in quick succession bound,
> Hips justle hips, the clashing hurleys sound.[1]

Some traditional festivals were annual events. Such was the Fair of Glen, held on the opposite banks of the Suir, at Glen in Waterford and at Ballydine on the Tipperary side. Revellers went back and forth across the river in boats to gain full enjoyment out of the day's entertainment. It was an occasion for high spirits with music and dancing and athletic displays by aspiring weight-throwers and jumpers who came to the fair to test their strength and skill against local champions. Although Davin did not take a serious interest in athletics until he was twenty-nine, his competitive impulse urged him to enter the contests and even in his teens he proved that he could hold his own with any of them.

Towards the end of the day the occasion was sometimes marred by faction fighting. The Shanavests and Caravats were particularly active in South Tipperary and County Kilkenny and it was common enough for members of these factions to come to the festival spoiling for a fight. When they had plenty of drink taken it was an easy matter to find a pretext for starting a row. In one of these outbreaks a man was seriously injured. Billy Cahill, one of the haulers at Deerpark got caught up in the affray and although he stoutly proclaimed his innocence he was sentenced to six months imprisonment in Clonmel jail.[2]

In the post-famine years when Maurice was growing up, young people had few opportunities to take part in active sports that would give an outlet for their youthful energies and enthusiasms. Due to public apathy in those traumatic years there was a marked decline in the native games of hurling and football. Carrick acquired a reputation for dog-fighting and bull-baiting.[3] Cock-fighting was also popular in the area[4] and heavy betting accompanied these activities.

The gentry enjoyed hunting and horse racing, pursuits which were practically exclusive to their own class at that time, although their tenants might be allowed to attend as spectators or helpers. Sir Richard Cox hosted the Castletown races, which lasted three or four days, on his demesne a few miles from Carrick in county Kilkenny. Lord Bessborough held an annual 'Barony Meeting' on his land every September. It was in the nature of a harvest thanksgiving when the people exhibited the produce of the land and the gentry presented a pleasing and benevolent aspect of landlordism.[5]

As for the labourer and his wife and the cottier tenant of a few acres, life consisted of unremitting toil from Monday to Saturday. Sunday was the only day for rest and recreation. These people were described by Davin as the bulk of the people, 'the humble and hardworking who seem now to be born to no other inheritance than an everlasting round of labour'.[6]

Boxing

Young men in the town of Carrick had an exceptional interest in boxing even from the time of the bare knuckle prize fighters. Champions of the ring who visited Ireland from abroad were drawn to the town where their exhibitions of the 'noble art' would be supported and appreciated. Amongst a number of pugilists who taught boxing before Davin was born was Bill Neat from Nottingham. He held classes in a store at the quay and as a consequence there was always a number of boxers in the town who had acquired some measure of competence and skill from professionals.

Opportunities to take part in sport of any kind were so limited that Davin was naturally drawn to test his boxing skill in contests with the local lads. He carefully studied the style of J.C. Heenan who gave exhibition bouts in 1864 and he took particular note of the speed and defensive methods of the old champion who had claimed the American title a few years previously.[7] Having established his superiority over all the local exponents, Davin proved too good for a number of British Army men who claimed to be champions of their regiments.

In 1866 when the great Jem Mace retired from the ring he came to Clonmel to give public exhibitions of his skills. Davin went there hoping to have a few rounds with the former welterweight champion who was known as the father of modern scientific boxing; but he was disappointed as the old champion was unwell that day and he was not prepared to fight.[8] He was also aware of Davin's reputation as a hard hitter and the powerful physique of the Carrickman would have daunted many a man who was not fighting fit. Maurice realised that boxing did not offer any further challenge for him. However, his boxing reputation lived on and a claim to have survived a few rounds with him was considered to be an achievement.

The political context

As Davin was approaching his twentieth birthday a new movement was launched in the United States and in Ireland aiming to revitalise the revolutionary ideal to break the connection with England and to gain national freedom. The powerful rhetoric of Kickham's articles in the Irishmen and later in The Irish People appealed to young people of generous spirit and many were attracted to the Irish Republican Brotherhood, or the Fenians as they were generally known. Carrick-on-Suir was considered to be a headquarters of Fenianism and a demonstration was openly held in the town on St Patrick's Day, 1861, featured by rousing speeches and the singing of patriot songs. Further public displays were held on Carraigmoclear and Sliabh na mBan where the people enjoyed the occasion with sports, dancing and music.[9]

Two events which occurred in 1861 were of considerable propaganda value to the Fenian movement. John O'Mahony, whose name bore a magical attraction as the hero of the '48 Rising, arrived home on a short visit to Mrs Jane Mandeville in Ballydine a few miles outside the town of Carrick. The presence of such a legendary figure created a stir amongst the supporters of the republican ideal in the locality and they used the occasion for recruiting purposes. Another Young Ireland veteran of '48, Terence Bellew McManus, died in America and when his remains were brought home the funeral procession in Cork and in

Dublin was used as a demonstration of public support for the IRB.

The spirit of Young Ireland was revived and in the national euphoria generated by these events thousands of young men were attracted to the Fenian movement. But spies were at work passing information to the constabulary. Acting on reports received, thirty-six constables raided a house in Lough Street in Carrick occupied by a newsagent and stationer named Meagher. Inflammatory documents, copies of *The Irish People* and twenty-five pike heads were discovered. Meagher and his sons were arrested and charged with 'Fenianism'. Others from Carrick lodged in Clonmel jail on a similar charge were William Ryan, John Kent, David Slattery, John Vale, J. Doherty and Con O'Leary.[10]

The 'secret' nature of the IRB makes it difficult to identify its members and it is not clear if Davin, a young man of patriotic outlook, had been influenced to support the movement. No hint of his involvement can be found in any of his papers, but in his obituary notice in the *Clonmel Nationalist* it is stated that 'while still a young man he joined the Fenian movement and took an active part in the work of that organisation.'[11] The writer of the obituary was Seán Ó Floinn who was then the Carrick correspondent of the Nationalist. He would have a reliable source for his claim since he was a close friend of the O'Hickey family whose father was Head Centre of the IRB in Carrickbeg. Ó Floinn was also friendly with Pat Davin and he would scarcely have made the claim if he had any doubt about it.[12] Furthermore, no disclaimer was entered in subsequent issues of the Nationalist. Pat Davin would surely have questioned the statement if he had doubts about it, being a man of strong views who from his young days regarded his eldest brother as his hero. The social and cultural expressions of the movement when sports, dancing and music were enjoyed at the gatherings at Carrick-on-Suir, Carraigmoclear and Sliabh na mBan would certainly have appeal for Davin. Whatever about this circumstantial evidence concerning his early involvement, evidence of his later life shows him as a firm cultural nationalist whose opposition to the Fenian element in the GAA was so strong that he 'would have nothing to do with business conducted by these people'.[13]

Rowing

At the time when Davin was becoming disillusioned with boxing, circumstances combined to change the direction of his athletic pursuits and brought him back to what was his first love, the river and its boats. Boat racing on the river was traditional in Carrick and in the early nineteenth century the regatta was a popular event enjoying the sponsorship of the local gentry.[14] But it was almost twenty years since the last successful regatta was held in July 1848, a casualty of the general depression following the great famine.

The upward trend in the economy in the 1860s brought benefits to farmers in improved prices for their produce and as a consequence more business for traders in the town. In this more prosperous climate the Waterford regatta was revived with some success in 1863 and in the following years it became firmly established with a wider range of events and a greater number of entries, including some from Carrick.[15] The example given by Waterford prompted a move in Carrick to revive its traditional regatta in 1865. Some enthusiasts, impatient at the delay, organised informal challenge races usually for £1 a side and in the class for four-oared gigs, Davin's *Robin* proved to be the best. *Robin* was again a winner in the Waterford regatta in 1866. Davin, now fully committed to rowing, decided to build his own boat for four oarsmen. Taking extreme care with the design and the selection of timber, he used rivets for the joinings, and his nine-year old brother Pat assisted him. When completed, the family and workforce had a hand in carrying the boat down to the river and amid great excitement it was launched, Mrs Davin naming it *Cruiskeen Lawn*. However, its performance on the water was not up to expectations; it was not responding as it should to the efforts of the crew. To correct what appeared to be an imbalance, the boat was returned to the shed and Davin fitted an extra four feet to the bow. The change brought a remarkable improvement in its performance.[16] At the Waterford regatta in August 1871 the silver cup event was won by *Cruiskeen*, stroked by Davin, with T. Quinlan, Tom Davin, J. Walsh as crew and Pat Davin as the cox. On the same day Davin's *Gypsy* won the race for two-oared wherries. *Cruiskeen* scored a long list of successes at subsequent regattas at Clonmel, Waterford and Carrick and even when Davin retired from active rowing his boat continued to lead the way with a new crew including Jack and Mick Carroll, Tom Torpey and Mick Roche, a grand-uncle of Mick Roche of Tipperary hurling fame.

Carrick regatta was firmly established by August 1868 and Davin stroked the *Robin* to win the main event with J.R. O'Donnell, J. Quinlan, W. Foley and J. Foley as cox.[17] Two years later he scored a remarkable treble at the home regatta, winning the canoe race in *Banshee,* the wherry race of one and a half miles in *Gypsy* and the gig event in *Robin;* the three Foleys rowed with him and P. Foran was cox.[18]

Some of Maurice Davin's Rowing successes.
August 2nd 1868.
Carrick-on Suir Regatta: Canoe Race, M. Davin second in *Water Lily.* Gig race for four oars: Robin won: M.Davin, stroke, J.R. O'Donnell, Jas. Quinlan, E. Foley and P. Davin, cox.

July 29th 1870.
Waterford Regatta: Canoe race, M. Davin in *Water Lily,* 2nd to E. Clibborn, Clonmel.
August 12th 1870.
Tramore Regatta: M. Davin in *Banshee* in canoe race.
August 1870.
Carrick-on-Suir Regatta: Canoe race won by M. Davin. M. Davin won two-oared wherry race with *Gypsy* and the four-oared gig race in *Robin.* M. Davin, stroke, with three Foleys and P. Davin, cox.
August 4th 1871.
Waterford Regatta: Wherry race won by M. Davin's *Gypsy*. Gig race won by *Cruiscin:* M. Davin stroke, J. Walsh, Tom Davin, T. Quinlan and P. Davin, cox.
September 1871.
Carrick Regatta: M. Davin's *Gypsy* won the wherry race. *Cruiscin* won the gig race by 3 lengths and M. Davin 2nd. in canoe race in *Mavourneen,* to E. Clibborn.
Notes: Wherry: Light shallow rowing boat for two oars.
Gig: Light rowing boat for racing, four oars.

From his schooldays Davin was interested in physical fitness; he was by nature competitive at work and at play. Whether it was in lifting a sack of corn or playing handball in the alley at William O'Shea's Academy, he wished to prove what he was capable of achieving, more for his own satisfaction than in self-glorification before his peers. His boxing experiences taught him the value of regular exercises in toning up and developing greater power in his muscles through using dumb-bells and clubs. He practised weight-lifting and in fact he fitted out what could be called a miniature gymnasium for use by himself and his brothers.

He neither smoked nor drank and his advice to young people was 'avoid the fags, anyone who uses them will never be any good'. He studied whatever fitness periodicals and manuals he could acquire and he worked out a strict diet for himself to be adhered to rigidly. In the morning he drank water from the Deerpark well, which was clear and free from pollution. This was followed by a bowl of porridge, a little bread and a small amount of beef or mutton cooked well on a gridiron. For the mid-day meal he had boiled mutton or roast beef with plenty of vegetables, but he used potatoes sparingly. His supper consisted of porridge, dry toast and milk. He avoided salty bacon and all fatty foods including butter.[19]

Athletics
It could be said that Davin's athletic career started by chance and that

he had no idea of where it was going to lead him. His first appearance at an athletic meeting as a competitor was at a sports in Gurteen in County Waterford in 1869.[20] He took part in the high jump and with a leap of 5 ft 4 ins tied for first place; he gained second place in the 100 yards sprint. This was the type of sports meeting common at the time in rural parishes. It was organised by local people, there was no system of handicapping and those competing had no organised training, so each contest was a test of natural talent. Very few competitors togged out in athletic attire but simply took off their coats and sometimes their boots and entered the contest mainly for the fun of it.

His experience at Gurteen encouraged Davin to go a step higher. A few weeks later he went to Tramore sports and won the high jump and came second in slinging the 56 pound weight. At this stage he began to give more attention to improving his technique in throwing the weights and jumping, although his interest in rowing remained at a high level. He was so emotionally attached to the river and the boats he had built himself that it would not be easy to break away. He had a number of successes in rowing during the regatta season in 1870 and 1871[21] and at the athletic sports in Cahir he was first in the standing hop, step and jump and also in putting the 28 pound weight, and he tied with his brother Tom in the high jump. This was to be a year for a decision, whether to continue rowing or to concentrate his attention on the athletic events in which he excelled.

Perhaps Maurice got some encouragement from his brothers Denis and Tom, both of whom had rowed with him and were also very interested in athletics. Tom at nineteen years was apprenticed to a solicitor, Mr Forsythe in Eustace Street in Dublin[22] and he had gained some valuable experience of athletic meetings in the city and the standards of achievement there. On Easter Monday 1870 he competed at Dunleary (Dun Laoghaire, then generally known as Kingstown) sports and won the high and long jumps and came second in the 220 yards hurdle race. When home on holidays he accompanied Maurice to the sports in Cahir where he came first in two hurdle races, first in the long jump at 18 ft 4 ins and he tied with Maurice in the high jump at 5 ft 4 ins.[23] These may appear to us to be moderate figures, but considering that there was no specialising in any one event, very limited training and having to jump from a grass take-off, the performances were full of promise. Denis at twenty-four was in the grain business in the town operating a corn store on the Quay and living on a farm close to the home place which Mrs Davin had bought some years previously.

Finally, in 1871 Maurice made the emotional decision to abandon active participation in rowing and to devote his spare time to weight-throwing. He was now twenty-nine years old. The muscular strength which he had developed was attuned mainly to the skill of rowing. To adapt to shot-putting, hammer-throwing and slinging the weights he had to change to a new regime of exercises. He designed his own hammer and weights with which he hoped to challenge the best in the country. One of the 16 pound weights for shot-putting was a cannon ball found at Clonmel and was reputed to have been used by Cromwell's forces at the siege in 1650. This ball had an emotional significance for the Davins because of the tradition that one of their ancestors had taken part in the defence of the town with Aodh Dubh Ó Neill's army and so the weight was lovingly preserved at Deerpark.

Davin was unhappy that traditional field events were not always included at athletic meetings and he had a special desire to promote hammer-throwing, which was frowned upon by those in charge of athletics in Dublin. The official attitude was expressed by a writer in the Irish Sportsman: 'The hammer has always seemed to us, in an athletic point of view at least, to be a very barbarous substitute for the elegant quoit or discus.' Subsequent experience has belied this prejudiced view; the hammer became popular as one of the most spectacular events on the athletic programme and Irishmen became its most successful exponents at the Olympic Games for many years.[24]

When in 1871 Davin took his first major step into the arena of the top-ranking athletes of the day at the Queen's College (now University College) sports in Cork, he chose the hammer event for his challenge and in taking first place he defeated one of the stalwarts of Munster, D.M. Kennedy of Queen's College. He failed by a narrow margin to match Kennedy in slinging the 56 pound weight.[25] He did not compete again until the Carrick-on-Suir sports the next year. Before the home supporters he was in fine form and won five events, the standing long jump and hop step and jump, throwing the 56 pound and putting the 17 pound and the hammer with a splendid throw of 93 feet.[26] Buoyed up by his performances at Cork and Carrick, Davin felt that he was now ready to challenge those in charge of athletics in Dublin. He entered for the Civil Service Club sports in June 1872 as a member of Carrick-on-Suir rowing club.[27]

The Civil Service Club which had been founded in 1867, confined its membership to the 'gentlemen class', including university people, the learned professions, officers of the army and navy, government officers, gentlemen of independent means and 'others who may mingle in society with them'.[28] There was no place for artisans, labourers or the lower ranks of the army or police forces. Maurice's entry was accepted presumably because he was considered to be a man of independent means. Moreover, his brother Tom, a professional man articled to a solicitor, was already competing at meetings in Dublin and Belfast.

Dublin was a new and exciting experience for Maurice. Going to local sports in a horse-drawn sidecar, accompanied by friends and neighbours he was amongst his own people, well-known and respected by the entire community.

His opponents in this new arena differed from him in background and experience, but shared his interest in athletics and his determination to excel. At the end of the day Maurice Davin had created a sensation among the elite athletes winning the acclaim of all present by his magnificent hammer throw of 93 ft 10 ins, more than 3 feet beyond the mark of M.M. Stritch, the Dublin hero. In slinging the 56 pound weight 26 ft 8 ins, he failed by a few inches to match Stritch's throw, but he had established his place in the top rank of weight throwers in the country. To complete a great day for the Carrick men, Tom Davin won three events, the high and long jumps and the 600 yards hurdle race.[29]

Athletic interest in 1873 was mainly focussed on the inaugural event of the Irish Championship Athletic Club (ICAC) held in College Park in July. Davin had taken a rest from active athletics that year, having to devote his full attention to family business and domestic affairs. The river trade needed to be re-organised to meet the growing dual challenge of rail transport and the introduction of steam-powered vessels. His youngest brother Pat was not making satisfactory progress in his studies, mainly due to poor attendance at O'Shea's Academy and serious consideration had to be given to the possibility of sending him to a boarding school. Pat was a lover of nature and spent much of his time with his pet birds or roaming the fields with his dogs and fishing down by the river. It came as a shock to him when he was informed that Maurice had made arrangements for him to continue his studies as a resident in Mount Melleray Seminary, and in spite of his protestations and promises of improved attendance at school and greater application to his books, he was packed off to Melleray where he was to spend two profitable years.[30]

Championship success

The high standard of Davin's performances in 1872 warranted an invitation to the first championships, although he had not competed in any meeting in 1873. Even the important sports at nearby Clonmel did not entice him, notwithstanding his favourite event, the hammer, being included on the programme. Unprepared, Davin made the train journey to the capital and joined his brother Tom in the arena. In view of his lack of training he performed creditably in three events, but failed to win a title. Stritch won the hammer and the 56 pound weight and Wadsworth of Queen's University, Belfast, won the 16 pound shot.

There was consolation, however, before the end of the day as Tom won the high jump with a leap of 5 ft 10½ ins, the best jump on record in Ireland up to then, and he was placed second in the long jump at 21 ft 1 in.[31]

Disappointment at his failure to win a national title made Davin determined to make amends in 1874 and he trained diligently for the Civil Service Club sports in June when he hoped to challenge the supremacy of Wadsworth and Stritch, the established favourites. It was his first appearance at the Landsdowne Road venue and he sensationally made a clean sweep of the weight events, winning the hammer with a one-handed throw of 108 ft 7½ ins, the 16 pound shot at 40 ft 5 ins, the 56 pound weight at 28 ft 7½ ins and the 42 pound weight at 20 ft 7 ins.[32]

The expected meeting of the giant weight throwers in the ICAC Championships a few weeks later was eagerly anticipated and there was much speculation about the possible outcome, but to the dis-appointment of the spectators Davin was unable to participate. His business commitments did not permit him to be absent from home for a second weekend within three weeks and so he had to forego the chance of winning a championship title for another year. Tom Davin was invited by the ICAC to represent the club in the high jump at the English championship meeting in March 1874. He cleared 5 ft 10 ins, coming second to Brooks of Oxford University who leaped a record 5 ft 11 ins.

Maurice returned to Landsdowne Road for the championships in 1875, having undergone a rigorous training schedule in his determi-nation to give of his best on this occasion. At thirty-three years of age he was at the height of his power as an athlete, scoring clear victories in the hammer at 113 ft 6 ins and the 16 pound shot at 40 ft 10 ins. These national titles were the first of many he was to gain over a five-year period during which he firmly established his reputation as the most popular and highly respected athlete in the country. His genial and friendly attitude to his opponents, his absolute honesty which never allowed him to take an unfair advantage of a rival and his superb performances achieved without a hint of boastfulness, won the admiration of opponents and spectators alike.[33] His pleasure in winning was derived more from satisfaction at having established the ability of a country athlete, a working farmer, a Carrick man, to attain pre-eminence in sport, rather than from any feelings of personal pride.

A newcomer to the Dublin athletic scene in 1875 was Michael Cusack, from Carron, County Clare, who had taken up a teaching post in Blackrock College at the end of the previous year. Cusack entered for the Dublin Athletic Club sports in May as a member of the French

College Cricket Club and his performances in the 16 pound and 42 pound weight events were welcomed by the Irish Sportsman. Two months later he competed at the Civil Service Club Meeting, this time representing the Dublin Amateur Athletic Club and he was placed second to M.M. Stritch in the 42 pound weight. Later that year he took part in the O'Connell Centenary Meeting in Landsdowne Road. There is no account of Cusack's having any connection with track and field athletics for the three following years. There are reasonable explanations for this. For some month in 1876 he was on the staff of Kilkenny College; in June he married Margaret Woods; later that year he was appointed to a post in Clongowes Wood College. He returned to Dublin in 1877 and in October he launched a new enterprise when he opened his Civil Service Academy, specialising in grinds for the Civil Service and other public examinations. He was aware, no doubt, of Davin's reputation but there is no evidence that the two had ever met at this time.

Popularity of athletics
The seventies were marked by the phenomenal increase in the number of organised athletic meetings held in the Dublin area and throughout the provinces. About the middle of the century exciting moves were afoot in England to codify and organise sports activities such as cricket, football and athletics and the Ascendancy in Dublin, taking a lead from across the Irish Sea, followed the trend. Trinity College, following the example of Oxford and Cambridge, formed an athletic club in 1857 and ten years later the Civil Service followed suit in setting up their own club. These elitist clubs adopted the rules of the English Amateur Athletic Association (EAAA) and their annual sports meetings were fashionable social occasions attended by the leaders of Ascendancy society in Dublin, but their membership was restricted to their own institutions. In the autumn of 1872 a group of enthusiasts founded the Dublin Amateur Athletic Club (DAAC) which offered membership to 'gentlemen' who did not qualify for inclusion in the two existing clubs. The DAAC organised a number of athletic meetings every year, adhering to the rules of the EAAA. It gave an opportunity to athletes who otherwise would have no chance of competing in Dublin.

A new concept was put forward in 1872 which envisaged the annual championship sports where the leading performers at the meetings during the year would contend for the national title in their particular event. The idea, promoted by H.W. Dunlop and Reginald Miller, was given practical effect early in 1873 by the launching of the Irish Championship Athletic Club which offered membership to eligible amateurs on payment of an annual fee of ten shillings, but reserved the right to decide on each applicant by vote.[34] It was an attempt to place athletics on a nationally organised basis, but it was severely limited in its scope since its officership and committee were dominated by a class mostly unionist in outlook who were not disposed to open their ranks to what they considered to be the lower classes. The seed of its ultimate failure lay in this narrow sectoral approach and it had a short and chequered existence. Yet it had considerable achievements; it provided an arena where the best talent in the country could contend for a national title; it spearheaded international contests with England where standards were tested against the best of the English; it acquired its own ground when it took a lease on some acres from the Earl of Pembroke at an annual rent of £70.[35] Having levelled the land, a running track was laid down and a pavilion erected; the ground, later to be known as Landsdowne Road, became the venue for many athletic sports until the club disintegrated at the end of the decade. Complaints were made that the ground was too far out from the city and consequently it failed to attract the public support that was expected.

Landsdowne Road was the scene of Maurice Davin's ten triumphs in the Irish Championships from 1875 to 1879, not counting the occasions when there was no contest because no one was prepared to oppose him. The championships of 1876 attracted the largest entry up until then, probably because interest in athletics was growing and the challenge of the Davins and such as Dr Daly of Borrisokane posed a threat to the dominance of the established favourites. Moreover, it was announced beforehand that performances in the championships would be taken into account when it came to selecting a team to represent Ireland in an international match against England on Whit Monday. Consequently the promoters were expecting an increase in the attendance, but their hopes were not realised because of a counter attraction in the Phoenix Park – a review in honour of the queen's birthday – was the first choice of many Dubliners. Developments had been carried out on the grounds at Landsdowne Road since 1875 aimed at getting better performances from the contestants and securing more efficient crowd control. The track, or path as it was called, had been improved and a strong barricade had been erected to prevent encroachments on to the course.

It was Pat Davin's first appearance at the championships and he and Tom dominated the jumping events; Tom took first place in both the long and high jumps and Pat was a close second in both. Competition in the weight throwing events was especially keen between Maurice and the two giants, Daly and Stritch. Maurice retained the hammer title with a throw of 128 ft 10 ins far ahead of his rivals, but Daly won the shot putt with Davin second and Stritch third.[36]

The three Davins were selected on the Irish team to oppose England in the first international athletics contest between the countries at Landsdowne Road on Whit Monday. Maurice threw the hammer 131 ft 6 ins, his greatest throw to date and far ahead of the best English throw. In the 16 pound shot he beat the English champion, Stone. Tom and Pat tied at 5 ft 7½ ins to win the high jump and Ireland's only other victory fell to J.D. Ogilby in the 100 yards sprint. It was an historic day for the Davins for although Ireland won only four of the fourteen events, three of the victories were gained by the brothers from Carrick-on-Suir.[37]

Tom now retired from serious athletics to devote his time to building up his practice as a solicitor in his home town. Pat at nineteen was embarking on a brilliant athletic career. He was tall, strong and athletically built, much lighter and less muscular than Maurice, yet lithe and sinewy, ideally suited to sprinting and jumping events in which he was to gain international acclaim. He was absent from the championship meeting in 1877 probably due to concentration on his studies. Maurice was there and won three titles, the hammer, the shot and slinging the 56 pound weight.[38]

Maurice went to the return international in London the following year and again won the hammer event with a throw of 126 ft 4 ins and although he heaved the 16 pound shot a distance of 41 ft 6 ins he was three inches short of Stone's best throw. By this time Pat was making his name as the most outstanding all-rounder in the athletic world, winning championship titles in the 100 yards sprint, the hurdles, the long and high jump and the shot-putt. In the ten years from 1873 to 1882, the three Davin brothers won a total of twenty-six Irish championship titles. This is a measure of their dominant position and in each event that they contested they set new record figures with one exception: Pat's 10½ seconds in the 100 yards sprint was equalled by J.D. Ogilby, one of Ireland's greatest sprinters and a specialist in this event.

The 1878 Irish championships attracted entries from Cork, Tipperary, Limerick, Clare and some northern counties, as well as from the capital, leading the press to claim that the contests were representative in the most liberal sense of the term, ignoring the fact that a large section of the population was debarred from taking part. Although many entered, no one came forward to challenge Davin in the 56 pound weight. The official explanation given was that his great reputation was sufficient to frighten off any opposition, but the controlling body could be accused of doing little to promote the traditional events at which the Irish excelled. Maurice retained his titles in the hammer and shot with throws of 123 ft 2 ins and 40 ft 6 ins respectively and Pat demonstrated his versatility by winning the long and high jumps and the 120 yards hurdle race.[39]

In the final years of the 1870s there were ominous signs that athletics in Dublin was in decline; abuses which threatened to destroy the spirit of sportmanship had not been eliminated; betting, fixing handicaps and money prizes were all too common; clubs were falling apart and even the ICAC was struggling under financial difficulties. Davin went to the championships of 1879 and again took the titles in the shot and hammer. Then at thirty-seven years of age he bade farewell to the athletic arena, except for one last challenge which he felt honour-bound to meet some years later.

References

1. Mandeville, E., *The Hurling*, Dublin, 1798.
2. Davin, P., op. cit., p. 83.
3. Kickham, C.J., *Knocknagow*, Dublin, 1953, pp 432-6.
4. Davin, P., op. cit., pp 39-40.
5. Ibid.
6. O'Sullivan, T.F., *The Story of the G.A.A.* Dublin, 1916, p. 7.
7. Fleischen, N. & Andre, S., *A Pictorial History of Boxing,* up-dated and revised by Peter Arnold, London, 1993, pp 41-51.
8. Davin, P., op. cit. p.40.
9. Maher, J., *The Valley near Slievenamon*, Mullinahone, 1995. p.155.
10. *Tipperary Advocate,* 23/12/1865, 17/2/1865, 3/3/1866.
11. *Clonmel Nationalist,* 30/1/1927.
12. Information from Hugh Ryan, 1984.
13. Maurice Davin's letter to Fr Moloney, Toomevara, November 1887.
14. *Tipperary Vindicator,* 2/7/1845.
15. *Irish Sportsman,* 7/9/1864, 11/8/1865.
16. Interview with Pat Walsh.
17. *Waterford News,* 7/8/1868.
18. *Irish Sportsman,* 25/7/1870.
19. Maurice Davin's papers in Deerpark.
20. Davin, P., op. cit., p.40.
21. *Waterford News,* 1/9/1871, and information from Paddy Callaghan.
22. *Directory of the Incorporated Law Society.*
23. *Irish Sportsman,* 25/5/1870; Davin, P., op. cit., p.40.
24. Irishmen who won the hammer event in the Olympic Games: John Flanagan, 1900, 1904, 1908; Matt McGrath, 1912; Paddy Ryan, 1920; Pat O'Callaghan, 1928, 1932.
25. Davin, P., op. cit., p.40.
26. *Sport,* 26/11/1887.
27. *Irish Sportsman,* 1/6/1872.
28. Lawrence, J. *Handbook of Cricket in Ireland*, Dublin, 1872.
29. *Sport,* 26/11/1887.
30. Davin, P., op. cit., p. 92.
31. Sport, 26/11/1887.
32. Ibid.

33. Ibid.
34. *Irish Sportsman*, 12/10/1872, 14/2/1872, 18/1/1873.
35. Ibid., 1/11/1873.
36. Ibid., 3/6/1876.
37. Ibid., 6/1/1877.
38. Ibid., 24/5/1877.
39. *Sport*, 26/11/1877; Davin, P., op. cit., p. 42.

Chapter 3

Restoring national consciousness

The parlous state of athletics in Dublin in the late 1870s drew many critical statements from people genuinely interested in the sport and anxious to bring about a reform of its condition. It is ironic that Dublin, which gave the lead in organising meetings in the early years of the decade, was now experiencing a decline in standards of control and witnessing the demise of the clubs that could be acknowledged as the flagships of athletics in Ireland.

On the other hand, athletic sports meetings were proliferating in the provinces, in towns and rural areas. In seeking causes for this phenomenon it becomes clear that the growth of cricket clubs in the 1860s had a marked influence on the promotion and popularity of athletics. *The Irish Sportsman* claimed that in 1870 there were at least 150 active cricket clubs in the country and that they were ideally placed to organise athletic sports for the community. The writer admitted that 'cricket is not what one might call indigenous to Ireland and although it has made great advances amongst us it is probably not destined to be our fate. Its large progress of late has been due more to high example and noble patronage than to any large amount of personal conviction.'[1] Another and more cogent reason was the decline of hurling and football in the post-famine years, leaving a vacuum in rural recreation which was filled by the cricket clubs. Contemporary provincial newspapers record the results of cricket matches between townland teams, bearing witness to the popularity of the game even in small communities. A correspondent in the *Nenagh Guardian* claimed that 'the English game of cricket is very much in vogue in Ireland. It has completely displaced the old athletic exercise of hurling so prevalent some years ago. Hurling is almost unknown to the rising generation'. Readers were left in no doubt about who were promoting the game. 'It is recognised by the upper ten thousand and patronised by the scions of royalty ... every town and village, every hamlet and populous nook has either its club or is in connection with some neighbouring one.' The claim was made that it was played by all classes and creeds: 'Men meet in community on the cricket ground and partake of hospitality together ... This genial blending of the different classes on the cricket fields reminds one of the harmony of the Masonic Lodge.'[2]

Although the writer does not attempt to hide his own prejudice in favour of cricket, nevertheless he acknowledges the attractions of hurling as an 'open air and manly exercise requiring much bodily exertion, calling every muscle into action, healthful and exhilarating, stimulating both physical and intellectual powers'. But cricket was the game in vogue and even committed nationalists took to it. Michael Cusack was a member of the French College Cricket Club in 1875 and even as late as 1882 he was extolling the fine qualities of the game in his articles in the Shamrock and encouraging young people to practise it. J.K. Bracken was a playing member of the Templemore Cricket team in the 1870s and Frank R. Moloney was secretary of the Nenagh Cricket Club at the time the GAA was founded. Maurice Davin was chairman of the Carrick-on-Suir Amateur Athlectic, Cricket and Football Club in the early 1880s, although the cricket section of the club fell away for lack of support. Davin's name does not appear in any newspaper reports of Carrick-on-Suir cricket teams.[3]

During the 1870s there was a dramatic increase in the number of cricket club sports meetings and this development was assisted by the work of the Dunbar brothers who gave ample publicity to athletics in the columns of the *Irish Sportsman.* V.J.R. Dunbar travelled extensively to meetings, advising on rules in accordance with the laws of the EAAA and acting as handicapper, referee or judge. Responding to the urgings of the Dunbars in the Irish Sportsman, many athletic meetings were grafted on to the existing cricket clubs, beginning in Leinster and gradually extending to the whole country. The annual athletic sports in places such as Portarlington, Monasterevin, Tullamore, Kilmallock, Macroom and Ballinasloe were colourful events enjoying landlord patronage and the support of local military bands.

Only 'gentlemen' were allowed to compete at those elite meetings and the definition of an 'amateur gentleman' was 'one who has never competed in an open competition or for public money or for admission money, or with professionals for prize money, and who has never at any period of his life taught, pursued or assisted in the pursuit of athletic exercises as a means of livelihood, nor as a mechanic, artisan or labourer.'[4] The general population, including astisans, labourers and their families, were allowed time off to attend as spectators, but there was no place for them in the track and field events unless by a special dispensation a race confined to labourers or policemen was included on the programme.

Rural traditional sports

Apart from the prestige meetings in the towns, another development of equal if not greater importance was gathering force. The rise in the popularity of athletics is reflected in the increase in what can be termed traditional sports meetings in villages and rural areas, especially in Munster and Connacht. For the most part these were independent of Dublin control and were a spontaneous response to the demand for community recreation that was influenced by the track and field achievements of the Davin brothers.

At these meetings, which were usually held on a Sunday, local athletes competed against each other without restrictions of class or creed and the traditional weight throwing and jumping events were prominent features of the programme. Typical of such local sports were those held at Mullinahone in a field given by T.P. Kickham, at Laffan's Mill near Killenaule in Feehan's field, at Drangan in Friend's field and at Grague where the field was provided by Patrick O'Shea.[5] All the arrangements for these meetings were in the hands of a committee of local people who made their own rules and appointed judges and starters from among their own members. Success at the local sports encouraged young athletes to concentrate on developing their natural talents and in time they would come to pose a challenge to the best in Dublin.

A twenty-six year old tenant farmer from Thurles, T.K. Dwyer, caused a sensation in 1878 by winning the mile title at the ICAC events from the cream of the country's milers, including C.H. Ford, the champion for the previous two years. Dwyer had a list of successes at local sports over the previous three years, at Drangan, Mullinahone, Cahir, Kilkenny, Callan and Kilsheelan, as well as winning the mile championship of Tipperary at Dovea.[6] In Mayo, P.W. Nally was performing exceptional feats on track and field at meetings at Castlebar, Swinford, Claremorris, Headford, Hollymount and Foxford. He won races over distances from 100 yards to a mile, and he was equally successful at jumping and weight throwing. He displayed remarkable versatility and stamina and it was normal practice for him to compete in seven or eight events at a meeting and to win most of them, which earned for him the title of 'Champion of the West'.[7]

Tom Malone from Miltown Malbay was an all-round athlete who specialised in sprinting and long jumps. He displayed his class at major sports meetings and in 1879 he won the Irish championship in the 100 yards and the quarter mile. Before emigrating to Australia in 1882, he captured the English title for the long jump.[8] Other athletes from rural clubs who won Irish championship titles were J. Tobin, Nine-Mile-House (hammer), J. Carmody, Comeragh, Waterford (mile flat), while

M. Tobin of Drangan and T. Kennedy of Poulacapple were examples of the new generation of powerful weight throwers whose performances were well up to championship standards.

Athletic power, which had resided with the university colleges and the city clubs, was moving to the rural-based clubs in a trend initiated by Maurice Davin and his brothers. Sensing the need for a single controlling body which would co-ordinate and unify the developments taking place and at the same time ensure the dominance of Dublin in athletics, the Dunbars took the initiative. They issued a circular to the clubs that were springing up all over the country, seeking views on their proposal to establish an Irish National Athletic Committee which would formulate a set of rules and exercise control over meetings. There is no record of the number of replies received, but Maurice Davin wrote welcoming the idea. 'We are very much in want of some governing body for the management of athletics in this country. Sending out rules for perusal, corrections etc., is the proper way to commence. I am afraid I could not attend a meeting, but some of us may be able to go when the time comes.'[9]

P.W. Nally also responded and at length. He remarked that problems existed in regard to handicapping, judging, stewarding and the general arrangements of events and he was willing to attend a meeting to deal with those matters. Michael Cusack did not show any interest because his personal commitments at that time absorbed all his attention and he was not in a position to take an active part in athletics. At least one meeting was held in Dublin to establish the Irish National Athletic Club (INAC), but it is not clear how many people attended. Some discussion took place about devising and promulgating rules for the proper discipline of athletes and clubs.

One of the rules proposed was 'if a gentleman runs at an athletic meeting in Ireland, not under the rules of the INAC, he is disqualified for all races under INAC rules'.[10] Such a ban would be unacceptable to many who might otherwise be in favour of the idea of a national club.

A provisional committee was appointed with representatives from the four provinces. Davin was one of the six chosen for Munster, but no place was found for Nally among the three chosen to represent Connacht. It was intended that this twenty-three man committee would advance the objectives of the club.[11] Davin was disillusioned because of the absence of any commitment to the traditional Irish field events on the part of those promoting the INAC and he attended no meeting. Due to the absence of active leadership and lack of sufficient support, the effort petered out within a few weeks.

Motivated by an obvious threat to their dominant position, the ICAC adopted this resolution on the proposal of V.J.R. Dunbar: 'That while sympathising with the class of mechanics and the rural population who meet for athletic exercises on Sundays from inability to meet on other days ... the holding of athletic meetings on Sundays is detrimental to the interests of amateur athletics in Ireland ... and that those who may take part in such meetings shall be disqualified to compete at any meeting held by the ICAC or under its rules.'[12] Such a restrictive law was seen by the majority population as being designed to have an adverse effect on the rural sports, and at the same time to exclude the humble and hardworking members of the community from the official athletic events that were to remain the reserve of an elite class.

Initiatives

The year 1879 was remarkable for individual initiatives taken by Nally, Cusack and Davin, each of which had a bearing on moves to establish the GAA. Nally, growing impatient with the class-bound group that was in control of athletics in Dublin and anxious to make a symbolic move away from their influence, established the National Athletics Sports of Mayo in September 1879. He also made a break with the custom of having landlord patronage and instead secured as patrons two Home Rule members of Parliament, Charles S. Parnell and the Mayo representative Lysaght Finnegan.[13]

Under his new banner he organised a sports meeting at his home place in Rockstown near Balla, in direct opposition to an event that was due to be held on the estate of the local landlord Sir R.L. Blosse. His initiative proved to be an outstanding success, attracted a crowd estimated at 3,000 and completely overshadowed the landlord's sports. Six years later a similar tactic was successfully adopted by the GAA in Tralee.

Nally's strong nationalist views were applied to athletics as a way of advancing his ideas of national independence. Although he was Head Centre of the IRB in Connacht he was also involved in land agitation and championed the cause of tenants who suffered harsh treatment at the hands of unsympathetic landlords. He was joint honorary secretary of a committee set up to raise finance in support of the Dempsey family who had been evicted from their holding.[14]

He repeated the Rockstown initiative successfully in 1880, but afterwards he devoted most of his time organising the Irish Republican Brotherhood in Connacht and in England. These activities led to his arrest, trial and imprisonment in 1883 and resulted in his untimely death in questionable circumstances as he was about to be released after serving his sentence.

Early in 1879 Nally had met Cusack in Dublin. Their conversation turned to the unsatisfactory condition of athletics and the need for a controlling association on national lines. Nally at twenty-two years of age was fired with youthful enthusiasm. He had a marked influence on the older man who acknowledged many years later that no one had encouraged him more than the 'Champion of the West' to take up the challenge to establish a national association.[15]

Cusack's Academy was flourishing at this time and it was generally accepted to be the finest of its kind in Dublin in academic excellence and in the promotion of an athletic spirit. He founded the Academy Rugby Club and he played with the team regularly until 1882 when he abandoned the game, but in articles in the *Shamrock* he continued to urge young people to practise cricket.

It is remarkable that in his conversation with Nally, no mention was made of Gaelic games such as hurling and football. Athletics in general was the subject of discussion between them. It appears that Cusack came to a decision that he must attempt to reform athletics from inside the existing controlling bodies in Dublin and with that end in view he became involved successively with three of the principal clubs in the city.

He accepted an invitation to join the committee of the Irish Championship Athletic Club which was then on its last legs as a viable club and when it eventually folded up he took a leading part in trying to clear off its debts although he was not responsible for incurring them. In a surprising move, he became a founding member of the City and Suburban Harriers, although he had a poor opinion of cross-country running. Furthermore, the club's constitution was based on the rules of similar clubs in London. When the Dublin Athletic Club was formed in 1882, he became a member of the committee and succeeded in pushing through a motion that the club's events would in future be open to all competitors.

He returned to the athletic arena as a competitor in 1881 and scored a victory in the Irish championship meeting when he won the title in the 16 pound shot. At a number of sports he shared the judging with Maurice Davin, so the two had an opportunity of discussing their ideas on athletics. When the *Irish Sportsman* renewed the call made five years previously for a national association to control athletics, Cusack replied expressing his

> unqualified approval of the move to form an association for framing the rules for the instruction and guidance of the promoters of athletic meetings and of amateur athletics in Ireland...It will be responded to by every gentleman interested in this department of sport. For my part I shall feel honoured in being permitted to assist the promoters of this very laudable object, pecuniarily or otherwise.[16]

Davin made no response to this new move. His experience of the attempt made five years previously did not suggest that such an initiative had any prospect of success. Even though a draft scheme for a code of rules was drawn up under the 'supervision of a gentleman who has some ten years experience in Irish athletics' and some meetings were held, the National Athletic Association went the same way as the former attempt and never really got off the ground. Cusack's experiences with the unionist-controlled bodies in Dublin over a four-year period led him to the conclusion that it was fruitless trying to broaden their perception of a national association. He was in and out of a number of their clubs seeking reforms in their rules. While he succeeded in achieving limited changes, he became convinced that they would never attract countrywide support. He abandoned his connection with them in 1883 and struck out on a new course that was to lead to Hayes' Hotel in Thurles in November 1884.

Athletic club in Carrick-on-Suir

Maurice Davin played an important role in the formation of a new athletic club in Carrick-on-Suir in 1879.[17] The prime mover was a local businessman, James J. Hearne, who was keenly interested in athletics. He had been connected with the sport during some years he had spent in America. The eminent position in athletics held by Davin and his brothers was certain to raise thoughts of starting a club in the home town. Hearne was backed by the Davins and before long he had sufficient support from other prominent people to ensure success.

The inaugural meeting was held in the Commissioners' Room in the Town Hall on 8 August, with an attendance of about sixty, described as 'an influential, highly respectable and representative assembly'. A popular local landholder, W.H. Briscoe of Tinvane, was appointed president and the other officers were Maurice Davin, perpetual chairman, J.J. Hearne, secretary and Joseph O'Ryan, joint treasurer with the secretary, who along with nine others formed the executive committee. The club was to be known as Carrick-on-Suir Amateur Athletic, Cricket and Football Club, having for its purpose the promotion of these manly exercises.[18] A suitable ground in Knocknaconnery was rented for an annual sum of £24 from Mrs Skehan of Cregg Road, who had to get premission to sub-let from the landlord, John H. Power of Mountrichard, who insisted that he must see the terms of the agreement before giving his consent.

As chairman, Davin grasped the opportunity to put into practice his considered views on the proper management and control of a club. His practical experience, combined with his study of methods at home and abroad, provided the necessary background for the position. He caused a table of rules to be drafted by a four-man committee which included his brother Pat and Joseph O'Ryan; printed copies were made available for the members. Membership fees were fixed and subscriptions were sought from well-wishers. In the first year, sixty full members paid ten shillings each and twenty-five associate members contributed five shillings each.

Under Davin's supervision a running track was prepared on the Knocknaconnery ground and a wooden paling seven and a half feet high was erected to enclose the arena. A pavilion was built to accommodate dressing rooms and a storage space for the club's equipment. Prominent members of the Ascendancy were requested to become patrons and subscriptions were received from the Marquess of Waterford and from Lord Arthur Butler, Lord Charles Beresford and Lord Bessborough and it was expected that they would be annual subscribers to the funds of the club.

The first athletic meeting was held on Easter Monday, 29 March 1880. The programme included track events as well as weight throwing and jumping. It attracted a crowd of a few thousand, most of whom were content with standing room outside the fence. Anyone willing to pay a higher admission charge was provided with a seat inside the enclosure. Traders paid a fee to the club for the right to carry on their business in the grounds on the days of sports meetings. A question was raised about whether it was appropriate to have alcoholic drinks on sale at an athletic contest and there were divided views on the issue. After discussion, a motion from Joseph O'Ryan was passed disapproving of such sales. However, in the following years the matter was raised again and the majority approved of a change of policy in regard to the sale of alcohol in the grounds.

Athletic meetings were held three times a year – at Easter, in July and in October. Membership was drawn mainly from the immediate vicinity of the town, but the high reputation of the club attracted athletes from Callan, Clonmel and Waterford and from well-known people such as Dan Fraher of Dungarvan and Joseph Kickham of Mullinahone. At the end of its first year's operation, the financial report showed a profit of ten pounds after all liabilities had been met.

A special sub-committee under the chairmanship of J.F. Quirke was appointed to take charge of the cricket section of the club. At some expense a cricket crease was laid down in the centre of the field. A local farmer paid a small charge for the right to graze the field, but he had to employ a man to keep the cattle off the crease and to remove the droppings they left. Because of complaints from cricket players, the cattle had to be removed and sheep were let graze there instead since they were considered to cause less of a nuisance. However, cricket received very poor support and the minutes of the club have no more than three references to the game during the four years of its existence – one of those was giving approval to the cricket secretary for the purchase of a Marylebone bag and two cricket bats.

Little attention was given to football of any kind. The only mention in the minutes refers to a four-a-side tournament played in connection with the athletic sports on Easter Monday 1882 and in that instance the competition was not completed. The committee, having discussed the matter, decided to award the trophies, four silver crosses, to the Kilcash quartet who were considered to be the most deserving team. No indication is given about the kind of football that was played, but the probability is that it was in line with some form of association rules.

Although cricket and football were included in the extended title of the club, its activities were almost entirely confined to track and field athletics. The general view, which is supported by Pat Davin, was that the cricket branch 'never seemed to succeed', which comes as a surprise considering that cricket was being popularly played in the area for some years. It is not surprising that football was poorly supported because interest in the football association had not penetrated to rural areas.

The most notable achievement in the club's history was Pat Davin's world record leap of 6 ft 2¾ ins at their sports on 5th July 1880. This remarkable feat was certified as follows: 'We the undersigned, hereby certify that Pat Davin did on July 5th 1880 at Carrick-on-Suir athletic sports clear the height of 6 ft 2¾ ins, same having been measured from the centre of the bar and the ground properly tested with a spirit level, Signed: H.W. Briscoe, L.P. Owen, R. Slack, R.M.W. Foley, J.P.T. Veale (Birmingham), T. Beary (Assistant County Surveyor), J.J. Hearne, Hon Secretary, V.J.R. Dunbar, judge'.[19] The *English Midland Athlete* accepted the certificate without reservation, but another English journal commenting on the presence of J.P.T. Veale wrote that they were glad one on whom they could rely was there, otherwise they might have felt inclined to doubt the measurement. This was typical of the attitude of some English commentators in regard to Irish performances and it was one of the factors which impelled Maurice and Pat Davin to prove their worth at the English championships in 1881.

Taking up the English challenge

Earlier in the year Davin had been extremely annoyed by disparaging remarks about Irish athletic standards in *The Field,* which claimed that performances were poor and that athletics were in decline. The latest derogatory references were a reflection not only on performances by Irish athletes, but on the honesty and integrity of the officials in charge and particularly on Davin himself as the chairman of a promoting club. The most effective answer to such remarks was to challenge them in competition in an English arena. Davin was fiercely proud of being Irish and he could never agree that an Irishman was inferior to an Englishman when competing on equal terms.[20]

He and Pat entered for the English championships due to take place in Birmingham on 16 July 1881. At that time Maurice was thirty-nine years old and had retired from competition, but he was a very fit man and with a few weeks' training he was confident of doing justice to himself and his native land. Pat Davin at twenty-four was at his peak as an athlete. They travelled by train to Dublin, then took a seventeen-hour boat trip to Liverpool, and boarded a train on the 'rocky line' to Birmingham where they arrived late on the evening of the 15th. Their appearance at the championships the following day caused a stir, especially among those who were sceptical about their achievements.

With their results the two Davins silenced the critics. They had fulfilled their mission satisfactorily and had taken four of the ten titles.[21]

Maurice Davin's victories in athletic championships

IRISH CHAMPIONSHIPS

16 pound hammer with wooden handle		Slinging 56 poundweight	
1875	113ft 6ins	1877	28ft 4ins
1876	128ft 6ins	1878	no opposition
1877	123ft 0ins	1879	no opposition
1878	123ft 2ins		
1879	100ft 6ins		

16 pound Shot

1877	38ft 5ins
1878	40ft 6ins
1879	41ft 3ins

ENGLISH CHAMPIONSHIPS

1881	16 pound Hammer	98ft 10ins
1881	16 pound Shot	39ft ½ ins

Maurice Davin's greatest recorded throw with the 16 pound hammer was 131ft 6ins at the international athletics match Ireland v England at Lansdowne Road on Whit Monday 1876; it was the longest throw on record.

The Davins came home to a rousing welcome in Carrick-on-Suir, but the story is told that Maurice slipped away quietly from the crowd and walked back along the railway line to his home in Deerpark, a very satisfied man. He and Pat had planted Ireland's athletic flag triumphantly and firmly in the international arena, setting a marker for future athletes to emulate.

The official Amateur Athletic Association (AAA) history records their achievements: 'One family from Ireland had taken charge of the field events. Pat Davin ... had set championship records for the high jump (6 ft. ½ in) and long jump (22 ft 11 ins), while his brother Maurice, at 39 the oldest man in the championships, had won the shot (39 ft 6½ ins) and the hammer (98 ft 10 ins). If the performances appear modest, it should be noted that the jumping was from a grass take-off on to grass and the hammer was wooden-shafted.'[22]

For Maurice, there was a tinge of sadness knowing that he had competed for the last time, but now he looked forward to even greater feats from Pat who over the next three years was to astonish spectators at sports throughout the country with amazing performances. He displayed exceptional versatility, sometimes competing in and winning six or seven events in one day on the track as well as in the field. Although when fully fit he weighed only 12 stone 4 pounds, he beat some of the weight-throwing giants in putting the shot and throwing the 56 pounds weight.

It was common for him to clear the high jump at 6 ft or more and in the long jump he had no equal. In August 1883 at Monasterevin his long jump of 23 ft 2 ins was the best on record and a few weeks later at Portarlington he cleared the same distance to reinforce his supremacy in this event. He enjoyed the great distinction, never since equalled in the history of world athletics, of holding the world records at the same time in both the high and long jumps. His high jump figure lasted for five years before being bettered by half an inch by the American, William Byrd-Page; his long jump distance from a grass take-off remained unchallenged for fifteen years. Although others could not be persuaded to compete against him for the all-round world championship experts agree that in his time there was no one fit to master him in such a test. At Monasterevin, when Pat had cleared six feet in the high jump, he believed that he could break the world record that day if the lath was raised to the appropriate height. Maurice refused to allow him to make the attempt because there was a favourable rise at the take-off: 'If I allowed this, anything I ever did in the way of honesty would be discredited.'[23]

The Carrick-on-Suir Amateur Athletic, Cricket and Football Club was brought to an abrupt end on 16 October 1883 when a well-attended general meeting reached a unanimous decision to wind it up, to dispose of its property and settle all outstanding accounts. An examination of the club's minutes yields no compelling reason why this should be necessary, although for some time difficulty was experienced in collecting membership fees, and monies due from traders and graziers, in spite of many calls for payment. The death in 1882 of the secretary and joint treasurer J.J. Hearne was a severe blow. He was the driving force who kept the wheels turning, ensuring that every detail was attended to efficiently. The other joint treasurer, Joseph O'Ryan, was engaged in his legal studies and was unable to give any time to the club for over a year.

In the four years of its existence the club had eighty-six meetings, and Maurice Davin, the chairman, missed only a few of them. His influence is seen in the rules and regulations on which the club was established and in the way its affairs were conducted and discipline imposed. The question remains as to why he would consent to bring it to a close, or was he constrained to do so by the prevailing circumstances. He was a stickler for correctness in all things and particularly in matters relating to financial accounting and he would have no hand in carrying on any business that was unable to meet its liabilities. Several times during 1883 he called on the committee members who were in charge of finance to collect the outstanding fees so that debts could be paid. They failed to get the response expected and the only way to pay what was owed was to sell off the club's property.

Domestic concerns occupied much of Davin's time and thoughts during 1883-'84. A disastrous fire which originated in the kitchen of their dwelling house while gruel was being prepared for the hauling horses, spread rapidly and completely gutted the building. Temporary accommodation for the family had to be prepared immediately. One of the outhouses was converted into a kitchen and bedroom for Mrs Davin and her daughter Bridget; a lofted barn in the farmyard was fitted out as a sleeping apartment for Maurice and Pat. The site was cleared and a contract for a new dwelling in a Victorian style was placed with a builder, Looby from Clonmel. The work was started immediately.

Mrs Davin had been in failing health for some time and the emotional shock of this traumatic event and the general disturbances that followed, did not help her condition. She had a presentiment that she would not see the roof completed on the new home and this proved to be the fact. She died on 13 June 1884. Since her husband's death twenty-four years previously, Mrs Davin had managed the family business with the co-operation and support of her eldest son. Decisions were reached after consulting together and Maurice benefited greatly from the accumulated experience and wisdom of his mother. His sister Bridget, who inherited her mother's practical efficiency, took her place as co-partner in the family business.

Although he had retired from active competition after his victories in the English championships, his interest in athletics found an outlet in his direction of the Carrick-on-Suir club. The failure of the club to survive was a severe blow to him. While an active competitor, he had displayed an interest in the concept of a national association for athletics and he was convinced that reforms were badly needed in sport. Within a few years he was ready to promote the idea of a new association to preserve and promote 'the characteristic sports and pastimes of the Gaelic race.'

Davin's national outlook

Davin was well-informed about what was going on in the world of sport through the national news media and journals from abroad. As a popular national figure he became the recipient of different points of view from acquaintances he met on the sports fields. Weighing these opinions against his own observations, he arrived at his considered viewpoint. He rarely made pronouncements to reveal his line of thinking, but he made no secret of his feeling for hurling and Irish football. He had seen both games played, but he was unhappy with what he saw because there appeared to be no established rules. He realised that both games held enormous potential if they were controlled by a code of practice.

Stories persisted amongst the workers in Deerpark about the feats of skill and strength that Davin performed and his prowess in various forms of sport. Many of these accounts concerned the hurling and football matches that he walked long distances to attend and his remarks about the rough and undisciplined quality of the games. These stories cannot be verified and must be accepted with some caution. However, they have been given support by the testimony of Davin himself in an interview with an American journalist in 1907.[24] William Fletcher of the *New York Daily* News visited Davin in his Deerpark home to talk to him of his athletic experiences. In the course of the conversation, Davin recalled a hurling game he attended at Glen on the south bank of the Suir. Teams representing Waterford and Tipperary were in contention. Thirty-five players were on each side and there was little order or control in the game. He was not pleased with what he saw and he came to the conclusion that suitable rules were needed in order to impose discipline on the game.

Another pointer to Davin's developing national philosophy is his interest in the Irish language which came to light recently in a series of Irish lessons for beginners found among his papers. They are numbered from one to eighty-five. Such lessons were prepared by members of the Society for the Preservation of the Irish Language (SPIL) and published in *the Irishman, 'The Teachers Journal, Irish*

People and Young Ireland. The Society for the Preservation of the Irish Language was founded in 1887 by Daithi Ó Cuimin, An tAthair Ó Nuallain and some others and within a few years they had published a series of booklets in simple Irish which proved to be very popular. The first *Irish Book* sold 20,000 copies and the society succeeded in having Irish (Celtic) admitted as a subject on the programme for secondary education.[25]

It would be no easy matter for a person to master the lessons privately unless he had some previous acquaintance with the language. In his youth Davin had certainly heard older people conversing in Irish on the boats and at the markets. Even after the famine years, the area around Carrick was bilingual to a considerable extent. According to the census figures for the barony of Iffa and Offa East for the year 1881, a total of 10,976 persons, that is 28.2 per cent of the population, were returned as Irish speakers. Although in the following years English was rapidly increasing as the spoken language and the number of Irish speakers had decreased to 3,402 or 15.9 per cent by 1891, yet Irish could be heard in the fields and on the streets.[26] The fertile plain between Slievenamon and the Comeraghs,with Carrick-on-Suir as its centre, retained a rich cultural heritage in literature and folklore in the Irish language up to the early years of the nineteenth century. Eoin Ó Néill in his study of the life and works of the Irish scholar Pádraig Ó Néill, has revealed the richness of this tradition.[27]

Furthermore, the workers from Sean-phobal and the Comeraghs who got seasonal employment in Deerpark were native Irish speakers and the Davin boys listened with fascination to their conversations and the stories and songs recited by Seáinín Gan Gruaig, Séamus Ceann Liath, Seán Gan Íosa and Micil Fada.[28] Here was a richness of cultural heritage in song and story and verse that was to a large extent closed to the boys until then. Maurice's continued interest in the Irish language is shown by his attendance at the first meeting of Conradh na Gaeilge held in Carrick-on-Suir.

References
1. *Irish Sportsman,* 14/5/1870.
2. *Nenagh Guardian,* 20/6/1873.
3. *Waterford News,* 25/8/1871; *Munster Express,* 9/9/1868.
4. Lawrence, J.H., *Handbook of Cricket in Ireland,* p. 155.
5. *Irish Sportsman,* 31/7/1875, 25/9/1875.
6. Ibid., 11/8/1877, 29/3/1879.
7. Ibid., 25/12/1875, 15/7/1876.
8. Dooley, W., *Champions of the athletic arena,* part I, Dublin, 1946, pp 13-15.
9. *Irish Sportsman,* 3/11/1877.
10. Ibid., 1/12/1877.

11. Ibid., 15/12/1877.
12. Ibid., 21/12/1878.
13. Ibid., 13/9/1879.
14. Ibid., 27/12/1879.
15. Ibid., 9/3/1899.
16. Ibid., 11/11/1882.
17. Minutes of Carrick-on-Suir Amateur Athletic Cricket and Football club in possession of Mr Gerard Quirke, Solr., Carrick-on-Suir.
18. Ibid.
19. Certificate amongst Davin's papers in Deerpark.
20. *Irish Sportsman*, 17/1/1880.
21. Davin, P., op. cit., p. 42.
22. Lovesey, P., *Official history of the Amateur Athletic Association centenary*, London, p. 36.
23. Dooley, W., op. cit., p. 25.
24. *The Nationalist*, Clonmel, 18/5/1921 copied from *Daily News*, New York.
25. Ni Mhuiriosa, M., *ReamhChonraitheoiri*, Baile Átha Cliath, 1968, pp 1-14.
26. Ó hOgáin, D., *Duanaire Thiobraid Árann*, 1981, pp 9-10.
27. Ó Néill, E., *Gleann an Óir*, Baile Átha Cliath, 1988.
28. Davin, P., op. cit., pp 78-81.

Chapter 4

The beginnings of the GAA

The cultural teaching of the Young Irelanders in the 1840s persisted as an influence on a nationally-minded people in subsequent decades. As the movement to preserve the Irish language drew its inspiration from the writings of Thomas Davis, so the exhortations of Thomas Francis Meagher to bring back the old game of hurling kept alive the idea of restoring the native games even in depressing times.

From time to time calls were made to stem the decline of native pastimes and to restore them to their former prominence in the lives of the people. The editor of *The Irishman*, Denis Holland, in October 1859 pointed out the connection between native games and national pride and in an article entitled 'The Sports of Manhood' he wrote: 'Our national pastimes, our grand athletic games, are dying and will inevitably cease to exist if we do not forthwith arrest this withering disease.' He lauded the hurling games of fifteen years previously and 'the brave sport of football in which the Irish excelled.'[1] But his message failed to produce any action at a time of depressed national spirit.

The efforts made in 1876 and 1881 to form an Irish Association for athletics failed. But in both instances the initiative came from a unionist source and lacked a popular appeal. The Ballot Act of 1872, in spite of its limitations, released tenants from the dominating influence of the landlord class at election time and left them free to express their opinions in the secrecy of the polling booths. It marked the beginning of the end to deferring to the 'master' and bowing to the upper class. This new spirit of independent action reached its dramatic expression when thousands of tenants gathered in Irishtown in Mayo in 1879 to voice their demands for a new deal. The resultant Land League and its successor, the Irish National League, united the people into a cohesive force with a sophisticated organisation with branches springing up in parishes throughout the land. Their regular meetings, conducted on efficient lines and without the patronage or permission of the landlords, gained widespread publicity in the national and provincial press. A modern historian has thus summed up this remarkable movement of popular expression: 'For the first time in Irish history the masses came on to the political stage as leading players rather than extras'.[2]

The early years of the 1880s were marked by heightened national expectations and uninhibited expressions of national aspirations. Organised agitation was inexorably moving toward the concept of tenant proprietorship through the Land Act of 1881 and the subsequent Arrears Act. The Home Rule movement, in tandem with the Land League and its successor the Irish National League, was gaining in momentum, with confidence that a Parliament in Dublin was close at hand. The Gaelic Union made a significant advance in its aim to restore the Irish language when it successfully launched the *Gaelic Journal*. This rising tide of national consciousness was illustrated by the enthusiastic reception given to the National Industrial Exhibition of 1882 which stimulated support for Irish industry and native products. The dramatic increase in the circulation figures for national and local newspapers reflected the rising rate of literacy in the population. In this uplifting atmosphere thoughts of reviving the native games and pastimes were sure to occupy the minds of at least some ardent nationalists. Justin McCarthy, the Home Rule MP, regretted that the hurling matches that were practised in his youth were not being played and he expressed the wish that Irish athletic sports be more independent of English organisation.[3]

Influence of the Irish language revival

Amongst those who came under the influence of the movement to revive the Irish language was Maurice Davin who was nearing his fortieth year when he undertook the study of the lessons prepared by SPIL. John Wyse-Power, who was later to be one of the founders of the GAA and a joint secretary, was an active member of SPIL and assisted John Fleming in editing the *Gaelic Journal*.[4] Michael Cusack, who was a native Irish speaker, appears to have taken no active interest in promoting the language until about 1882 when he was attracted to the Gaelic Union. He became a committee member and treasurer and was prominent in the launching of the *Gaelic Journal*. It seems fair to conclude that the language movement had much to do with shaping the outlook of those three founders of the GAA This was more especially the case in regard to Cusack, because it was in the last days of 1882 that he began to show an interest in reviving hurling, when he was already immersed in work for the language. Up to that time Cusack had displayed keen interest in sports other than hurling. His vision of athletics was sharply limited to what he termed 'pure athletics' which in his view was confined almost entirely to field events. He voiced his strong opposition to the policies of the unionist dominated clubs in Dublin in excluding labourers, artisans and such people from their competitions and for neglecting to include traditional events in their programmes. Yet he was successively an active member of the Irish Champion Athletic Club (ICAC), the City and Suburban Harriers and the Dublin Athletic Club up to the end of 1882 and as late as November 1882 he was fully in support of an athletic association as proposed by the Dunbars in the *Irish Sportsman.*

Cusack joined a small group in the city to set up the Dublin Hurling Club in the early days of 1883.[5] The apparent aim of this initiative was to restore the national game of hurling. Meetings were held, but the effort petered out within a short time. Although the Dublin Hurling Club was a failure, it marked a step forward for Cusack in that it revealed his new interest in hurling and over a few months in 1883 his weekly contributions to *the Shamrock* advised young people to practise the national game and he gave useful hints on how it should be played. Furthermore, he realised that he should turn his attention to the provinces if he was to make worthwhile progress in reforming the athletic scene.

Cusack went south in May 1883 for the Cork Athletic Club sports where he competed in the weight-throwing events and it is most likely that he was hoping to gain some support from the Cork athletes for his ideas of reform. However, the trip did not turn out to be successful mainly due to his own aggressive attitude. Because he was not allowed to use his own weight in the shot-putt event, an argument arose between himself and the secretary of the sports, J.F. O'Crowley. There was also a difference of opinion between the pair regarding the eligibility of one of the competitors. The argument did not end on the day but led to a heated controversy in the press between the two. Cusack, in a rather abrasive manner, suggested that the officials in charge of the sports were not competent and were like overgrown schoolboys. This drew a stinging response from O'Crowley who claimed that Cusack's attitude as displayed in Cork was not helping the cause of athletics in Dublin where he was highly unpopular and furthermore that his purpose in coming south was to promote his 'Gaelic Mission.'[6]

Cusack denied the latter accusation and stated that he had not mentioned to anyone that he was in Cork on his 'Gaelic Mission.' He suggested that Mr. Maurice Davin should act as a referee between them and if he should be proven wrong he would hand five pounds to Mr Davin to be used for the promotion of the 16 pound shot event. He also stated that he was opposed to the system of handicapping in vogue and that he had discussed an alternative plan with Mr. Davin by which a special medal would be awarded to any competitor who reached a certain standard in his event. For many years Davin and his brother Pat had been objecting to the way in which the best men were being handicapped in field events resulting in ridiculous outcomes, such as a man who failed to jump 5 ft 4 ins being placed first over one who had cleared 6 ft. Consequently they had promoted the idea of 'standards' as an alternative and fairer system.

It was astute of Cusack to bring the name of Davin into the debate and particularly to mention him as an associate who shared his views. It added strength to his case. Doubtless the two were on friendly terms, otherwise Cusack would not have presumed to propose Davin as a referee. How close the friendship was one cannot say, yet there is no question about Cusack's admiration for the Carrick man who was highly esteemed on all sides.

The two had met on a number of occasions since Cusack first made his appearance at an athletic sports in Dublin. Both were judges at the ICAC championships in 1880 and three years later Davin was a judge when Cusack was a competitor in the shot event. They had a common interest in reforming athletics and each had backed separate moves to form a national committee of control. Davin and Cusack had ample opportunity of discussing the best means of preserving and promoting the national pastimes. How far such discussions were pursued in the years before 1884 is a matter for conjecture.

Later in January 1885 when Cusack was naturally elated that the GAA had been established and was already gaining support, he referred to 1881 as a year of some significance in developing the concept of a Gaelic association. He had won the championship of Ireland in putting the shot and Maurice Davin had won two English titles in weight-throwing and he concluded 'since then we have been watching for an opportunity of establishing in Ireland an athletic association for the preservation of that marvelous strength, skill and agility for which our forefathers were so remarkable.'[7]

Modest beginnings

As the athletic season was drawing to a close in September 1883, Cusack gathered a few kindred spirits and commenced weekly hurling practice in the Phoenix Park.[8] This practical step was the logical outcome of what he had been promoting in his articles in *the Shamrock*. Others, attracted by the unusual spectacle of the ancient game being played with all its glorious simplicity and without the restraints of inhibiting rules, joined the select group and heartened by this support Cusack formed the Cusack Academy Hurling Club. As the numbers grew, the Metropolitan Hurling Club was founded in

December and the practices continued for some months into the new year.

This modest beginning involving no more than about forty players was in reality the seed from which the revival of hurling developed and in effect the first practical move that led the way to the foundation of the GAA. The game was not altogether extinct since there were pockets of hurling activity in places such as Galway, Tipperary, Cork and Waterford and although the national press ignored the Phoenix Park practices, the news of what was happening in Dublin filtered to Galway where it was warmly welcomed. In East Galway a number of teams were active and Killimor was recognised as the champion team of the area. To test their strength against the Metropolitan Club, some people in Ballinasloe put up a championship cup for a game between the two teams to be played on Easter Monday 1884. The Metropolitans accepted the challenge and led by Cusack they travelled by train to Ballinasloe for the match.

The opposing captains agreed beforehand on the rules to be observed, but in the course of play, after the Galway side had scored a goal, some disagreements developed regarding the rules and Cusack's team retired, their captain complaining that their opponents were too rough.[9] Killimor claimed the victory and although the game had an unsatisfactory conclusion it marked an important stage in the evolution of a code of rules for the game. The Killimor rules which may have been formulated many years previously, were concerned with the actual play, but did not specify the layout of the pitch nor the penalties for minor offences; gradually they gave way to the official rules drawn up by Davin and adopted by the GAA at the Thurles meeting on 17 January 1885.

Killimor rules

1. Each team when hurling must wear a different colour for the purpose of distinction.
2. Three umpires to be appointed on each side, who have power to order any hurler to cease playing, who in their opinion is under the influence of strong drink, who loses his temper or strikes any of his opponents intentionally. Should the hurler refuse to do so the opposing team may claim the prize that is being played for.
3. Should any hurler, when jostling, use his hurl [sic] so as to bring it into contact with his opponent, with a view to injuring him, he must cease hurling when told to do so by any of the umpires. Penalty same as Rule 2.
4. No hurler can get a substitute except he meets with an accident which in the opinion of the umpires renders him unable to play.
5. No hurler is allowed, when playing, to handle the ball, which must, in order to secure a count, be hurled through or over the goal.
6. Should the ball go outside the goal posts it is to be taken back by one of

the umpires and placed at a distance of not more than thirty yards from the said goal.

7. The time and number of goals to be agreed on by the captains before commencing play; the majority of goals constitutes the winner.

8. Bystanders to have no voice in any of the decisions and should they interfere with the hurlers in any way that may be considered by the umpires and judges as preventing the game being fairly played, the aggrieved hurlers may claim the prize.

9. In cases of dispute, the umpires and/or three of the judges combined must decide by ballot. From this decision there is no appeal.

10. On the decision being declared, the stake holder must hand over the prize to the captain of the winning team.

(Taken from Ó Caithnia, L.P., *Scéal na hIomána,* An Clochómhar Tta., 1980. p. 756. With acknowledgements to Pádraig Puirséal).

Athletics subject to English rules

Meanwhile, developments were taking place on the athletics arena that were causing concern to Davin, Cusack and their supporters and diverting their attention away from the hurling fields. The first indication that something new was afoot was contained in an editorial in the unionist *Irish Sportsman* in January which called for 'Home Rule' in athletics in Ireland. The use of the term 'Home Rule', an emotive slogan, was sure to have an appeal for the nationalist population, but the unionist *Irish Sportsman* 'Home Rule' in athletics meant having a select body in Dublin, acting in conformity with the rules of the English AAA, which would decide on all athletic matters in Ireland.

During the summer months a concerted and well-planned drive was directed at sports meetings throughout the country to bring them under the control of the English rules. This move was spearheaded by two Dublin weekly sports journals, the *Irish Sportsman* and *Sport,* which enjoyed a wide readership and were on sale in most provincial towns. P.B. Kirwin of *Sport* made it known that he was prepared to appoint members of his staff to officiate as starter, handicapper, timekeeper or referee at any sports in the country. He had the rules of the AAA published in his paper and he warned that anyone competing at a sports not under its rules would be disqualified from taking part in AAA meetings. V.J.R. Dunbar of *the Irish Sportsman* was available to act as handicapper or starter wherever he was needed and he travelled long distances to meetings, even in remote places, imposing discipline and control under the rules of the AAA.

The clubs in the larger towns continued to take their lead from the city clubs as they had been doing for years, but the traditional rural meetings where the majority of country athletes first entered competition, were to be outlawed and anyone who took part in their events was debarred from competing at the sports adhering to the rules of the AAA. There was no recognised athletic association in Ireland at that time, but the promoters of sports in Dublin invoked the authority of the English Association in support of the ban. The more promising of the rural-based athletes were placed in a quandary. Their sense of loyalty to their local sports conflicted with their ambitions to test talents in competition with the established performers at the prestigious meetings. According to P.B. Kirwan of *Sport,* several athletes were applying to him for reinstatement and the rural clubs were experiencing difficulty in resisting the pressure to conform to the AAA rules. By the end of the athletic season the majority of meetings, even in small villages, were accepting the new regime and athletes such as F.B. Dineen, William Real and James Mitchel were entering competition with W. Barry, J.C. Daly and representatives of the Dublin clubs.

Dunbar, Kirwan and their colleagues were genuinely interested in developing athletics and the publicity which they gave to the meetings in their weekly reports added interest to the events and contributed to popularising the sport nationwide. However, their acceptance of direction from the English Athletic Association ran counter to the rising tide of national re-awakening which was finding popular expression in the movement for political Home Rule and in the growing support for the campaigns to revive the Irish language and Irish industry.

The GAA established

Cusack devoted all his journalistic talents in trying to combat this trend in athletics. Week after week in *Shamrock* during the summer months he criticised the failure of the AAA meetings to give proper recognition on their programmes to the 'pure athletic' events which were traditional to Ireland; he claimed that their system of handicapping was unfair and that abuses such as betting and 'roping' were generally practised. In order to gain wider readership than *the Shamrock* could command, he succeeded in getting articles on to the front page of the more popular *United Ireland.* He warned readers that athletic meetings were being steered on the lines laid down by promoters who wanted everything managed from London and that Irish people "should not submit to such a denationalising system".[10] To counteract the trend, action was urgently needed to set up a new association that would have the approval and full support of the national leaders.

Davin, engaged for much of 1884 in supervising the building of the new house in Deerpark, suffered a grievous loss in the death of his mother in June. Nevertheless he was in contact with Cusack ragarding the launching of the new association. In August he received a letter from Cusack:[11]

Dear Mr Davin

The Irish Assn. with its rules etc. must be formed before the end of this year. The Assn. could organise the whole country within the year 1885. We could then safely hold the projected mass gathering in 1886. The business must be worked from Munster. Suppose we held a meeting of delegates in some central place in Tipperary on the 1st of Nov. next.

Don't bother your head about Dublin. The place couldn't well be worse than it is. We'll have to look to the provinces for men. Dublin will have to fall in, or keep up the connection with England.

I have written to Cork this day telling them that you have responded most heartily. I am sure W. Stack of Listowel will look after north Kerry. Although I am not a member of the Natl. League, I think I am not without influence with several of its leading members. The Natl press will give me room for squibs when I am ready. The Shamrock is also at my disposal. I hope to see it enlarged in about a month and then the education of the people could start in earnest. The paragraphs on athletics in United Ireland are exploding like shells in the enemy's ranks. Of course they know it is my doing and that therefore the paper is not likely to hang fire soon.

I have found it to be utterly hopeless to revise our natl. pastimes without the assistance of the leaders of the people; and I have not hesitated to urge my claim with a persistence that brooks no refusal. After a protracted struggle I won all round. Our business now is to work together caring for none but the Irish people and quietly shoving aside all who would denationalize these people.

I'll write to you again when business is a little further advanced.

With many thanks,
I am, Yours faithfully,
Michael Cusack.

Contrary to the general belief that Thurles was chosen because of Davin's influence, the letter conveys the impression that the Carrick man favoured Dublin as a central venue; otherwise why would Cusack advise him not to bother his head about Dublin because 'the place couldn't well be worse than it is. We'll have to look to the provinces for men. Dublin will have to fall in or keep up the connection with England.' Munster and Tipperary offered the best prospect of support, especially during the very important initial stages when the association would be finding its feet.

No trace has been found of any previous letters from Cusack to Davin, nor of a later one which he had promised to send, and neither has any reply from Davin come to light. As he reported in the surviving letter, Cusack was busy making other contacts because he had come to the conclusion that it would be 'utterly hopeless to revive our national pastimes without the assistance of the leaders of the people.' The letter was written in a highly optimistic mood consequent on his success in gaining the support of the leaders of the National League; he had received encouragement from Cork, and from the old Kerry Fenian, Moore Stack, who was also active in the land agitation, could be relied on to look after North Kerry, which in fact he did when the time came.[12]

There was good news also from Galway where an important meeting had been held in Loughrea on 15 August 1884 in the home of John Sweeney in Dunkellin Street. Also present were two other Loughrea men, William Duffy and J.P. McCarthy, Peter Kelly of Killeenadema and Michael Glennon of Kilchreest. All five were connected with the land agitation. Following a discussion, they approached Dr. Duggan, the Bishop of Clonfert, to request his patronage of the new association. The Bishop considered himself to be too old and recommended a younger man, Dr Croke, Archbishop of Cashel. Because no contemporary account of the meeting exists, some doubts have been expressed as to whether it did take place. John Sweeney's grandson, Pat Finnegan, lived in the Sweeney home and preserved intact the room where the meeting took place and the table around which the men sat during their discussion. He had the story from his grandmother, Mrs Sweeney, who lived on into the nineteen forties, and according to his account Cusack was present at the meeting. William Duffy's son was also adamant that the meeting took place and that Cusack was present.[13]

An explanation offered for the absence of any report of the meeting on the Galway papers was that the local correspondent, T. Cunningham, was on court business in Galway that day, but it is also likely that those present were not anxious for publicity. If a doubt remains about Cusack's attendance, there is no doubt that the meeting was initiated by him through his friendship with William Duffy and that the message he received assured him of the support of East Galway.

Echoes of the Loughrea meeting are found in Cusack's subsequent statements. Almost immediately he abandoned the idea of working the new association from Cork and instead chose some central place in Tipperary as the most suitable venue for the meeting.[14] In the lead-up to 1 November 1884, he considered Thurles as most convenient because it was central for the majority of the best athletes in the country, but he added that 'it was fitting that the second Synod of Thurles should be held under the patronage of the Archbishop who resides there' and who would be favourable to any movement directed to provide native pastimes for the people of Ireland.[15] Early in January 1885 he wrote that Thurles had been chosen because of its proximity to the Archbishop's residence.[16] It seems clear that in this matter Cusack was acting under the influence of the message that came from the Loughrea meeting.

A claim subsequently made that a sub-committee of the IRB Council had conceived the idea of a national athletic association and that they chose Michael Cusack as the best man to organise it has not the ring of truth.[17] Cusack was a man of strong and independent mind, open and outspoken and not a person to engage in any underhand business; no more than Maurice Davin, a highly principled individual, would not devote his considerable talents to any undertaking without being completely satisfied that it was above board and in conformity with his own thinking. It is inconceivable that Cusack would approach the national leaders of the constitutional movement seeking their support for an association which unknown to them was actually sponsored by the IRB.

Early in October the way was clear for the final drive to 1st. November in Thurles, although even then Cusack was suggesting that the society for the 'preservation and cultivation of our national pastimes' could be worked from Cork.[18] His appeal to the Irish people published in *United Ireland* on the 11 October left little time for the general public to respond in a positive manner, although his message was clear and he had driven it home to his readers all during the summer. He emphasised the principles underlying the movement to restore the native pastimes and condemned the corrupting influences which had been devastating the sporting grounds of the cities and town and were fast spreading to the rural population. His immediate concern was to counter the growing dominance of the English rules in Irish athletics and he urged the people to take the management of athletics into their own hands.[19]

Davin's response to the *United Ireland* article came promptly in the next issue of the paper.

> Deerpark
> Carrick-on-Suir
> October 13, 1884

Dear Sir,

I am much pleased to see that you take an interest in Irish Athletics. It is time that a handbook was published with rules, etc., for all Irish games. The English Handbooks of Athletics are very good in their way but they do not touch on many of the Irish games, which although much practised, are not included in the events or programmes of athletic sports. Weight-throwing and jumping appear to be going out of fashion in England, but such is not the case in Ireland, although these events are too often left out of the programmes of what might be called leading meetings. I have some experience of these things, and see numbers of young men almost daily having some practice. It is strange that for one bystander who takes off his coat to run a foot race, forty strip to throw weights or try a jump of some kind.

Irish football is a great game and worth going a long way to see when played on a fairly laid out ground and under proper rules. Many old people say just hurling exceeded it as a trial of men. I would not care to see either game now, as the rules stand at present. I may say there are no rules and therefore those games are often dangerous. I am anxious to see both games under regular [sic] rules.

I cannot agree with you that Harrier clubs are a disadvantage, as I believe they are a good means of bringing out long distance runners, and we want some more good men at this branch of sport. I am sorry to hear that it became necessary to make some other remarks which appear in the article on 'Irish Athletics' in *United Ireland* on the 11th. I thought we in Ireland are pretty free from the abuses you mention. I know they are said to be a great blot on the sport in England, but I understand the management there are doing all they can to remedy it.

If a movement such as you advise is made for the purpose of reviving and encouraging Irish games and drafting rules etc., I will gladly lend a hand if I can be of any use.[20]

> Yours truly,
> Maurice Davin.

Cusack gave an enthusiastic reply to Davin's letter:

> Sir,
> My friend Maurice Davin has spoken. I am very glad he has. Through him a leader who is spotless in the midst of the speckled has spoken. He has had very considerable experience of Irish and English athletics. His modesty, which is as well known as his big Tipperary heart, and his physical and moral strength and courage will not allow him to say that jumping and stone throwing declined in England after he and his brother had totally eclipsed the best specimens of the English athletes in Birmingham in 1881. In obedience to the call of duty I should offer my humble advice as publicly as Mr. Davin has done, in the event of a meeting being held to draft laws for the promotion and conservation of every form of Irish sport. It seems to be the general feeling that a meeting should be held in Thurles on Saturday, 1st of November. Accordingly steps are being taken to summon by circular representative Irishmen for that place and time.'[21]

The circular was issued on Monday 22nd, October 1884:

> 4 Gardiner's Place
> Dublin
>
> Dear Sir,
> You are earnestly requested to attend a meeting which will be held at

Thurles on the 1st of November to take steps for the formation of a Gaelic Association for the preservation and cultivation of our national pastimes and for providing rational amusements for the Irish people during their leisure hours. The movement which it is proposed to inaugurate has been approved of by Mr Michael Davitt, Mr Justin M'Carthy MP, Mr William O'Brien MP, Mr T. Harrington MP, and other eminent men who are interested in the social elevation of the race. The place of meeting will be determined on at the Commercial Hotel, Thurles, at two o'clock on the day of the meeting.

Maurice Davin, Carrick-on-Suir.

Michael Cusack, Dublin. Hon. Sec. pro tem.

In *United Ireland* of 30 October, two days before the date of the meeting, Cusack issued another notice to the public:

Circulars have been issued by Mr Maurice Davin and myself calling a meeting to be held in Thurles on next Saturday for the purpose of inaugurating a movement which, I sincerely hope — may be the means of providing rational and national amusements for the humbler and more neglected sections of our race. To the circulars I have received a shower of replies which have burst on me in a storm of overwhelming welcome, which has swept aside any doubts I may have been tempted to entertain on the success of our movement.

Meeting at Hayes's Hotel

When Maurice Davin arrived at Hayes's Hotel at the appointed time on Saturday, he must have felt some disappointment that so few had come, but neither he nor Cusack expressed any misgivings about proceeding as planned. The billiard room provided for the meeting by the proprietor, Miss Hayes, was small but adequate for the seven men who went in there. In addition to Davin and Cusack, the others were:- John Wyse Power, John M'Kay, James K. Bracken, Joseph O'Ryan, Thomas St George McCarthy. John Wyse Power was a native of Waterford who was a journalist with the *Leinster Leader* in Naas. He was an enthusiastic supporter of the Irish language movement, being associated with the work of SPIL and the Gaelic Union and certainly had become acquainted with Cusack through the latter body. He became chairman of the Dublin County Board of the GAA and filled that office for a few years. He remained a keen supporter of the GAA all through his life.[22]

John M'Kay, a native of Belfast, was a journalist with the *Cork Examiner*. He had a keen interest in athletics and was a prominent member of the Cork Athletic Club which was one of the leading clubs in Munster. Through his paper and the *Cork Evening Herald*, he gave valuable publicity to the Association during its early formative years.

James K. Bracken was a building contractor and stonemason from Templemore.[23] According to police reports, he was an advanced member of the IRB, but he was also active in the land agitation. He was interested in athletics and football and he is said to have taken up a caman at one of Cusack's practice sessions in the Phoenix Park, which probably earned him an invitation to Hayes's Hotel from Cusack.

Joseph O'Ryan, a recently qualified solicitor, was born in Main Street, Carrick-on-Suir in 1857. He was interested in athletics and had been an active member of the Carrick-on-Suir Amateur Athletic Football and Cricket Club during its short life from 1879 to 1883. He was a friend and an associate of the Davin brothers. After qualifying, he lived in Callan for a time and practised there and in Thurles. Maurice Davin was probably responsible for inviting him to the meeting, but subsequently he was not active in the Association. [See Appendix 2]

Thomas St George McCarthy was a native of Tipperary and an RIC inspector stationed in Templemore. He was a former pupil of Cusack's Academy and a team-mate of his on the rugby team. The probability is that Cusack influenced him to attend the meeting. He took no further part in the Association's affairs, although he regularly attended games in Croke Park up to his death in the early nineteen forties.[24]

The small attendance may be explained by the fact that the first public announcement that the meeting was to be held on 1st November 1884 was published a mere week beforehand in the United Ireland of 25 October. Certainly Cusack had been in communication with some prominent people previous to the announcement, but the circular which he distributed widely was not sent out until the Monday before the meeting.

The general impression remains that the preparations for the launching of the Association were pressed forward with a high degree of urgency. Davin would have been expected to counsel a few extra weeks notice, but Cusack's impulsive nature was bent on proceeding immediately; in his view no time should be lost in breaking the grip of the EAAA on athletics in Ireland.

Cusack's insistance on 1 November appears to have had a special mystical significance for him. An explanation is persuasively put forward by one of his biographers that it was under the influence of the Gaelic Union and the ancient traditions of the Irish language that Cusack was inspired to form an association for the preservation and cultivation of the national pastimes. Lá Samhna, November 1st, was a special festival day in the ancient Gaelic sagas and furthermore it was reputed to be the day when the great battle of Gabhra signalled the end of the Fianna.[25]

It was three o'clock in the afternoon when the historic meeting in the billiard room of Hayes' Hotel was set in motion. Maurice Davin, having been elected to the chair, briefly explained the object of the meeting.[26] He pointed out that the rules under which athletic sports are held in Ireland were designed mainly for the guidance of Englishmen who promote the sports of their own country; that as far as they go these rules are good in their own way, so long as they are observed, but they do not deal at all with the characteristic sports and pastimes of the Gaelic race. It therefore became necessary to form an association which would resuscitate our fast-fading sources of amusements and draft rules for the guidance of those who are patriotic enough to devise schemes of recreation for the bulk of the people and more especially for the humble and hard-working labourers who seem now to be born to no other inheritance than an everlasting round of labour. Cusack followed, urging the necessity to form a Gaelic Association.

Because the sporting press were giving no publicity to native sports he had asked for assistance from the national weekly press and William O'Brien had promised to help, but had warned against the movement being political in any sense. Cusack then read about sixty messages from people approving of the objects of the promoters. In his letter, Michael Davitt regretted he could not attend, but he would be willing to lend a hand. He suggested an effort should be made to revive the Tailteann Games, the great national festival. Cusack reported that Mr Davitt believed that such an event would cost £1,000, but he would guarantee that half that sum could be raised in America.

Cusack then proposed Davin as President of the Association. M'Kay seconded the motion saying that there was no meeting of athletes that would not rejoice to have the opportunity of ratifying such a selection. The name of Davin was respected by all Irish athletes. The Cork club he represented looked with favour on the new association, provided it was properly carried out. He had at first intended to oppose any business being done because of the small attendance, but he had changed his mind when he heard the nature of the proposition. The formation of the Gaelic Association was only one step in reaching the goal they aimed at, which was a general athletic association for Ireland. He objected to Irish affairs being managed by Englishmen, especially in athletic matters. He suggested that no committee be appointed until a later date. Cusack, Wyse Power and M'Kay were appointed joint Honorary Secretaries, with power to add to their number.

It was agreed that the objects of the Association should be submitted to Archbishop Croke, Charles S. Parnell and Michael Davitt, inviting them to be patrons. The meeting adjourned to give the elected officers time to draft the laws under which the work of the Association was to be carried out.

Although the accounts of the meeting supplied to the press by Cusack and M'Kay name the seven who were present and took part in the proceedings, other reports give the names of thirteen participants. The Freeman's Journal named six in addition to the seven. This report was written by Mr Dunbar, of the *Daily News*, who was not present at the meeting.[27] His account was copied by the *Irish Sportsman*. The extra six are also included in the account published in the *Tipperary Advocate*.

The six names are: John Butler, D (or Dwyer), C Culhane, M Cantwell, William Delahunty, all from Thurles and William Foley from Carrick-on-Suir. It is generally accepted that D or Dwyer refers to T.K. Dwyer, the mile champion of 1878.

Thomas F. O'Sullivan, the historian of the GAA was a prominent official at national and county level and he was in close touch with people involved in the early years. In the preparation of his history he did considerable research in the files of the national and provincial papers and gleaned information from official and unofficial sources to ensure accuracy. Regarding the attendance at the foundation meeting, he states: 'Notwithstanding the fact that Mr Cusack placed a few etceteras after the names of those attending the meeting in Thurles only the seven persons whose names are given were present'. There appears to be no doubt about the other named six being at the hotel on that day, having come to meet Davin and to express their support for the movement, but they did not take part in the meeting in the billiard room. Yet their names merit being recorded.

References

1. *Irishman*, 22/10/1859.
2. Lee, J., *The modernisation of Irish society 1848-1918*, Dublin, 1973, p. 72.
3. *The Shamrock*, 11/10/1884.
4. O'Neill, M., *From Parnell to De Valera*, Blackwater Press, 1991, p. 53.
5. *Irish Sportsman*, 24/2/1883.
6. Ibid., 19/5/1883, 26/5/1883, 23/6/1883.
7. *United Ireland*, 4/1/1885.
8. O'Sullivan, T.F., *Story of the G.A.A.*, Dublin, 1916, p. 19.
9. O'Laoi, P., *Annals of the G.A.A. in Galway,* Galway, 1983, p. 6.
10. *United Ireland*, 19/6/1884, 5/7/1884. *The Shamrock* 5/4/1884, 18/10/1884.
11. The letter is preserved in Davin's papers.
12. Gaughan, T.A., *Austin Stack*, Dublin, 1977, pp 11-16.
13. In conversation with Patrick Finnegan in 1970.
14. Letter from Cusack to Davin 26/8/1884, in Davin's papers in Deerpark.
15. *Shamrock*, 25/10/1884.
16. *United Ireland*, 3/1/1885.
17. *Irish Press Golden Jubilee Supplement* 1934, p. 56.
18. *Shamrock*, 11/10/1884.

19. O'Sullivan, op. cit., pp 4-5.

20. Ibid.

21. O'Sullivan, op. cit., p. 6.

22. O'Neill, M., *From Parnell to De Valera*, 1991.

23. Murphy, N. in *Nenagh Guardian*, 19/8/1982.

24. De Búrca, M., *Michael Cusack and the G.A.A.*, Anvil Books, 1989, p. 105.

25. Ó Caithnia, L.P., *Micheál Cíosóg*, Baile Átha Cliath, 1982, pp 194-195.

26. O'Sullivan, T.F., op. cit., pp 7-9; *Cork Examiner* 3/11/1884; *Leinster Leader* 8/11/1884; Shamrock 15/11/1884.

27. *Chicago Citizen,* 19/9/1888, copy amongst Davin's papers.

Chapter 5

The introduction of rules for Gaelic games

Positive replies having been received from the three invited patrons the way was now clear for the second meeting which was called for Cork on December 27th 1884. Again the notice was short and M'Kay claimed that this was responsible for the small attendance.[1] Only four of the seven founders were among the sixteen who were present; the rest were from Cork, except for M.J. O'Callaghan from Dublin. There was an echo of Cusack's previous visit to Cork in May 1883; as he entered the Victoria Hotel he was warned: 'Cusack, my boy, you'll meet with opposition here today'. When Davin arrived, Cusack enquired if he was afraid to go in, 'if I have to speak roughly and plainly to Cork people to get them into line with us.' Davin's reply was typical of his independent outlook: 'Michael, I am not afraid of anything.'[2]

It was a strange and somewhat confusing meeting, or possibly two meetings, although the published reports convey the impression that there was only one. It was dominated by members of the National League or Home Rule party which was founded by Parnell when the Land League was suppressed. Surprisingly Alderman Madden, the Lord Mayor elect of the city, presided instead of Davin; and more surprising that the Parnellite John O'Connor succeeded with his proposal that the Organising Committee of the National League be elected to the Central Committee of the GAA along with the officers of the association and a representative from every recognised athletic club in the country.

In spite of the warning given to Cusack as he entered the hotel, the meeting was without rancour. Cusack could not raise any objection to John O'Connor's proposal; in his letter to Davin the previous August he had expressed the view that it would be hopeless to try to revive the national pastimes without the assistance of the leaders of the people. Neither would Davin object as he was a supporter of the Home Rule movement. The decision amounted to an alignment of the new association with the National League and gave rise to the charge that the GAA was founded on political lines. A motion in Bracken's name was adopted requesting that the president and honorary secretaries draft the new rules.

Davin's influence was seen in a letter from his brother Thomas issuing a challenge from twenty-one footballers in south Tipperary to play a team from any other county under Gaelic rules. The letter indicates that the president was already working on the rules and that they were being applied in games in the Carrick-on-Suir area.

There is no way of knowing whether there was agreement that Davin should take on the responsibility of framing the rules, or that as president he felt that it lay with him to do the work seeing that he had emphasised so strongly the importance of drawing up rules. Although Cusack in private conversation shortly before his death is reported to have said that he consulted with leading footballers before drafting the first rules,[3] it is generally agreed that Davin was the draftsman. Writing in 1902, Cusack recorded that the sub-committee met in Thurles in January 1885 to consider rules for hurling, football and athletics which Mr. Davin had drafted.[4] P.J. Devlin had no hesitation in saying that Davin had written the rules.[5] Liam Ó Caithnia is equally definite that Davin drafted the first rules of hurling and football that were adopted at the January meeting in Thurles.[6] Davin was well equipped by temperament, experience and interest to undertake the task. He had supported a call for a code of rules to govern Irish athletics while still actively participating in competitions,[7] and the rules of the Carrick-on-Suir Amateur Athletic, Cricket and Football Club, of which he was chairman, reflect his insistance on the maintenance of order and control in all its activities.[8]

The intensive study of the rules of field sports undertaken by Davin is revealed by the entries which he made in his notebooks over a number of years and the numerous cuttings which he made from newspapers and magazines. He kept in touch with the progress in athletics at home and abroad and he noted the developments that were taking place in field games in England, recording the emerging rules of rugby and association football (soccer) as they appeared in the press. He was a recognised expert on the rules of track and field athletics, but his main concern was to establish definite rules for the traditional Irish sports of weight-throwing and jumping (the events which Cusack claimed were 'pure athletics'), and the field games of hurling and football.

Hurling rules

When Davin sat at his desk in Deerpark to prepare a draft for the rules of hurling he was not starting from a blank page. Scholarly research into ancient Irish manuscripts[9] has established the antiquity of hurling. The romantic tales of the Red Branch and the Fianna, the Brehon Laws and the works of the classical poets of medieval Ireland have references to hurling matches (baire chomortais and imirt baire) to the hurley (caman) and the ball (liathroid). Although the references do not enlighten us about the nature of the game, and give no details regarding the conventions or rules, if any, that were observed, there is sufficient evidence to conclude that hurling in some form was an elite game in ancient Ireland.

A major work of research into all the available sources from the seventeenth to the nineteenth century has proved more fruitful in uncovering the hurling practices during that period. In this monumental study, the author establishes the incidence of the game throughout the country and the conventions that were generally observed while allowing for local or individual differences or deviations. Chapters deal with specific aspects such as the layout of playing areas, the number of players engaged in matches, their functions and placings on the pitch and the different types of sliotair and hurleys that were in use; each section is dealt with in exceptional detail and supported by commentary and analysis by the author.[10]

Although no written code of rules has survived from that period and it is doubtful if any such ever existed, nevertheless it can be deduced from the evidence available that some form of rules relating to games practices and modes of conduct survived in folk memory and were understood and accepted as part of the traditional game.

Davin may not have had access to the accounts of the great hurling matches that were common in the eighteenth century, but the folk memory could recall the great inter-barony match played at Brittas near Thurles in 1770 when twenty-seven hurlers from the two Ormonds met a like number from the baronies of Eliogarty and Kilnamanagh. The game was properly conducted on a field that was prepared and roped-off, probably due to the attention of Mr. Langley, the owner of Brittas. Old story-tellers would speak eloquently of the inter-county games played on the Green of Urlingford between teams representing Tipperary and Kilkenny. Such contests could not have taken place unless there was agreement between the sides in regard to the nature of the game and that they accepted an unwritten code of practices.

Hurling was an integral part of the rural community as shown in this description from the unpublished autobiography of Michael Doheny.[11]

He is bare of foot, with knee breeches girt at the waist by a belt or string, a short flannel waistcoat and cap or light straw hat. Another, and another, and another follow all equipped alike, inspired alike and impassioned alike. Twenty-one at a side are now stripped. They divide into two wings and a centre. In the centre are the heaviest and strongest men, on the cord the most dexterous, and on the scriob the fleetest of foot. Thus arranged, they come face to face with their opponents, and take each other's hurlies as boxers take each other's hands. Some experienced old hurler is appointed to throw up the ball. See it rise in the air glistening in the setting sun. The fourteen men that constitute both centres close where it is to descend. It comes, the hurlies clash, the men clutch as if for a death wrestle, and some are sent sprawling, heads, limbs, ball and hurlies are now in one entangled mass. How it happens that heads and legs and arms and ribs are not marked in so reckless a melee is almost a miracle, and yet they are no sooner down than up, no sooner up than down. The ball is now here, now there, now in the air, now driven before some one of unmatched fleetness. The crowd become as excited as the performers, cheering, encouraging, exulting, as the fortunes of the hour incline.

Doheny noted the reasons for the decline in the popularity of hurling;

> ...the sport is fast passing away. Its decay is owing to several causes, among which three are leading: First, the introduction of the dance drew down on the hurling the opposition of the priest. In some instances, too, of late, family and faction fights were renewed at the hurling, which still more imperatively called for the reprobation of the clergy. And finally there was yet another cause which operated more effectually than any or perhaps all others, namely the disinclination of the farmers to allow the hurlers on their grazing lands....That evils were growing up with the sport is undoubted, but the evils could be averted or crushed out by the same power and agency that was sufficient to put down the hurling itself. And putting down the hurling was so far crushing out the national heart. Woe to those who lend themselves to the unholy work of unnerring a people and accommodating them to the fetters of their masters. A few feeble attempts have been made in this country to revive hurling, but without success, because politicians seek to make it subservient to their selfish and most unworthy purposes.

In November 1884, Tom O'Grady hailed with delight the revival of our native games and made the claim that Moycarkey parish had never abandoned the national pastimes.[12] In south Galway, hurling was being played in almost every townland and the Killimor rules drawn up by Peter Larkin provide evidence regarding the nature of the game and how it was played. Three umpires from each side were empowered to deal with misconduct on the field of play, even to the point of sending off a serious offender. No mention was made to the size of the pitch or the goal area, nor to the number of players on a team. In Cork, several challenge games were played in the 1870s between teams from Blackrock, St Finbarrs, Aglish, Carrigaline, Shanbally, Cloughroe and Ballygarvan.[13]

The Dublin Hurling Club made the first practical attempt to revive the ancient game of hurling in Dublin. Michael Cusack was among the members appointed to formulate rules for the game and they were published in 1883. It can be claimed that these rules owed something to the rules of hurley drawn up a few years previously by Trinity College. Hurley was more closely related to hockey than to traditional hurling; its rules were strong on the offside regulations, probably due to the influence of hockey, but they made provision for the puck-out by the goalkeeper, the throw-in from the side-line and the measurements for the goal area and the crossbar.

The Dublin Hurling Club took example from the last mentioned provisions when they came to decide on their rules. Strangely they included the term 'bully' which is used in hockey and they did not allow striking with 'the back of the hurl' in a melee when two or more players were in direct play with the ball. The Dublin Hurling Club rules seem to have been in the nature of a compromise between hurling and hurley and they lasted only a short while. Cusack did not feel happy with them even though he had been on the drafting committee. No record exists of the rules the Metropolitan Hurling Club played to, but the type of game was directed in accordance with Cusack's understanding of how hurling should be played.

Davin had little to learn from the Trinity College game, but the Dublin Hurling Club had some rules that needed to be critically examined, particularly those relating to the measurements of the pitch and the goal area. Cusack did not favour too many restraining rules and this view had to be balanced against Davin's determination to eliminate any dangerous practices. Consideration had also to be given to the experience in Ballinasloe on Easter Monday 1884 when Cusack's Metropolitan team and the Killimor side failed to arrive at full agreement about the rules to be observed.[14]

The twelve rules drafted by Davin and adopted at the meeting in Thurles on 17 January 1885 have been criticised as lacking in detail and as being without distinctive form or substance.[15] Davin chose a wise course in refraining from introducing too many rules at the one time which would certainly have caused some confusion and probably have sparked off opposition.

Davin's hurling rules were adopted at the meeting in Thurles on 17 January 1885:

1. The ground shall, when convenient be 200 yards long by 150 yards broad or as near that size as can be got.
2. There shall be boundary lines all around the ground at a distance of at least five yards from the fence.

3. The goal shall be two upright posts twenty feet apart with a crossbar ten feet from the ground. A goal is won when the ball is driven between the posts and under the crossbar.
4. The ball is not to be lifted off the ground with the hand when in play.
5. There shall not be less than fourteen or more than twenty-one players a side in regular matches.
6. There shall be an umpire for each side and a referee who will decide in cases where the umpires disagree. The referee keeps the time and throws up the ball at the commencement of each goal.
7. The time of play shall be one hour and twenty minutes. Sides to be changed at half time.
8. Before commencing play hurlers shall draw up in two lines in the centre of the field opposite to each other and catch hands or hurleys across, then separate. The referee then throws the ball along the ground between the players or up high over their heads.
9. No player is to catch, trip, or push from behind. Penalty, disqualification to the offender and a free puck to the opposite side.
10. No player is to bring his hurley intentionally in contact with the person of another player.
11. If the ball is driven over the side lines it shall be thrown in towards the middle of the ground by the referee or one of the umpires, but if it rebounds into the ground it shall be considered in play.
12. If the ball is driven over the end lines and not through the goal the player who is defending the goal shall have a free puck from the goal. No player of the opposite side to approach nearer than twenty yards until the ball is struck. The other players to stand on the goal line, but if the ball is driven over the line by a player whose goal it is, the opposite side shall have a free puck on the ground twenty yards out from the goal posts. Players whose goal it is to stand on the goal line until the ball is struck.
N.B. Hitting both right and left is allowable.

Football rules

The argument that Davin invented a new football game can hardly be sustained in view of his statement in October 1884 that he considered Irish football to be a great game and worth going a long way to see when played on a fairly laid-out ground and under proper rules. He had discussed the merits of the game with old people who said that only hurling exceeded it as a trial of men, but his own view was that both games were dangerous unless revived under regular rules.[16]

Football cannot lay claim to an equal status with hurling in traditional Irish life, yet it may boast of an honourable pedigree at least from the sixteenth century. It has not featured in literature, documentation or reports as hurling has. The probability is that football was introduced to Ireland from England sometime in the seventeenth century, although the Statutes of Galway in 1527 prohibiting hurling made the following reference to football: 'at no time to use the hurling of the little ball with hockey sticks or staves ... but only the great football'. Rough and tumble football was played in England for at least 2,000 years. It was dominated by brute force. The players jostled and heaved and wrestled and punching and kicking opponents was an accepted part of the game.[17]

Rugby football was introduced to Ireland by Trinity College where a club was formed in 1854 and other Dublin clubs were attracted to play the game which enjoyed the patronage of the British army, the public schools and the ruling class. No uniform system of play existed for a number of years until two men of Trinity College drafted a code of rules which was adopted in 1868.[18] The game received publicity in the sports papers of the time and it was taken up in the provinces, although for a period there was confusion regarding some of the rules until the Irish Rugby Football Union was founded in 1880. While rugby and soccer were developing, traditional Irish football was in decline and the promise of previous centuries was not realised. Surviving accounts of games in the seventeenth and eighteenth centuries indicate that there was a basis for the development of a distinctive Irish game.

The Gaelic poet Séamus Dall Mac Cuarta who was born in 1647 and lived until 1733, composed a poem in Irish entitled 'Iomáin na Bóinne'. Though 'iomáin' normally signifies hurling, here it is clearly used to mean 'football'. The poem celebrates in twelve verses a football match played on the south bank of the river Boyne between two local teams, one from the valley of the Boyne against a similar number representing the basin of the Nanny river. It appears that there were twelve players on each team and that the ball could be caught and carried or thrown, but there is little information on the actual play. It was probably played in an enclosed field and each side attracted its own supporters. Such games were played in the stretch of country between Lough Erne and the Irish Sea, usually once a year, on some special occasion in winter time.[19]

John Dunton, an Englishman travelling in Ireland about 1699, saw hurling played and wrote a very clear description of the play, but gave only a short reference to football:

> They do not play often at football, only in a small territory called Fingal near Dublin ... the people use it much and trip and shoulder very handsomely. These people are reckoned the best wrestlers of the Irish.[20]

An eight-a-side football match in Omeath in 1750 is the subject of an Irish poem, 'Iomáin Leana an Bhabhdhúin', written by Reamonn Ua Murchadha. The game lasted from midday until sunset without any goal being scored. The account gives some evidence of how the game was played. Six from each side opposed each other in a 'bulk', shoulder to shoulder, contending for the ball, while two wingers awaited their chance to snatch the ball and run with it towards the goal until obstructed by the opposing wingers.[21] Wrestling was allowed and play was rough. One of the players was thrown heavily on a heap of stones beside the field and seriously injured. He died two weeks later as a result of his injuries, and since he was a relative of the poet, his death may have been the inspiration for the poem.

A football match between Swords and Lusk played at Oxmantown Green on the outskirts of Dublin city in 1720 is described in a long and at times humorous poem written by Matt Concanon and entitled 'A Match at Football'.[22] The poet presents a lively and revealing picture of the scene and the play between teams of six-a-side 'on a wide expanse of level ground.' The pitch was enclosed by a barrier and men on horseback controlled the crowd. The poet described the ball thus:

'To outward view, three folds of bullock's hide,
With leathern thongs fast bound on ev'ry side,
A mass of finest hay concealed from sight,
Conspire at once to make it firm and light.'

The ball could be caught in the air, kicked, carried or rushed along the ground towards the goals which were formed by boughs of sally at either end of the ground. In the struggle for the ball the players tugged, pulled and grappled at each other. Tripping was allowed and admired and when two opponents engaged in a bout of wrestling no other player was allowed to interfere. A piper escorted one of the teams on to the pitch and a carnival air pervaded the whole scene. Reflecting the friendly spirit of the day, prizes were awarded to both victors and vanquished.

During the nineteenth century native football deteriorated considerably (as hurling did) due to social and economic pressures. The game as described by Concanon in 1720 held promise of developing into a more disciplined form, but one looks in vain for any evidence that his promise was being fulfilled in the years prior to 1884. In fact it had degenerated into a rough and tumble maul, described as 'the greatest curse that ever came on the country. The ball was set in motion and before ten minutes every two on the pitch were at each other's necks.'[23]

The decline of hurling and football is usually ascribed to the effects of the famine of the forties and doubtless it had a debilitating effect on the spirit of the population, especially in the rural areas, where the game had been most popular. The fall in the population through famine, disease and emigration left those who survived at home in a dispirited condition with little taste for engaging in sporting activities.

There were other causes for the decline which had to do with the land system and the rise of nationalism. The authorities, including the government, the landlords and their agents, viewed the gatherings of hurlers and footballers with suspicion and outright opposition, seeing them as occasions for inciting sedition.

In giving evidence before a select government committee, a witness named Barrington stated that he had heard that gangs wishing to establish an association got people to assemble at hurling matches and proposed an oath to them. He believed that hurling matches were exceedingly popular in Tipperary and openly held; but he added that if they hurled in a field and had not got the owner's permission for entering there, they would be liable to be transported. These matches became unpopular with the Church of Ireland landlords and clergy because they were used also for organising opposition to the payment of tithes.[24]

In south Tipperary, around Clonmel, football was the most popular game, as it still is. Pierce Nagle, a teacher in Powerstown close to Clonmel, had some knowledge of Fenian activity in the area. When he turned informer he reported to Dublin Castle on what was going on. At the trial of Fenian prisoners in 1865, he testified that football matches were used as a cover for their meetings. He had been at four such matches on Sunday afternoons in the early sixties, and after football had been played, instructions were given on military tactics by a militia man named Ryan.[25] Nagle himself had been involved in the manoeuvres. Considering the national outlook of the Fenians, it is reasonable to conclude that the game they played was some form of native football.

Nationalists organising games were kept under close observation by the RIC. A report from Tarbert in Kerry in 1866 alleged that the Fenians were busy organising football matches on Sundays in the townland of Kilpadoge. A large number of young men were accustomed to assemble by previous arrangement to play at football, but all the local Fenian sympathisers attended.[26] The implication was that the football game was used as a cover for rebellious activity. Such police surveillance proved to be a restraining influence on playing or publicising native games during the middle nineteenth century. On the other hand cricket and rugby were receiving every encouragement and both these games were growing in popularity, even in places where the native games had been strong such as in Kilkenny and Tipperary.

Football of an indeterminate character was being played with wide variations in the play from one area to another. In Kerry the game was called 'caid' which was played either in an enclosed field or across country. The latter version was from parish to parish with old and young taking part and there were no restrictions as to numbers. It was played in winter time when the crops had been removed from the land. Carrying the ball, wrestling, holding and pulling an opponent were allowed. The field version of 'caid' was played in an enclosed pitch with boughs for goals. Both games could be classed as rough and tumble. The ball, also called 'caid', was formed of an animal's bladder and covered with a hide.[27]

An account book of the Kilruane Football Club[28] for the years 1876-1880 records a membership of over fifty paying fees of half-a-crown to three-and-sixpence each. Two footballs were purchased and over the five years nine matches were played against neighbouring sides, Carrigatoher Cricket and Football Club, Killeen Football Club, the 53rd Regiment stationed in Nenagh and the Nenagh Cricket Club. In the games against Nenagh Cricket Club, the teams were fifteen-a-side, but in the other matches twenty or twenty-five players were included on each team. No account of the play is given, nor is it clear what type of football was played although there are indications that it was some form of rugby, since the club had secured a 'Book on Football' and at that time the rules of rugby had been established. It is more than likely that the British regiment in Nenagh would be favouring the rugby game which was being promoted by the army and the ruling class.

The Carrick-on-Suir AACFC devoted little attention to football of any type.[29] A large crowd assembled at the festival of Glen to watch a football match a few years before the GAA was founded. It was played in a field provided by Bob Hurley and by all accounts it was a rough and tumble affair with little evidence of any rules. The basic form of football in west Cork in the early years of the GAA had only three recognised positions on the pitch – goalkeeper, full-back and out-rushin' (forward).[30]

It was not a simple matter to bring a degree of control and discipline to the confused and diverse practices of Irish football. To achieve a transformation in the game within a short space of time seemed to be out of the question. The most pressing need was for a referee to take control with powers to impose penalties for breaches of the rules. Davin's main concern was to eliminate the more serious fouls and to regulate the layout of the playing area.

Football Rules adopted at the meeting in Thurles on 5 January 1885:

1. There shall not be less than fourteen or more than twenty-one players a side.
2. There shall be two umpires and a referee. Where the umpires disagree the referee's decision shall be final.

3. The ground shall be at least 120 yards long by 80 in breadth and properly marked by boundary lines. Boundary lines must be at least five yards from the fences.
4. The goal posts shall stand at each end in centre of the goal line. They shall be 15 feet apart with a cross-bar 8 feet from the ground.
5. The captains of each team shall toss for choice of sides before commencing play and the players shall stand in two ranks opposite each other until the ball is thrown up, each man holding the hand of one of the other side.
6. Pushing or tripping from behind, holding from behind, or butting with the head shall be deemed foul, and the player so offending shall be ordered to stand aside and may not afterwards take part in the match, nor can his side substitute another man.
7. The time of actual play shall be one hour. Sides to be changed only at half time.
8. The match shall be decided by the greater number of goals. If no goal is kicked the match shall be deemed a draw. A goal is when the ball is kicked through the goal posts under the cross-bar.
9. When the ball is kicked over the side line it shall be thrown back by a player of the opposite side to him who kicked it over. If kicked over the goal line by a player whose goal line it is, it shall be thrown back in any direction by a player of the other side. If kicked over the goal line by a player of the other side, the goal-keeper whose line it crosses shall have a free kick. No player of the other side to approach nearer than twenty-five yards of him till the ball is kicked.
10. The umpires and referee shall have during the match full power to disqualify any player, or order him to stand aside and discontinue play for any act which they may consider unfair, as set out in rule six.
   No nails or iron tips to be allowed on the boots. (Strips of leather fastened on the sole will prevent slipping).
   The dress for hurling and football to be knee-breeches and stockings, and boots or shoes.
   It would be well if each player was provided with two jerseys, one white and the other some dark colour. The colours of the club could be worn on each. Then when a match was made, it could be decided the colours that each side should wear.

The rules for track and field athletics followed more or less the accepted practice in those events. In regard to running events on the track, limits were imposed on the handicaps allowed and these were observed up to recent times. Special provisions were adopted for the traditional Irish weight-throwing and jumping competitions and they all bear the stamp of Davin's wide experience in these events. He had been strongly opposed to any handicapping in field events and consequently the new rules did not allow handicaps in jumping or weight-throwing.

Some authorities in recent years have been less than generous in their criticisms of Davin's first attempt to bring order and control into the games. L.P. Ó Caithnia contends that the rules failed to provide for certain elements of hurling.[31] He finds this surprising considering that Davin could have drawn from the five previous attempts to establish a code of rules. W.F. Mandle dismisses the football rules as 'bordering on the farcical' and concludes that on the basis of the rules 'the games were almost entirely without distinctive form or substance'.[32]

The course that Davin chose to follow was fully vindicated when the rules were widely adopted in games throughout the country in 1886 and in the following year inter-club competitions and All-Ireland championships in hurling and football were played. Looked at from any viewpoint this was a remarkable achievement for the young association that was starting off from a situation where scarcely any rules existed. The progress made in the space of a few years is in striking contrast to the decades required to reach acceptable codes for rugby and association football in England.

The dissemination and acceptance of the rules were facilitated by a number of positive factors. They were published without delay in the national newspapers; they were printed in booklet form and made available to clubs at a few pence each; Davin and Cusack attended games explaining the rules and seeing to their enforcement; the dramatic spread of the association created a demand for copies of the rules by the newly formed clubs. In addition, club officials sought clarification of the rules in letters to Cusack or to the newspapers which created a lively debate as to the merits of some of the measures adopted. The rule which outlawed wrestling, especially in football, was not taken too kindly in some quarters where it was deemed to be an essential part of the traditional game. For some years there were local problems because rules were not always observed. But provision was made for changes at the annual convention in the light of the experience to be gained.

At this second meeting on 17 January 1885 on Cusack's proposal it was decided that no handicapper, starter, judge or official of any description from outside the district in which the sports is held could be allowed to act. This was intended to debar Dunbar, Kirwan and others of the 'foreign faction' from acting at GAA meetings.

To counteract the ban imposed by those promoting the A.A.A. rules, the following resolution was adopted: 'That after 17 March 1885, any athletes competing at meetings held under other laws than those of the GAA shall be ineligible for competing at any meeting held under the GAA.'[33]

References

1. *C.E.*, 29/12/1884.
2. *The Irish Athletic and Cycling News*, 24/4/1888.
3. Mehigan, P.D., *Gaelic football*, Dublin, 1941, p. 19.
4. *Irish Weekly Independent*, 13/12/1902.
5. Devlin, P.J., *Our Native Games*, Dublin, 1934, p. 24.
6. Ó Caithnia, L.P., *Scéal na hIomána*, B.A.C., 1980, p. 102; *Bairí Cos in Éirinn*, B.A.C., 1984, p. 174.
7. *Irish Sportsman*, 27/10/'77.
8. Minutes of Carrick-on-Suir Amateur Athletic, Cricket and Football Club, in possession of Mr G. Quirke, Solicitor, Carrick-on-Suir.
9. Ó Maolfabhail, A., *Camán, 2,000 years of hurling in Ireland,* Dundalk, 1973, pp 55-85.
10. Ó Caithnia, L.P. *Scéal na hIomána.*
11. Doheny, M., 'Autobiography of An Agitator', *Irish American,* 19 Feb. 1859.
12. O'Sullivan, T.F., op. cit., p. 26.
13. MacCárthaigh, S., *Irish Press* Golden Jubilee Supplement, 1934, p. 58.
14. Ó Laoi, P., *Annals of the G.A.A. in Galway*, p. 6.
15. Ó Caithnia, L.P. op. cit., p. 622; Mandle, W.F. *The Gaelic Athletic Association and Irish nationalist politics 1884-1914*, London, 1987, p. 27.
16. O'Sullivan, T.F. op. cit., p. 5.
17. Reason, J. & Carwyn, J., *The world of rugby*, London, 1979, pp 9-11, 18.
18. Van Esbeck, E., *The story of Irish rugby*, Dublin, 1974, pp 14-15.
19. *Gaelic Journal*, vol x, p. 550.
20. MacLysaght, E., *Irish life in the seventeenth century*, Dublin, 1939, p. 364.
21. *Gaelic Journal*, vol x, 1900, pp 521-523; Mehigan, P.D., op. cit., p. 16.
22. Mehigan, P.D., op. cit., pp 16-17, 145-155; Ó Caithnia, L.P., op. cit., pp 30-42.
23. Mehigan, P.D., op. cit.
24. *Select Committee on the State of Ireland 1831-2*, vol xvi.
25. De Búrca, M., *Our Games Annual*, 1964, pp 77-78.
26. *Kerry Archaeological and Historical Journal, 1970*, p. 139.
27. Mehigan, P.D., op. cit., p. 15.
28. MS. 9515, Manuscript Room, N.L.I.
29. Minutes of Carrick-on-Suir AACFC.
30 Downey, P., *Irish Times*, 2/2/1991.
31. Ó Caithnia, L.P., op. cit., pp 622-3.
32. Mandle, W.F., op. cit., pp 26-7.
33. O'Sullivan, T.F., op. cit., p. 11.

Chapter 6

Confronting the Opposition

In the weeks immediately following the foundation of the GAA on 1 November 1884, the sporting press in Dublin gave little attention to it. *The Irish Sportsman* referred to the three distinguished patrons Croke, Parnell and Davitt, but did not think it worthwhile to publish their letters, using the plea that they had already appeared in other organs.

The first blast of criticism came from the *English Daily Telegraph* which claimed that the new society had been founded on political lines by Parnell, Dr Croke and Davitt, and also suggested egregiously that an agrarian offence would be no disqualification for membership.[1] The anonymous writer 'Pendragon' delivered a lampoon against the Archbishop and his letter, but Wyse Power considered that it failed in its purpose because, he commented, if anything was needed to complete the success of the GAA it was the fact that a leading English newspaper looked on the project with disapproval.[2]

No adverse response to the new Association came from the clubs that favoured the AAA until after the new rules had been adopted at the second Thurles meeting on 17 January. Within five days, a meeting of the Irish Cyclists Association called on all athletes to unite to quash the 'Gaelic Union' before it would destroy athletics in the country.

The Irish Sportsman urged the athletes not to allow their rights to be infringed by any clique or party; they could scarcely believe that a self-constituted junta of seven individuals would come together in a small provincial town and try to impose their arbitrary dicta on the followers of athletics in Ireland.

This paper was spearheading the attack on the GAA and its tactics included reprinting from the *Daily Telegraph* the Pendragon article and publishing a satirical poem holding Cusack up to ridicule.[3] But the paper was no match for Cusack when it came to the use of language and he was successful in countering their most vicious attacks and furthermore he succeeded in a suit for libel against *the Sportsman*.

Such venomous assaults on the GAA and on Dr Croke were not allowed to pass without appropriate replies. Wyse Power described the 'Pendragon' piece as a wanton, cowardly and scandalous attack on the most loved and esteemed of the hierarchy. Cusack warned that the GAA would use every legitimate means to resist the pernicious influence of those who encourage nothing but what is foreign to the Irish people.[4]

Davin defends the Association

Maurice Davin, as President, eschewing the bitterness that marked the controversy up to then, issued a strong but reasoned exposition of the GAA position.[5] Employing facts rather than rhetoric and drawing on his vast knowledge and experience of the world of athletics, he refuted the arguments of the AAA adherents. He declared emphatically that the GAA would not offer cash prizes to amateurs and their rules in regard to amateurs, betting and malpractices were similar to those obtaining in England. He had in his possession several programmes of English meetings showing that amateur and professional events were advertised for the same sports, where amateurs competed against amateurs and in another area professionals contended against each other for money prizes.

He pointed out that the Association's rules for athletics were administered and controlled by Irishmen, but the AAA claimed to make rules for the whole world as if no one knew anything about athletics except Englishmen; athletic rules were observed long before the AAA was thought of; they were simply adopted by the AAA, as they now have been adopted by the GAA.

He referred to additional rules dealing with games that are customary in Ireland, but are not touched on by the AAA and he added that the GAA had framed sensible conditions in regard to handicapping. In weight-throwing and jumping, handicaps were not allowed, but the competitors were arranged in classes; he once saw a man getting first prize for jumping 4 ft 11 ins, being placed above another who had cleared 6 ft; in foot races, limits were set to the handicap allowed. All their rules were compulsory until the first General Meeting, when it could be seen how they worked and whether changes should be made.

He made it clear that no change had been made in the rules by which cyclists regulated their races and they had not made any reference at all to the harrier clubs. He strongly denied that GAA athletes would be disqualified in England and prevented from winning honours there and he would like to see the best Irishmen entering for English events.

He repeated his conviction that Irish football was a fine manly game and superior to rugby; according to press reports he had read about the latter game; it was not one to be encouraged; the cyclist and harrier clubs had said that they would not be bossed or dictated to by any association, but they had allowed all these things to be done for years by adopting the rules of the London clubs; when any changes were made in the rules, they, i.e the Irish clubs, had not been asked for their opinion. He made the logical observation that if these people start an association, it would be for the purpose of accepting the rules of the English Association and being bossed by them. He concluded by declaring that the GAA had made rules for national games played in Ireland by members of the Association and anyone who did not like these rules need not take part. He stated his firm belief that 'the GAA would not be so easily quashed as some people think.'

The moderate but firm line taken by the President added to his stature as leader of the Association. J.A.H. Christian of the Dublin clubs lost no time in replying to assure Davin that they had no intention of opposing the GAA, but would afford them every help in reviving native pastimes so long as they did not encroach on the athletic scene. He added that of the seven who attended the GAA meeting, only two, Davin and O'Crowley, were connected with athletics; the others were of small account. He concluded that 'we Dubliners would be happy to help – but neither Dubliners nor country clubs will submit to the GAA.'[6]

Cusack could not let this slight on his athletic career pass without commenting on Christian and the 'characteristic, idiotic insolence of his class,' and he made the point that he possessed a championship cross which he won for weight-throwing in 1881 and that was more than Christian could boast of.[7] As the bitter controversy continued, Christian pursued the political charge against the GAA and Cusack countered that the AAA clubs were run by loyalists and extreme conservatives.

All athletic clubs were invited to a meeting in the Wicklow Hotel on 21 February 1885 to form an Irish Amateur Athletic Association. Davin received an invitation, but he declined to attend because he could not approve of the purpose of the meeting. However, he asked Cusack to go if he thought well of it. He also informed J.G. Beatty, the Secretary and added that there should be no ill-feeling between athletes who could hold different opinions and yet be friends.[8]

J.A.H. Christian presided at the meeting and he welcomed the conciliatory tone of Davin's letter. Cusack's presence was less pleasing to the Chairman who could hardly relish the prospect of being confronted face to face with his rival. He ruled that only a club representative or a pressman could remain. Cusack was not prepared to be taken as representing the GAA at such a meeting; he had come at the request of the President to clear up any difficulties that might arise, but as he was on the staff of the *United Ireland* he would remain as a pressman.

John M'Kay and J.F. O'Crowley represented the Cork Athletic Club, which though not then affiliated to the GAA was leaning towards it. Both questioned the motives of those who had convened the meeting. O'Crowley bluntly told them that they were attempting to crush the GAA, and he could not understand why they were blindly following the English rules when they could form their own rules as the GAA was doing, with the result that they were rousing the spirits of the people. M'Kay denied that the new Association was run on political lines and he maintained that the National League was not a controlling power when compared with the voting strength of the clubs.[9]

Only twenty clubs attended the meeting, and when the motion was put to establish the IAAA the representatives of five of them refrained from voting. Thus the IAAA was founded by the representatives of fifteen clubs, almost entirely drawn from the Dublin area. Their subordination to the English body was now being challenged by the GAA that was more in tune with the nationalist, self-reliant spirit of the mass of the people.

After the second Thurles meeting of the GAA had adopted the new rules, the leaders lost no time in buckling down to the task of promoting the objectives of the Association. They concentrated their efforts in two main directions; (i) The existing athletic clubs were targeted to win them over and secure their acceptance of the rules and control of the GAA, (ii) Simultaneously they embarked on a campaign to revive the games of hurling and football and to establish new clubs for that end.

The emphasis by the GAA in its first year or two on athletics rather than on hurling and football is due to the prevailing circumstances. As it set about wrestling control of the existing athletic clubs from the IAAA the GAA met with virulent opposition from the officers of that association which sparked off a long and tedious controversy in the newspapers. This generated an amount of public attention on the athletic clubs and how they would react to the opposing conceptions. The great majority of clubs in the southern provinces gradually turned to the GAA, adopted its rules and its national stance.

Athletics dispute
During the summer months, a lively propaganda contest waged between Cusack in *United Ireland* and the spokesmen for the other side in the *Irish Sportsman*. The latter claimed that the principal clubs had thrown in their lot with the IAAA, counting among their gains Queen's College, Cork, Ulster Cricket Club, Mallow, Ballinasloe, Drogheda, Mitchelstown and Portarlington.[10] But the tide was definitely turning against them as the GAA message filtered down to the clubs.

The change of allegiance from the IAAA to the GAA did not involve any great structural alterations in the clubs. They continued to function as before, organising their meetings and athletic contests, but operating under a new regime and adopting a new banner. Gone was the patronage of the titled gentry as democracy ruled in the clubs and the common people took control. The trend was set even before the new rules were drafted when on 11 November 1884 the organisers of a sports in the village of Toames near Macroom declared for the GAA and on 11 January the sports at Tulla, County Clare followed suit.

As the athletic season proceeded, more and more sports meetings opted for the GAA and when the prestigious meetings at Clane, Carbury, Monasterevin, Portarlington, Blarney and Cork took their stance with the Association, the GAA had established a firm footing in the country. The Blarney meeting in May attracted many of the best athletes in Munster, including the champion sprinter F.B. Dineen of Ballylanders. Thousands of spectators attended the Cork Sports in the Mardyke in June, and among the outstanding performers were the weight-thrower J.S. Mitchell of Emly and the great quarter-miler T.J. O'Mahoney, the Rosscarbery 'Steam-engine'.[11] A feature of these meetings was the prominence given to the traditional field events on the programme which was in strict accord with the new rules.

Clubs were instructed to submit a draft programme for their Sports to Maurice Davin before finalising it in order to ensure that it was in keeping with the spirit of the rules. When Archbishop Croke's famous letter was read at the meetings, it produced an inspirational effect on the attendance, leading to boundless enthusiasm for the Association.

Although the IAAA had failed to maintain their control over clubs outside the Dublin area, they were reluctant to acknowledge the success of the GAA. They could not accept that Thurles was a proper place to hold an athletic conference, or that a rural-based association was capable of organising athletics. The *Irish Sportsman* declared in July that the GAA was 'semi defunct', although all the evidence pointed to its robust health.

A dramatic confrontation between the two associations took place in Tralee on 17 June, the date fixed by the County Kerry Athletic and Cricket Club for their annual Sports under the rules of the IAAA. The GAA supporters, led by B. O'Connor Horgan, Solicitor, Michael Power, Moore Stack, Maurice Moynihan, Patrick Clifford and Fr McMahon PP decided to hold their Sports on the same day in opposition. It attracted four hundred entries and an attendance estimated at ten thousand to Rathone Paddock, while the rival event was poorly patronised.[12]

The *Irish Sportsman* viewed the occasion in a different light. It commented: 'It was most unfortunate that the few malcontents who for all practical purposes form the GAA – as the outcome of the factious spirit – decided to hold a counter demonstration. Yet a large and fashionable gathering of spectators attended.'[13]

One of Ireland's leading athletes, F.B.Dineen of Ballylanders, made a strong public appeal for support for Davin, Cusack and the three patrons. He had been a regular competitor at AAA meetings previously and his call to abandon subservience to English rules had a marked influence on his fellow athletes.[14]

The outcome of the Tralee confrontation left no room for any doubt about popular support for the GAA in Kerry and in the ensuing weeks Cusack drove home the message with obvious delight in the columns of *United Ireland.*

Archbishop Croke wrote to Cusack in September expressing his pleasure at the way the Association was bounding ahead and how the national sports were once more being patronised by rising manhood. He offered a cheque for £10 to provide a trophy for some event at the national championships which were to be held the following month in Tramore.

The decision to hold the first GAA athletic championships at a rural venue rather than in Dublin where previous championships were held, was prompted by the fact that little progress had been achieved in the city, but it was also an illustration of the independent outlook of the leaders. The weather in Tramore on 6 October was wretched, but that daunted neither spectators nor competitors. Maurice Davin was present to supervise the proceedings, supported by the two honorary secretaries, Cusack and M'Kay, the two vice-presidents Bracken and Kennedy and J.F.O'Crowley the official handicapper. Among the new champions who won the Association's gold medals were Mitchell of Emly, Pat McGrath of Aherlow, O'Mahoney of Roscarbery, P.S. Kenny of Carrick-on-Suir, J.J. Manning of Sixmilebridge, Dan Fraher of Dungarvan, T. Ryan of Clonmel and J. Hennessy of Blackpool in Cork. The Archbishop Croke Challenge Cup for the hammer-throwing event was won by Jim Mitchell.[15]

The campaign to revive hurling and football in the country was launched at the same time as the movement to gain the support of the athletic clubs, but it did not receive anything like the publicity that athletics received in the press. Unlike the athletic situation, no club structure or organisation existed which could be used as a launching pad for either hurling or football.

Davin was very active in south Tipperary, Kilkenny and Waterford, organising games, explaining the rules, refereeing matches and acting as judge whenever a dispute arose about interpretation of a rule. Cusack continued to promote hurling in Dublin, attracting more players to sessions in the Phoenix Park and at the same time propagating the message of the hurling revival in the weekly column in *United Ireland*. Elsewhere some exceptional individuals interpreted the call from Thurles as a matter of personal responsibility to give the lead in promoting the national games in their own community.

Hurling and football revived

Early in December 1884, F.R. Moloney, a nineteen-year-old businessman in Nenagh, presided at a meeting in the town for the revival of the national pastimes and there and then it was agreed to arrange a hurling match for the following Sunday. It took more time than was anticipated to prepare for the game, which did not take place until late March 1885, when Silvermines provided the opposition to Nenagh in a game under GAA rules, played in a field outside the town. It ended in a scoreless draw and the replay a few weeks later was a colourful event that attracted three thousand spectators and the scene was enlivened by music provided by the Nenagh Brass and the Silvermines Fife and Drum Bands. The venue, Captain O'Carroll's field in Lisenhall, was bedecked with green and white flags and a banner at the entrance proclaimed 'God Save Ireland'. Again the result was a draw.[16]

This was the beginning of the hurling revival in North Tipperary and F.R. Moloney was the driving spirit responsible for it. With three other representatives of Nenagh Hurling and Football Club, he attended the second Thurles meeting on 17 January 1885 and subsequently acted as an agent for the distribution of the book of GAA rules. As a result of Fr Moloney's organisational ability, the North Tipperary district could boast of ten affiliated clubs by December 1885.[17]

Galway was one of the exceptional areas where hurling was being played in 1884 before the GAA was founded. Early in January 1885, east Galway signalled that they were ready to move with the new Association. Mr Lynch of Killimor indicated that Thomas Rogers of Eyrecourt had twenty one men who would take up Tom Davin's challenge issued on behalf of the footballers of South Tipperary, but instead of football they opted for hurling, so nothing ever came of the challenge.[18]

Activity on the hurling fields of Galway increased considerably after the publication of the new rules and from March to December 1885 records show that at least fifteen hurling matches were played. By the end of the year over twenty clubs were playing hurling in the county.[19] A few of them did not immediately conform to the new rules, preferring to stay with the Killimor rules that they were accustomed to, but gradually there was a general acceptance of the authority of the Central Council.

Newspaper references to hurling matches during 1885 are sparse, but they are sufficient to show that the game was spreading extensively throughout the country. The hurlers of Clare were early in the field with a match in Tulla in January and the following month Clonard and Falls Road crossed camain in Belfast.[20] Hurling in Wexford was given a major stimulus in March when Mr Barry, M.P. presented a cup valued £25 for competition among the teams in the county.[21] It was customary to include a hurling match on the programme of athletic meetings promoted under the auspices of the GAA and on the occasion of a hurling match, the game was often followed by athletic events. The same was equally true of football matches.

Hurling matches were played in conjunction with the Sports in Glanmire, County Cork and also as part of the day's activity in Desertmartin in County Derry.[22] A huge crowd witnessed a hurling match in Tralee which was described as graceful and active. Many came from Kilmoyley, the home of hurlers.[23] At Killarney Sports, the spectators were entertained by the usual spectacle of a hurling match.

In Limerick, St Michael's Temperance Club could boast of fifty active hurlers before the end of the year.[24] Their match with Shamrocks at Rosbrien was the first in the county under GAA rules. In Dublin, Faugh a Ballagh (Fag a' bealach) Club played both football and hurling every Sunday in the Phoenix Park and the games were spreading to Inchicore and Drumcondra. Gorey drew up a programme of hurling, football and weight-throwing for the winter.[25]

Due to Davin's influence, the Association made a promising beginning in football, particularly in the Carrick-on-Suir district. Before the new rules were sanctioned, a report on a football match between Kilkenny and Bamford, states that the players were often at grips and there is no way of knowing what kind of football was played. Neither is there any detail about a match between Whitegate and Ballyanna played late in January 1885. Callan was the venue for the first recorded football match under the new rules when twenty one local men opposed a side from Kilkenny. Three weeks later they renewed the rivalry in a return game and the next Sunday Kilkenny played Danesfort. In April, Maurice Davin was the referee when Callan played Ballyneale, a parish bordering Carrick. He appears to have ruled out wrestling during the game, but when the game was over he allowed an exhibition by chosen wrestlers. In May, Callan's second team proved to be superior to Mullinahone.[26] In the first year, football was more popular than hurling in parts of Kilkenny.

In Kildare the first football match under GAA rules was played in February between Sallins and Naas,[27] and Straffan lined out against Clane on St Patrick's Day. In Offaly, Fr Gleeson was in charge of a football match between Coolderry and Killyon. In Kilmacduagh near Gort, four football matches were arranged for a day in November, and at Drogheda Sports a football match was included on the programme.[28] In November the Grocers' Assistants founded the Michael Davitt Football Club and similar clubs were established in Waterford and in Ballyrush, County Sligo.[29]

The new football rules were introduced to Limerick early in 1885 and the first game in which they were applied took place in April between Rathkeale and Kilmeedy. During the year the famous Commercials Football Club appeared and they arranged games with teams in Tipperary and Cork.[30]

The prevalence and character of the games in both hurling and football and the extraordinary enthusiasm that they called forth wherever they were played, gave assurance that they were destined to sweep through the country. The sudden success attending the games created the need for a form of local organisation capable of giving permanence, stability and guidance to the movement.

In setting up a local system of control, the GAA followed the organisational structure of the National League which was based on a network of branches or clubs throughout the country. The National League like the Land League before it was a highly sophisticated development with 1,200 branches in operation by 1885.[31] Each club had its officers, its roll of members with membership cards, regular meetings and recorded minutes and persistent exposure in the press helped to cultivate a favourable public opinion. The emerging GAA clubs followed this example and in many cases their members had acquired organisational experience in the National League clubs.

The official link between the GAA and the National League, which was forged in Cork in December 1884, was finally severed in the wake of the Tralee Sports in June. On that occasion, Mr Ed. Harrington, MP supported the IAAA meeting in opposition to the popular GAA event and as a result he was dismissed from the presidency of the Tralee branch of the National League. Subsequently Mr T. Harrington, MP, national secretary of the National League, declared that his organisation had no connection with the GAA. At a meeting of the GAA in Thurles on 18 July , J.K. Bracken proposed and J.F. O'Crowley seconded a motion which was adopted, declaring that the GAA was not a political association but a thoroughly national one and that while they did not need support from any association, they disclaimed any intention of interfering with or injuring any existing Irish national association.[32]

Although the official link between the two organisations no longer existed, they were closely connected at local level. Dr Croke took a strong line in advocating support for both the National League and the

GAA, giving a lead that influenced both clergy and laity which was of considerable help to the infant GAA. E.J.Walsh, president of the Wexford National League, addressing a large meeting of members in November, 1886, strongly urged the formation of GAA clubs in every parish in the country and thereupon the Wexford Gaelic Athletic Club was inaugurated for the town. Instances of co-operation such as this were common enough, and both organisations gained from it.[33]

As the time for the first annual Convention of the GAA was drawing near, the athletic controversy in the press flared up again with renewed intensity. Realising that they were losing popular support, the IAAA banned from their meetings from 1 September any athlete who competed under GAA rules.[34] This purported to be in retaliation for the GAA ban in operation since St Patrick's Day. In reality it was a restatement of the general ban imposed by the AAA dominated clubs in 1883 before the GAA existed.

Seeing that the GAA was firmly established and had nothing to fear from its opponents, a view was finding favour in some quarters that the ban had achieved its purpose and ought to be reconsidered. This view found its most public expression in a leading article in the *Freeman's Journal* on the eve of the Annual Convention. It urged the GAA to end its ban and allow all bona fide athletes to compete at its meetings regardless of whether they had taken part in events under the rules of another association.

Cusack responded immediately in a letter to the Freeman published on the morning of the Convention. He refuted inaccuracies in the editorial: the GAA was in existence before the IAAA was founded; it had not initiated the boycotting of athletes; it was not a political body. But he refrained from commenting on the question of dropping the ban, which was the main thrust of the article. When the delegates met in Hayes's Hotel for the first Annual Convention on 31 October 1885, the proceedings were overshadowed for a time by the ongoing athletics dispute.[35] The assembly went into private session to consider some delicate matters, including the *Freeman* article.

A letter was read from John Wyse Power, who was unable to be present, suggesting that a modus vivendi should be sought between the GAA and the other sports associations. A decision on this contentious matter was deferred. A delegation from Cork presented an alternative code of rules for football, but they were ruled out as being entirely foreign to the objects of the Association. Davin explained that according to their constitution, members of clubs playing under another code were not on that score debarred from competing at GAA sports, but as football clubs they could not be regarded as branches of the GAA. A motion was adopted binding all affiliated clubs and holders of office to observe the rules and regulations of the Association. The financial state was reported as prosperous and after a three-hour private session the meeting was declared open.

Davin addresses the first Convention

Maurice Davin, the president, addressing the Convention said that the whole country, so far as he had time to test its feeling, was with them. Besides an enormous number of hurling matches, football matches and parish meetings, the official handicapper had assisted in carrying out more than a hundred meetings. Of course he was not able to be everywhere his services were required, and altogether the number of important meetings held under the auspices of the Association during the year fell little short of one hundred and fifty.

A subject of the utmost moment was at present engaging their attention. Davin continued, they had seen in the principal daily newspaper of the country *The Freeman's Journal,* an article on the eve of the meeting and another that morning strongly counselling union between the different athletic associations now before the Irish people. They could not but appreciate the kindly and sympathetic spirit in which those articles were written; on behalf of the Association he, as one of its founders, wished to give expression to his appreciation of the good feeling displayed. He felt therefore that it was incumbent on him and due to the paper exercising so commanding an influence, to refer briefly to this matter.

Previous to the establishment of the GAA Davin stated, all athletic sports in Ireland were held under the rules of the AAA, an English body governing English athletics.

> 'It counts on its executive council 101 members of whom two are Irish and these are members of a Belfast cricket club. This association admits Americans like Myers to its competitions, although American athletes have nothing to do with English laws, but Irishmen are not eligible to compete in England if they compete under any laws save those of the AAA. The GAA was established twelve months ago exactly; its members cannot compete in England nor can any person competing under its laws.'

The IAAA, Davin continued, was established on 21 February with the object of smashing the GAA. Now the GAA had been accused of boycotting them. In that case the GAA could point to the example of the English Association which was turning athletics into ridicule.

The president then read a passage from an English sporting paper *The Referee,* ridiculing the squabbling that was occurring among athletic bodies in England. He said that the English Associations and their representatives in Ireland should settle their squabbles in the first instance. It would then be for the GAA to consider what course to adopt.[36]

The convention passed a motion bearing Davin's stamp on it, directing that where records are claimed in weight-throwing or jumping events, the ground must be proved level, or the performances must be done both ways and in the case of weights they must be proved to be the correct weight. All the officers were re-elected and the proceedings of this first Convention were conducted with admirable control in an atmosphere of satisfaction with what had been achieved. There was a marked reluctance on the part of both Davin and Cusack to make any definite response to the plea from the *Freeman* that 'some steps should be taken to put an end to the split'. Were they happy, Davin asked, to defer making a decision until further consideration could be given to such an important matter at the adjourned Convention on 27 February, or had this been the feeling expressed by the general body during the private session?

Dr. Croke urges moderation

The whole matter of the ban took a turn on Monday morning 2 November when the *Freeman* published a letter from Dr Croke:

My dear Sir,

As one of the patrons of the Gaelic Athletic Association I suppose I may be allowed to say, through your columns what I think of the unfriendly feeling which has hitherto existed and which judging from recent manifestoes in the public papers, appears to be more pronounced now than ever, between the two leading athletic associations in Ireland. When I ventured to connect my name with the Gaelic Athletic Association I really felt pained and so had felt for many a long day previously, at seeing all our fine national sports and pastimes dying out one by one, and English or other non-native games introduced and almost universally patronised instead. Not that I was or am in the least opposed to foreign games as such, if manly and becoming, but only in so far as they favoured by a certain class of our people, to the utter exclusion of those well-known Irish exercises which were formerly so common here and in which, when young, I was proud to take a part myself.

It did not therefore occur to me when becoming a patron of the GAA that there was to be any substantial, much less a bitter and persistent antagonism except on the point just referred to, between it and any similar body already in existence, or that may be called into existence afterwards. All I wanted and aimed at was, to encourage and thus revive national games; but it did not strike me at all at the time nor does it strike me now, or form any part of my design, absolutely to discourage,

84

and even denounce, all sports and pastimes that are not national. Still less did I think that a society or association formed for the promotion of one class of games, should boycott all other similar bodies, to the extent, at all events, of not allowing a man who had competed for a prize or championship under one set of rules to contend for a like prize, if offered by an athletic association whose rules were different.

Indeed so little did I dream of or contemplate any such thing that until very lately I was not aware of the very discreditable fact that the elder association of athletes had boastfully and spitefully boycotted its junior brother, simply, it would appear because of the Hibernian complexion of the latter, and the practical encouragement it was proposed to give to purely Irish games.—— Anyhow, as patron of the Gaelic Athletic Association, a lover of fair play all round and the enemy of every species of needless strife and estrangement amongst Irishmen, I would respectfully suggest to the committee of management of the GAA the advisability of modifying their rules in the above particular, so as to allow all qualified athletes to compete for their prizes, without any regard whatever to the fact of their having previously entered the lists for the prizes given by other athletic associations whose rules and views differed in some points from their own. This will set an example of tolerance and moderation to all other athletic schools and let us hope that they may have the manliness and good-feeling to follow suit.

I am, my dear sir, Your very faithful servant,

T.W. Croke, Archbishop of Cashel.

Dr Croke's enormous prestige in the country and his commanding influence on the general body of the GAA, demanded that his letter should have an immediate response and could not be delayed until the adjourned Convention in February. Obviously hurried consultations were held among the principal officers and an agreed decision reached to accede to the Archbishop's proposal. In Cusack's letter to the *Freeman* on 5 November, he acknowledged the Association's indebtedness to the paper for its part in helping to remove 'the pernicious system of boycotting' from the sporting grounds of Ireland and said he was in a position to state that the founders of the GAA accepted the Archbishop's plan and that it would be submitted for formal approval at the next meeting of the executive.

Although the report of the Convention in the *Freeman's Journal* suggests that Dr Croke's letter had been read during the private session, that could hardly have been the case. The letter was dated 1 November and was not published until Monday the 2nd. If it had been before the Convention, Davin would not have failed to give it due notice when he addressed the meeting, as he did in the case of the Freeman's article.

It appears that the publication of the Archbishop's letter on Monday 2 November had taken both Davin and Cusack by surprise and hence their hurried but deferential response. Croke's anxiety to eliminate all needless strife amongst Irishmen was to some extent motivated by his deep concern to demonstrate unity of purpose at this crucial stage in the movement for Home Rule which appeared to be close to reaching a successful outcome. However, the ban was not formally removed until the adjourned Convention in February 1886.[37]

References
1. *Daily Telegraph*, 8/11/1884.
2. *Leinster Leader*, 15/11/1884.
3. Irish Sportsman, 24/1/1885, 31/1/1885.
4. O'Sullivan, T.F., op. cit., p. 16.
5. *Freeman's Journal*, 13/2/1885.
6. Ibid., 14/2/1885.
7. Ibid., 17/2/1885.
8. O'Sullivan, T.F., op. cit., p. 16.
9. Ibid., pp 16-17, *Freeman's Journal* 20/2/1885.
10. *Irish Sportsman*, 4/4/1885, 11/4/1885, 18/4/1885, 25/4/1885.
11. O'Sullivan, T.F., op. cit., p. 21.
12. Ibid., p. 22.
13. *Irish Sportsman*, 20/6/1885.
14. *Tipperary People*, 17/4/1885.
15. *Freeman's Journal*, 6/10/1885.
16. *Tipperary Advocate*, 28/3/1885, 18/4/1885.
17. Ibid., December 1885.
18. *United Irishman*, 17/1/1885.
19. O Laoi, P., *Annals of the G.A.A. in Galway 1884-1901*, pp 13-22.
20. *United Irishman*, 17/1/1885, 19/2/1885.
21. O'Sullivan, T.F., op. cit., p. 19.
22. *United Irishman*, 6/6/1885, 4/7/1885.
23. *Freeman's Journal*, 30/7/1885.
24. Ó Ceallaigh, S., *History of Limerick G.A.A* Part 1, Tralee, 1937, pp 32-34.
25. O'Sullivan, T.F., op. cit., p. 26.
26. *Kilkenny Journal*, 19/1/1885, 28/1/1885, 21/2/1885, 14/3/1885, 21/3/1885, 11/4/1885, 27/5/1885.
27. *Leinster Leader*, 14/2/1885.
28. *United Irishman*, 28/3/1885, 2/5/1885, 4/7/1885, 14/11/1885.
29. O'Sullivan, T.F., op. cit., p. 26.
30. Ó Ceallaigh, S., op. cit., p. 32.
31. Curtis, L.P., *Coercion and Conciliction in Ireland*, London, 1963, p.47.
32. O'Sullivan, T.F., op. cit., pp 22-23.
33. Ibid., p. 26.
34. *Freeman's Journal*, 19/8/1885.
35. Account of Convention based on reports in *Freeman's Journal* and *United Irishman* and O'Sullivan, T.F., op. cit., pp 24-26.
36. *Freeman's Journal*, 2/11/1885.
37. Ibid., 27/2/1886.

Some of the weights used by Maurice Davin, in training and in competition.

Davin's violin.

Chapter 7

Davin as President of the GAA

The example of tolerance and moderation set by the GAA when, under the influence of Dr Croke, they declared their intention to remove the exclusion rule at the forthcoming adjourned convention in February 1886, did not receive a positive response from the IAAA. Instead they interpreted the conciliatory statements made by Davin and Cusack as a sign of weakness in the GAA's opposition to the Dublin based association and were convinced that a compromise settlement could be reached. When they met at the Wicklow Hotel, their president J.H. Christian reiterated his old conviction that the IAAA should control athletics and that the GAA should confine its activities to promoting hurling and native games. The remarkable success of the GAA in gaining widespread support from athletic clubs prompted the majority of those present to recommend amalgamation between the two associations. This was most unlikely because of Cusack's unequivocal statement published a few days before their meeting that 'we have made no overtures nor are we prepared to make overtures to the IAAA or to receive overtures from them.'[1]

The IAAA was not prepared to accept this as the official policy of the GAA so they directed a query to John M'Kay. He replied that he was not interested in amalgamation but in absorption of the IAAA. In spite of these rebuffs they wrote again to Cusack requesting that he place their resolutions for a settlement before a general meeting of the GAA. His reply that he had 'read the letter and burned it' was an indication of his deep-rooted antipathy for the rival association.[2]

At the adjourned convention of the GAA in Thurles in February 1886, Cusack presented his first annual report outlining the great achievements of the year and on the President's proposal it was unanimously adopted.[3] Davin referred to Archbishop Croke's request to withdraw the boycotting rule and stated that they would honour his wish.

Cusack moved that all duly qualified athletes be permitted to compete at sports held under the rules of the GAA. John M'Kay was doubtful about the wisdom of passing such a resolution without entering a condition that the opposing association should withdraw its similar rule. Davin counselled that any such condition would amount to entering into an agreement with the other party whom they did not wish to recognise at all. On that advice M'Kay withdrew his proposal and the motion was adopted unanimously. The president pointed out that since the boycotting rule was deleted there ought to be no obstacle to GAA athletes competing in England and he hoped that many would do so.

Referring to the proposals being put forward by the IAAA Davin stated that he was against any scheme of amalgamation with those who had not the remotest idea of the changes that the GAA had introduced among the Irish people. Resolutions to that effect had been adopted at numerous club meetings around the country and Davin was expressing the will of the general body of the membership of the Association.

Under the new rule allowing a duly qualified athlete to compete at GAA sports, an individual affiliated to a non-GAA club was allowed to take part in a sports under GAA control, but his club could not be affiliated to the GAA. The Lee Athletic and Football Club in Cork, which played rugby under the rules of the Munster National Athletic and Football Association, applied for affiliation to the GAA.[4] An official of the club, J. Murphy, who was one of the vice-presidents of the GAA, supporting the application claimed that the GAA football rules were not suited to a city club. Davin, on the grounds that the rules of the club were foreign to the objects of the GAA, ruled that as a football club they could not be regarded as a branch of the Association. On a proposal from John Cullinane, J.F. Murphy's name was erased from the list of vice-presidents and F.R. Moloney was elected in his place.

The Lee club called a meeting in Cork to protest (1) against the removal of J.F. Murphy's name from the list of vice-presidents of the GAA and (2) against the refusal of the Association to accept the affiliation of the Lee club. Present at the meeting were GAA officials M. Cusack and John M'Kay secretaries, and O'Crowley, handicapper. M'Kay defended the Association's decisions in regard to the points at issue stating that the Lee club members had misinterpreted Davin's rulings and as a club playing under rugby rules they were not entitled to affiliate to the GAA. The maturity and unity of purpose displayed by the officers and delegates in dealing with the business of the adjourned convention added considerably to the prestige of the association.

Under the surface however, a rift was developing between Cusack and some of his colleagues, particularly M'Kay and Wyse Power, his two joint secretaries. At the conclusion of a great tournament at the Corporation Grounds on the North Circular Road, Dublin in June 1886, there was a heated argument between Cusack and the treasurer John Clancy, mainly concerning finance. Cusack experienced difficulty in adjusting to the constraints imposed by a committee system. His propensity to make decisions on his own and to take action without consultations with his colleagues was irksome to his fellow secretaries. On the other hand Cusack kept closer in touch with Davin during the early months of the year.[5] In April he visited Deerpark where he and Davin attended hurling and football matches and explained the rules to the players. The claim of a second club in Athenry to affiliate was brought before a committee meeting in Dublin in May. In the absence of the president, John Clancy, treasurer, took the chair. To decide the issue, Cusack quoted Davin's ruling: 'Clubs may be formed in every parish and there shall not be more than one club in any parish unless with the sanction of the central council.' In June Cusack was again in Deerpark where he and Davin were reported to be working on the preparation of the second edition of the pamphlet on the rules of the association.[6] On these visits Cusack would not have missed the opportunity of discussing with the president the immediate problems confronting him.

The Tipperary resolution

Early in March 1886, Archbishop Croke in replying to an address of welcome from Dungarvan GAA club spoke in praise of what the GAA had achieved in reviving native games. He expressed his complete opposition to amalgamation with the IAAA and feeling fully confident that Home Rule was imminent he declared in reference to the opposition 'we will beat them out of the field of manly exercise as we have beaten them out of the field of politics'.[7] The *Freeman's Journal* report of the Archbishop's speech and of John M'Kay's statement at the Lee club meeting in Cork, did not find favour with Cusack. Within a few days, F.R. Moloney, secretary of north Tipperary GAA, submitted to *the Freeman* for publication a copy of a resolution adopted by the fourteen clubs in his area.

> To Mr E. Dwyer Gray, M.P.   15/3/1886
> 1. That the *Freemans Journal* and all the sporting papers in Ireland boycotted the GAA at its inception.
> 2. That the *Freeman's Journal* falsely stated in its report of the last hurling match between north Tipperary and south Galway that the rules as printed were thrown to the winds.
> 3. That the *Freeman's Journal* falsely represented Mr M'Kay as stating in Cork last Sunday that two Gaelic footballers had been carried off the field injured.
> 4. That the *Freeman's Journal* delayed and cut down the speech delivered by our esteemed patron, the Archbishop of Cashel in replying to the address presented to him in Dungarvan.[8]

Cusack's influence was clearly evident in this resolution. His antagonism to Dwyer Gray, the owner of the *Freeman* and its companion paper *Sport*, dated from the early days when he needed to get his message across to the public and he received no assistance from that quarter. He had made use of Moloney to score against Gray, a matter that the Nenagh man was to regret later on.

Two letters promptly appeared in *the Freeman* justifying the actions of the paper and rejecting the north Tipperary resolution.[9] Dwyer Gray, recognising that Cusack was the real author of the resolution, strongly rejected the charge that his papers were hostile to the association and stated that he found one of the GAA officials almost intolerable. He could not see that such statements as made by that person could serve the national pastimes.

The Archbishop wrote to the editor of the *Freeman* on 19 March 1886:

Dear Sir,

I have seen a resolution in this morning's *Freeman* purporting to come from the members of the north Tipperary branch of the GAA and, as one of the patrons of the society, I am pained to be obliged to say that as far as the *Freeman's Journal* is concerned, I believe the chief charges made against it in that resolution, to be utterly and absolutely without foundation. I am bound in honour to declare that, to my certain knowledge, it was I myself who supplied the report in question which, having been posted in Dungarvan on Sunday evening 7th, could not possibly be published in the *Freeman* earlier than Tuesday the 9th. I see no good can come to this association from public contentions of this kind.

T.W. Croke,
Archbishop of Cashel.

The Archbishop's letter did not deter Cusack from pursuing his confrontational course, although in deference to Croke he refrained from answering him in the public press. Instead he immediately wrote to him claiming that he could justify every clause in the Nenagh resolution and repeating his charge that the association had been handled vilely by Gray. Then as if associating Croke and Gray as his two opponents he concluded, 'as you faced the Pope and Errington so I will, with God's help, face you and Gray'.[10] It was a dramatic statement recalling the way the Archbishop had stood firmly to his convictions when he was called to Rome by the Pope as a result of connivance by George Errington, the unofficial agent of the Liberal government to the Vatican.

Cusack had overstepped the mark in challenging Croke's statement. The Archbishop immediately wrote to *the Freeman* revealing the substance of Cusack's letter and quoting verbatim the sentence above. He repeated that before going to Dungarvan he had asked *the Freeman* not to publish a report of his speech there until he supplied a summary of it himself, because he would 'not depend on unskilled amateur hands reporting it correctly.'

He concluded that although he had a deep interest in the GAA, he could not continue to be a patron 'if Mr Cusack is allowed to play the dictator in its councils and to run a reckless tilt with impunity against me or anybody who happens to disagree with him.'[11] This revelation gave rise to immediate widespread reaction against the terms expressed by Cusack. John M'Kay condemned the offensive tone in the letter, which was written without reference to the views of the association. He repudiated the use of intemperate language to further the cause of their great popular movement that did not need such advocacy. He praised Cusack's great work for the GAA, much of its success was due to his efforts. He believed that the present case could be met by an expression of regret. As for the inaccuracies in *the Freeman* report of his own speech in Cork, M'Kay rather generously accepted that they were the result of errors in telegraphing the report to the paper.

An editorial in the *Freeman* went much further than M'Kay did, declaring that Cusack was not suited to the position of secretary since he lacked the courtesy and discretion which were essential for the post; his quarrelsome nature and constant use of abusive language would ruin the association, the editorial claimed. The pent up feelings of annoyance with Cusack's aggressive and insolent manner were now released and criticisms of his actions poured in from the provinces, some of them demanding an apology and others calling for his resignation. The Dungarvan Club considered there was an obligation on them to make their views known to the public because of their association with Dr Croke's speech. Their feelings were expressed in a motion proposed by Dan Fraher in strong disapproval of the 'disgraceful attack on the Archbishop.' From Nenagh the central branch of the north Tipperary G.A.A. dissociated themselves from Cusack's insolent letter to his Grace of Cashel. Similar resolutions were adopted by clubs in Newmarket-on-Fergus, Bray, Sligo, Dunleary, (Dun Laoghaire) Wicklow and Cork.

Davin was dismayed by all the controversy and to bring the matter to a head he wrote to the press:

> Dear Sir,
> A meeting of the GAA will be held at an early date to consider its present position and future management. While I entirely disapprove of Mr. Cusack's action in writing such a letter to the Archbishop of Cashel

(a matter on which the executive of the Association was not consulted) yet I am in hopes he will do the right thing and try his best to make amends.

Yours truly,
Maurice Davin.
President G.A.A.[12]

Dr. Croke intercedes

In the meantime the Archbishop considered that the controversy had been blown out of proportion and he wrote to Davin advising an end to the matter:

The Palace
Thurles
March 26th 1886

My Dear Mr Davin,
I have seen your letter in this days *Freeman*.

This unpleasant affair has already gone far enough if not too far. So in the name of God, let it be forgotten.

Mr Cusack did not weigh his words sufficiently, but we all know he would not deliberately insult me.

Yours faithfully,
✠ T.W. Croke.

When Davin opened the proceedings at the meeting in Thurles on 5 April about fifty clubs were represented as well as all the officers with the exception of vice-president J.F. Kennedy of Cork.[13] Before commencing the business, the president asked for the views of the delegates as to whether the representative of the Lee Athletic and Football club be allowed to take part in the proceedings and vote. After strong feelings had been expressed for and against, it was finally agreed on the proposal of M'Kay that since the representative had been invited to the meeting it would be unfair to exclude him, but the Lee Club would cease to be affiliated after that day.

Remarking that they had to deal with an unpleasant business, the president said that they would hear Mr. Cusack's explanation. M'Kay read a short statement signed by Davin, Bracken, O'Crowley and Wyse Power to the effect that they had called to Dr. Croke and that in the course of the interview the Archbishop had made it clear that he did not wish to give any opinion or make any pronouncement that might influence the decision of the meeting on the important issue to be discussed. However, he suggested that the rule allowing money prizes in some circumstances should be rescinded or modified.

The pitch being cleared for a fair hearing, Cusack made his case clearly and effectively, presenting the facts as he saw them and displaying his exceptional powers of expression in the English language. He revealed that he had drafted the resolutions for the Nenagh clubs and that he had informed Dr Croke, Davin and Gray by telegram on the matter. He had written to the Archbishop by post because he understood that His Grace deprecated public controversy. At the time he wrote he was extremely irritated by what appeared to him to be the systematic omission from the *Freeman* of matters that would place the association in the best light before the public. He never intended insulting the Archbishop, but he agreed that the last sentence in his letter, if taken on its own, could be interpreted as insulting, yet the letter in its entirely would hardly justify so violent an interpretation.

Twice the president reminded Cusack that he was wandering from the subject. On the second occasion Davin called on him to withdraw or qualify the expressions he used in the letter. Cusack's response was that if he conveyed his message too bluntly or too plainly to the Archbishop no man living regretted it more than he did. The majority of delegates were favourably impressed by the open and direct manner in which Cusack had spoken, but some dissenting voices were raised calling on him to resign. Davin pointed out that Mr Cusack had withdrawn the offensive expression and had stated his regret for it, to which Cusack replied: 'Yes, and you may put it as strongly as you can in the presence of this great meeting.' When the poll was taken, thirty-six were in favour of accepting Cusack's apology, among them all the officers present. Fourteen voted for his resignation.

Davin's skill in controlling the meeting ensured that the business was transacted efficiently and democratically and to the satisfaction of all sides present. The principal business of the meeting having been decided, a number of motions were discussed. The rule permitting the award of money prizes at Gaelic sports had been the subject of controversy in the press for some time. M'Kay moved a motion to expunge this provision from the rule book and it received unanimous approval.

Another motion calling on members and branches to give preference to Irish manufactured goods was unanimously adopted. In an effort to place a curb on Cusack's impulse to write without consultation, a resolution was passed that in future all communications written on behalf of the GAA should be signed by the president and at least two of the secretaries. Such a restriction, although well-intended, would be almost impossible to operate in practice and Cusack's reaction to it was to refrain from writing any letters at all, and that did nothing to serve his case with the general body of members. While he could claim that the check imposed on him was unworkable, members and clubs that were left without communication from the executive had a serious grievance that was mounting day by day and would eventually precipitate drastic action.

Some confusion persisted regarding club affiliation, although Davin had laid down the conditions at a number of meetings. The question was raised at an executive meeting in Thurles on 5 June 1886 when Cusack and the other two secretaries attended.[14] The president pointed out that affiliations could be accepted only from hurling, football, handball and athletic clubs, but no club could be accepted unless it numbered at least twenty-one playing members. Wyse Power proposed that three handicappers be appointed on account of the increase in the number of meetings, but the president ruled that a change could not be made without a previous notice of motion. On a majority vote P.B. Kirwan was appointed to handicap the Grocers' Assistants' and the *Freeman's Journal* Club's meetings. The decision gave rise to serious differences later. Nothing untoward marked the proceedings at this meeting to give forewarning of the contentious nature of the next meeting in July.

Cusack ousted

Criticism of Cusack mounted in the following weeks and the other officers were receiving regular complaints about his neglect of administrative duties. He must have been aware of this through his loyal friends in some of the Dublin clubs. When he and Davin met at the great tournament in Dublin on Whit Monday, 14 June 1886, the president could hardly have refrained from mentioning the growing disquiet amongst the clubs. A special meeting of the executive, which Cusack failed to attend, was held the following day in the Imperial Hotel to consider what action to take. A decision was reached to call a general meeting on 4 July and notification was published over the names of M'Kay and Wyse Power. A week later Cusack reported that he and Davin were hard at work by the Suir arranging the contents of the second edition of the booklet of rules and determining as best they could how the association could be saved from the dangers that threatened it.[15]

A question arises as to the real purpose of Cusack's visit to Deerpark so soon after the Whit Monday meeting. Although the two men were in general agreement on the aims to be achieved, their personalities were distinctive and different. Cusack could not hold back from controversy. He regarded as personal enemies any who did not support the GAA from its inception, and even genuine members who did not fall into line with his ideas of how the association should function received the lash of his tongue. Davin was more lenient with lapses, treating them as part of the transition stage in the movement. He was reserved and even aloof at times and he considered controversy among members as useless and even counter-productive. It was a recurring theme with Davin that the association was founded to end dissension and not to perpetuate it. The individual views of the two leaders on what constituted the 'dangers that threatened the association' could not run in parallel.

One may ask whether the discussion between the two at Deerpark had anything to do with Davin's absence from the decisive meeting on 4 July. That meeting at Thurles attracted sixty-three delegates representing thirty-six clubs, seventeen of them from Tipperary, along with six of the officers. Maurice Davin, John Wyse Power and John Clancy were absent.[16] The large attendance was drawn in the expectation that a serious decision was about to be made. From the outset Bracken and Cusack were at loggerheads regarding every issue that was raised. When Cusack proposed Frewen for the chair, citing his considerable experience on Poor Law Boards, Bracken responded that there were vice-presidents in the room and Frank Moloney was appointed chairman for the day. Moloney who was only twenty-one at the time lacked the experience to effectively control a meeting of that size.[17]

Cusack questioned the appointment of P.B. Kirwan to handicap the Grocers' Assistants' Sports claiming that Kirwan was hostile to the GAA Bracken objected saying that such matters had nothing to do with the meeting whereupon Cusack left the room, but he was prevailed on to return. M'Kay read a letter from Wyse Power to Maurice Davin:

> With great regret I find it entirely impossible for me to attend the Executive meeting in Thurles and as one of those who signed the requisition which led to its being convened I think it is only due to the Association that I should set down briefly and plainly the reasons which compelled me to consider the calling of the meeting as an absolute necessity. The conviction has forced itself upon me that the manner in which the affairs of the Association are managed should be looked into without delay.
>
> From our friends everywhere come complaints of administrative neglect and charges of a serious kind. I send you a few letters of this nature which I received within the past week. They are fair examples of the complaints that are reaching me. I understand that you and most of my fellow officers have been similarly favoured. All this correspondence is to the same effect: it is one universal complaint that the gentleman who has most persistently made himself known to the public as the secretary of the GAA will not answer the letters that arrive, in consequence of his judicious advertising, addressed to him. Clubs complain that the receipt of their affiliation fees are not acknowledged

by him and that no notice is taken when they beg him to pay attention to their communications. Those who won medals at last year's championships complain that they have not yet received them and that their letters to the gentleman responsible have not been answered.

As a result of this unaccountable neglect of important business, the Association is suffering. How could it escape the result of all this mismanagement? Mr Cusack undertook that these medals should be delivered to the winners at Tramore in October last, but they have not been delivered yet. And when the successful competitors, who regarded themselves defrauded of what is rightly theirs, complain of this treatment they are not vouchsafed a reply. This may appear a trivial matter, but I hold it is more important than the framing of rules, the arranging of championship meetings or any other business that could occupy the attention of the Executive. The best rules will be useless unless they are properly administered. An Association, in order to succeed, must be managed with the same regard for its interest that any one of us would exhibit in the transaction of private affairs.

As a matter of fact the affairs of the GAA are utterly neglected by the gentleman who at the start took them into his hands. Is it not the naked truth that the work of the officers of the Association is for the most part apologising to correspondents for his remissness. In short we have one chief secretary who neglects his duty, and two secretaries, an assistant secretary, a president, four vice-presidents and a treasurer whose business it is to answer the complaints provoked by the chief secretary's carelessness. The sooner this state of things is remedied the better. If it is not put an end to at once we may say farewell to the prosperity of the Association.

John Wyse Power.

Bracken proposed that each speaker be confined to five minutes, but Cusack protested that he needed more time to answer the accusations. Bracken replied that the limitation did not apply to him and that he could have half an hour. Cusack accepted that he did not acknowledge the receipt of affiliation fees because he did not know what to do with them: in some cases two clubs from the one parish had applied for affiliation. With that he produced from his pocket a bundle of cheques and money orders and threw them on the table, thus refuting any suggestion of misappropriation on his part. He stated that he had asked the advice of a gentleman in whose judgement he had the greatest confidence, and his recommendation was that he should bring the money orders to the meeting. The indications are that he received this advice when he visited Davin. He agreed that he did not answer letters for some time because his hands had been tied behind his back by a resolution passed a few months previously.

M'Kay read a letter from the treasurer John Clancy whose duties as city sheriff prevented him from being present. He had, he claimed, endured many insults from Cusack; he had not received the accounts from him and when he wrote asking for them his letter was unanswered. After further exchanges Bracken enquired why the accounts had not been audited. This led Cusack into an attack on Clancy for purchasing some cups as prizes for the Whit Sports without getting previous approval from the executive. For this reason Cusack would not hand over money to pay for 'Clancy's cups,' but Bracken claimed that Clancy had bought and paid for the cups out of the gate money from the sports.

M'Kay speaking as one of the secretaries, stated that in his view Mr Cusack had arrogated to himself the working of the association from the very beginning; he was never consulted by him on any matter of importance and although he had written dozens of letters to him he had never received a reply. Mr Cusack had been offensive to him and to any other officer who disagreed with him and in his articles in *United Ireland* for the past three or four weeks he had attempted to besmirch him and other officers. Without any help from Mr Cusack he had worked hard for the association and he believed they had a duty to put an end to the bickerings which had been brought about by the actions of Mr Cusack.

Cusack recounted what he had done for the GAA. He had been abused by a hostile press and he had to defend the association against its enemies. He was stoutly supported by his friends, especially L.C. Slevin and T. Molohan. The discussion drifted into the area of gossip, about who said what and to whom during the Whit weekend. Gradually it deteriorated into unseemly wrangling among the principal speakers in the course of which it was claimed that Bracken called Cusack a liar, whereupon Cusack left the room for the second time. A few speakers, notably Mr Brennan, Dungarvan, and Mr Washington, Faugh a Ballagh, pleaded for moderation in the interest of the association. E.M. Walsh of Nenagh proposed and Thomas O'Grady, Moycarkey, seconded a motion that it be imperative on Mr Cusack to answer all communications addressed to him within three days of delivery. An amendment in the names of W.G. Fisher, Waterford and Mr M'Ginnis, Freeman's Journal Athletic Club declared that it was the opinion of the meeting that Mr Cusack had not properly discharged his duty as secretary to the GAA and that he be requested to resign.

On a division the amendment was carried by forty-seven votes to thirteen.

When the nature and extent of the complaints made against Cusack are taken into consideration it must be concluded that his dismissal was inevitable. His treatment of his colleagues, apart from the president, was inexcusable. His reluctance to delegate responsibility to his co-secretaries is difficult to understand. Their sincerity could not be questioned. They had both answered his call at the beginning, as the other officers had, when there was no prospect of material gain nor public acclaim for them, no more than for Cusack or Davin. Neither was there any assurance of the subsequent success that attended the movement. Both men had talents that could have been employed more as the Association spread and developed and the organisation and management became more demanding.

In such circumstances it is doubtful if even Davin's presence could have saved him, although the moderating influence of the president would have imposed a check on the exchanges. As it was, the conduct of the meeting added nothing to the credit of the association; it was in sharp contrast to the unity of purpose that marked the adjourned convention in February.

Before dispersing, the delegates adopted a motion proposed by vice-president Kennedy, and seconded by W. Fisher, instructing the secretary Wyse Power to request the editor of *United Ireland* 'to ensure that the G.A.A. should not be traduced in the columns of his paper by one of the former secretaries of the association who has been asked to resign.' The effect of the motion was to deny Cusack the only medium that was open to him to project his views to the public and it left him without a voice until he brought out the *Celtic Times* in the new year. It was a cruel and regrettable termination to his term as secretary of the association he had inspired and nurtured.

Popularity of games in 1886

The long drawn-out controversy about the control of athletics and the turbulent disputation in the council rooms, occupied the time and thinking of the leading figures in the Association in the first half of 1886, but they do not appear to have put a brake on the progress of the games. On the contrary, hurling and football had taken such a grip on the imagination of the mass of the population that they created their own momentum leading to an astonishing wave of enthusiasm for the organisation of Gaelic games.

Young and old thronged to the playing fields in the lengthening evenings of spring and on Sunday afternoons. Colourful tournaments dramatically presented with banners and bands were a major influence in attracting the crowds. The forerunner of such displays was a match played in Dublin between north Tipperary and south Galway, two areas where hurling organisation was more advanced than in other parts. Frank Moloney was at the head of affairs in the Nenagh district and in preparation for the big challenge he arranged a practice session in Ardcroney on 3 January and another in Borrisokane a few weeks later. From those taking part a team of twenty-one players was chosen drawn from Silvermines, Knigh, Nenagh, Lorrha, Youghalarra, Carrigatoher, Ardcroney and Kilbarron.[18]

Dan Burke of Gort was the chief organiser of the south Galway team that was selected from Gort, Kilmacduagh, Kiltartan, Peterswell, Kilbeacanty and Tubber. Their leader took great care in providing an attractive outfit for the players so that they might create a good impression on the Dublin onlookers. He had them dressed in green caps, white jerseys, knickerbockers and shoes.[19]

The game was fixed for Tuesday 14 February 1886 and both teams travelled by train on Monday, but on different routes. Moloney's team arrived at Kingsbridge where they were welcomed by Cusack and other officials and straightaway they went to the Broadstone station to welcome the arrival of the Galwaymen. The teams spent the night in the Clarence Hotel and received instructions on the rules of play. On Tuesday the players lined up four deep with hurleys on their shoulders and marched to the fifteen acres in the Phoenix Park. The pitch was laid out and stewarded by members of the Dublin and Wicklow clubs under the supervision of vice-president J.E. Kennedy. Cusack was the referee and the game lasted eighty minutes. In the first half they played with the Tipperary sliotar which the Galway men considered 'big and awkward,' and they changed to the lighter and smaller Galway ball in the second period. The spectators were impressed by the skill and fitness of the players and the game earned a lot of favourable comment. Victory rested with the Tipperary side who scored the only goal.

When the teams returned home the next day they were greeted by enthusiastic crowds with bands and torch bearers at the railway stations in Gort and Nenagh. They had given a lead that was followed by a series of monster tournaments at Thurles, Athlone, Kilkenny, Cork and Dublin. These exhibitions offer proof that clubs had the faith and expertise to undertake organisation on a large scale and make a success of it. Special trains were booked to bring thousands of spectators from distant centres; it was estimated that 15,000 attended the Thurles games at Easter. Such exhibitions inspired confidence in the ability of the GAA and they proved to be a major influence in popularising the games nationwide.

Three hurling and three football games were played in two fields in Turtulla, Thurles on Easter Sunday.[20] Five of the teams accompanied by their supporters and bands came by special train from Dublin. The Metropolitans lost by one goal to Holycross, Faughs beat Two-Mile-Borris and Moycarkey and Nenagh finished level in hurling. In football the contests were between Davitts, Bray Emmets and Dunleary in opposition to the local teams from Thurles, Rosanna and Templemore. All the arrangements were in the hands of a Thurles committee under the leadership of Hugh Ryan. It was a day of extraordinary excitement and enthusiasm unequalled in the affairs of the association up to then.

At the conclusion of the day's sport Maurice Davin led a parade of the teams with their supporters and bands to the Archbishop's house where Dr. Croke addressed the assembled crowd. His Grace congratulated the Gaels on a memorable day that gave an impetus to their national sports which up to then were for too long lying in the dust; all that was changed and they had become the favourite games in the country.

Thousands were present in Athlone on that same Easter Sunday to cheer for their favourites when Athenry representing Galway and Connacht played Clara, the Offaly and Leinster representatives.[21] According to the reports of the day all the business in connection with the game was conducted in Irish. In Kilkenny on 23 May 1886, three football games ended in draws, Callan and Waterford, Kilkenny and Dalkey, Castlecomer and Carrick-on-Suir; the Metropolitans travelled from Dublin to challenge Carrick-on-Suir in a hurling game but it had to be cancelled owing to the lateness of the hour.[22]

The tournament bears out the claim that Kilkenny favoured football rather than hurling in the early years of the GAA. Cusack refereed the games and afterwards he remarked that the southern teams were inclined to wrestle with their opponents. Wrestling in football was abolished at the meeting on 4 July on a motion put forward by Hugh Ryan, Thurles. A meeting of Waterford clubs criticised this change on the score that it was subversive of the Gaelic rules. Cusack subsequently supported that Waterford objection stating that the change had been made in the absence of the founders of the association, obviously referring to himself and Davin, but the president had made it clear that he favoured the change.[23]

At a tournament in Davin's field in Deerpark on April 18th, 1886, one hurling and two football matches were played. Davin and Cusack officiated at the games and explained the rules to the players.[24]

The dramatic success of the major tournaments raised the question of organising a display of the full range of Gaelic activities in the capital city. An exhibition of hurling, football and track and field athletics was planned for the Whit holiday weekend, 4 June 1886, in the Corporation grounds on the North Circular Road. The time and venue were specially chosen for the convenience of citizens so that the association would gain the maximum advantage. Davin, Cusack and the other leading officials took charge of the arrangements to make sure that the events ran smoothly. The lord mayor, Mr T.D. Sullivan and the lady mayoress attended and the musical entertainment was provided by the Artane Boys' Band who were making their first appearance at a GAA function.

Dublin Metropolitans beat Holycross by a goal and Nenagh scored over Athenry by a point. In football Davitts overcame Dunleary and the Templemore and Faughs game was undecided. It seems that Faughs were accused of getting assistance from another club and the award of the match to Templemore led to a lively exchange of letters in the press. The sports continued until late in the evening, the prizes were presented by the lady mayoress. The lord mayor, Mr T.D. Sullivan, addressing the crowd complimented the GAA on their achievements in reviving the old spirit among the people. At the conclusion the Artane Band played God Save Ireland and the great crowd sang the chorus.[25]

To outward appearance the day's events were an outstanding success and added considerably to the prestige of the association. Discord developed among some of the officers, whether it was the result of an undercurrent of ill-feeling of long standing, or on the other hand, an immediate reaction to inconsiderate remarks, it was an ominous sign for the association and had a direct bearing on the unhappy meeting on 4 July 1886.

The traditional attraction of hurling matches between Cork and Tipperary had its beginning at the great tournament in Cork on August 29th, 1886.[26] Three hurling teams and two football teams from Tipperary travelled by train to Cork where they were escorted to the Park by the Cork teams and three bands. J.K. Bracken was the referee and J.F. O'Crowley acted as timekeeper.

In hurling Aghabullogue struck the first blow for Cork by overcoming Killenaule, but Holycross levelled the score with a narrow victory over St Finn Barr's. The outcome of the first Cork/Tipperary test rested on the final match between Moycarkey and the Cork Nationals which O'Grady's men from Moycarkey won by one goal and one over (cúilín) against four overs. In football Fethard were leading Glanmire by four overs when the excitement got the better of the crowd and they invaded the pitch, so the match had to be abandoned. As the pro-gramme was running behind time the football match between Thurles and Aghabulogue could not be played.

Such major tournaments were the highlights of the Association's second year and their example was followed by smaller clubs in little towns and villages. Challenge games between parish teams became the norm and the local rivalries added to the excitement. Hurling and football superseded the attractions of athletics and the effect was seen in the way popular support gradually shifted to the matches. It is obvious too that Davin, whose background would suggest a leaning towards athletics, devoted more of his time popularising the games and bringing about standardisation of the rules. That is not to say that athletics were on the decline. Week after week the issues of *Sport* gave long lists of athletic meetings under Gaelic rules, giving proof that track and field events at local level were holding the interest of the public, but there is no denying that the games were assuming the premier place in the Association's activities. However, the national athletic championships at Ballsbridge on 11 September were poorly supported and were run at a financial loss. The argument that a Dublin venue was not suitable cannot hold up considering the huge crowd that attended the North Circular Tournament and the Freeman's Journal Sports earlier in the year.

Abuses at athletic meetings were increasing, events were being 'fixed' and the rule requiring a minimum number of field events on the programme was often ignored. To combat such infringements the executive at a meeting on 1 August, with Bracken presiding, insisted that the official handicapper must be in charge at all meetings except when special permission was granted and the programme had to be approved by either of the secretaries, John Wyse Power or John M'Kay.

Problems of indiscipline

Davin, although pleased with the dramatic progress made in hurling and football during the year, was painfully aware of the problems that were exposed all too often and urgently needed to be corrected or eliminated. It happened that advertised programmes could not be completed due to poor organisation and the lack of punctuality. There was a call for more efficient stewarding at games. Sometimes a match had to be abandoned before full-time when the crowd invaded the pitch. Betting or gambling on the result was one of the more serious abuses and at times was responsible for the disruption that occurred. Differences about the interpretation of playing rules were common enough and led to bad feeling between opponents.

The Association looked to Davin to give a lead in solving much of the problems that arose. He was acknowledged as the expert on the rules and his word was accepted as the law because of the respect he commanded. He was preparing a revision of the rules and a new constitution for presentation at the Annual Convention in November, but in the interim he made rulings on specific points that needed clarification. In regard to affiliations he confirmed that only hurling, football and athletic clubs could be accepted; in regard to players he announced that it was proposed to add a rule that persons playing under rugby or any other non-Gaelic rules cannot be admitted as members of any branch of the GAA.[27]

Having repeatedly made it clear that only one club could be affiliated from a parish, he became annoyed when local disputes were aired at executive meetings and he commented:

> 'The meeting was no place to bring up old quarrels. The GAA was started for the purpose of putting down such things and not perpetuating them. If a parish could not agree within itself it should be cut off until it agreed'.[28]

To deal with betting he proposed that vigilance committees should operate at GAA fixtures and clubs were asked to co-operate in eliminating this abuse that was a threat to amateurism in athletics.

The Freeman's Journal's weekly paper *Sport,* as if making up for its neglect in the past, praised the gigantic strides that hurling and football had made during the year. The GAA had started from a small base with thinly scattered clubs at the beginning of the year and by December the number had grown to nearly six hundred. 'Thus', reported *Sport,* 'the games were in the forefront of the Gaelic movement.'

But dark clouds were looming ahead. The association had not been far removed from political influences from the start. The principal Home Rule leaders gave it their patronage and at local level it enjoyed a harmonious relationship with the National League clubs. The defeat of the first Home Rule Bill in June cast some doubts on the efficacy of the constitutional movement to achieve any measure of independence. The Fenian tradition of physical force was still alive although dormant to a large extent since the adoption of the 'New Departure.' Some activists seized the opportunity to reactivate the IRB and the popular success of the GAA offered an opening to reach out to the youth of the country. Two weeks before the date appointed for the annual convention a meeting of the association was held in Thurles. Maurice Davin presided, two vice-presidents, J.K. Bracken and J.E. Kennedy, as well as J.F. O'Crowley the handicapper, were present. Neither of the two secretaries, J. Wyse Power and J. M'Kay, attended. About fifty clubs were represented. After a discussion on the rules the president announced the following revisions:

(i)   That persons playing under rugby or other non-Gaelic rules cannot be admitted as members of any branch of the GAA.

(ii) That only hurling, football, handball and athletic clubs could be affiliated to the association.

(iii) That no unaffiliated club be allowed under any circumstances to hold sports under the rules of the association.

Davin explained that they were determined to have their games played under old Irish rules in accordance with the spirit that inspired the foundation of the GAA.

P.T. Hoctor, an active IRB man, was elected vice-president and J.B. O'Reilly also reputed to be a member of the Brotherhood, was elected honorary secretary in place of Michael Cusack. It was the first time that either had attended a general meeting of the association. Timothy O'Riordan of Cork was appointed secretary in succession to John M'Kay who had resigned. James Butler of Thurles was appointed to the new post of recording secretary. The meeting elected the old Fenian John O'Leary as the fourth patron on a proposal by James Wise of Tipperary supported by J.K. Bracken.[29] The influence of the IRB was plain to be seen in the decisions made at this meeting and as preparations were being made for the second Annual Convention the president, Maurice Davin was the only non-IRB man on the executive. The changed situation raised fears in some quarters that the association might be used against the National League. A number of Dublin clubs came together the day before the Convention and adopted a motion deprecating any action that would tend to bring the GAA into conflict with the National League. But they were too late in realising the danger.

References

1. *Freeman's Journal*, 22/11/1885.
2. Ibid., 12/12/1885; *United Ireland*, 12/12/1885.
3. Report of Convention, *Freeman's Journal*, 27/2/1886, *United Ireland*, 6/3/1886.
4. O'Sullivan, T.F., op. cit., Dublin, 1916, pp 24-29.
5. *United Ireland*, 24/4/1886, 8/5/1886, 26/6/1886.
6. Ibid., 22/6/1886.
7. *Freeman's Journal*, 8/3/1886.
8. *Sport*, 21/3/1886.
9. Ibid., 21/3/1886; *Cork Examiner*, 24/3/1886.
10. Ibid., 21/3/1886.
11. Ibid., 21/3/1886.
12. *Freeman's Journal*, 27/3/1886.
13. *Cork Examiner*, 7/4/1886; O'Sullivan, T.F., op. cit., p. 30.
14. O'Sullivan, T.F., op. cit., pp 32-33.
15. Sport, 10/7/1886; *United Ireland*, 22/6/1886.
16. Report of meeting, *Cork Examiner*, 5/7/1886; *Freeman's Journal*, 6/7/1886; *Sport*, 19/7/1886.
17. Murphy, N. in *Nenagh Guardian*, 29/12/1984,
18. *Tipperary Advocate*, 2/1/1886, 30/1/1886, 20/2/1886.
19. O Laoi, P., *Annals of the G.A.A in Galway 1884-1901*, pp 23-25.
20. O'Sullivan, T.F., op. cit., p. 3; Fogarty, Canon P., *Tipperary's G.A.A. Story*, Thurles, 1956, p. 22.
21. O'Sullivan, T.F., op. cit., p. 31.
22. Ibid., p. 32.
23. *Freeman's Journal*, 9/7/1886; *United Ireland*, 24/7/1886.
24. O. Sullivan, T.F., op. cit., p. 31.

25.   Ibid., p. 32.
26.   Fogarty, Canon P., op. cit., p. 23.
27.   O'Sullivan, T.F., op. cit., pp 32-35.
28.   *Freeman's Journal*, 28/9/1886.
29.   O'Sullivan, T.F., op. cit., p. 35.

Maurice Davin Esq., Deerpark, Carrick-on-Suir.

Chapter 8

Davin's constitution adopted. IRB assume control

Maurice Davin presided at the second Annual Convention in Hayes's Hotel on Monday 15 November 1886.[1] The other officers present were J. Wyse Power and T. O'Riordan, the honorary secretaries, J.K. Bracken, F.R. Moloney and P. Hoctor, the vice-presidents and James Butler the recording secretary. Approximately eighty clubs were represented and about three-quarters of them were from Munster. Wyse Power's report on the year was adopted although it conveyed bad news on the financial position. The national athletic sports which should be the main source of income incurred a loss. Financial problems were to become a major cause of worry in the early years of the association.

The resignations of two officers, John Clancy, treasurer, and J.F. O'Crowley, handicapper, opened the way for new appointments and Patrick Hassett and F.B. Dineen were chosen to replace them; both were from Limerick and were supporters of the IRB. John O'Leary's letter consenting to be a patron of the Association was read:[2]

Dublin
12 November 1886

Gentlemen,

I need scarcely say that I am grateful to the Gaelic Athletic Association for the honour they have done me – an honour the more highly prized in that I am in such thorough sympathy with the aims and objects of the Association.

There are many societies and associations in Ireland about which good Irishmen may perhaps fairly differ, but your society appears to me one about which there can be no difference of opinion amongst right-thinking and well-feeling people. The main object is, as I understand, to make our young Irishmen healthier and stronger and to seek, by the attraction of manly Irish sports, to prevent young men from devoting their leisure time to less manly and possibly, less moral pursuits. It is, of course, a very great additional merit in my eyes that the Gaelic Athletic Association devotes much of its energies to the cultivation (and sometimes, I believe, the revival) of special Irish sports as hurling and the like.

One word, however, of warning before I have done. I do not know that you heard it, but you may. In England there was some time ago, and perhaps still is, a most complete cultivation of the body. Muscles were thought to be everything, and heart and brain were held of comparatively small account. I do not understand, or think, that there is any danger that your hearts will go far astray, but you should take care that in feeding your muscles you do not starve, or at least, imperfectly nourish your brains. In this, as in all matters that concern our national well-being, we can always get 'light and leading' from the pages of our prophet and guide, Thomas Davis:

'Mind will rule and muscle yield, in Senate, ship and field,
When we've skill our strength to wield, let us take our own again.'

Sincerely yours,
John O'Leary.

Davin, although he did not agree with the physical force movement, accepted that his fellow officers were sincere in their political beliefs, and he felt sure that they would co-operate fully with him for the advancement of the GAA. He placed before the convention for adoption the constitution he had drafted:[3]

1. ***Name:*** That the association be called the Gaelic Athletic Association for the preservation and cultivation of national pastimes.
2. ***Affiliations:*** That it shall consist of hurling, handball, football and athletic clubs; these clubs to pay an affiliation fee of ten shillings per year towards the funds of the association, the fee to fall due on the 1st of November, payable before the first of January.
3. ***Central Executive:*** That a central committee or executive be appointed annually; that it consist of a president, four vice-presidents, three secretaries, one record secretary, a treasurer and four members of the general committee; vacancies to be filled up by the executive at the first quarterly meeting held after the vacancies occur.
4. That two members from each affiliated club form the general committee.
5. ***General Committee:*** That the general committee meet in Thurles on the 1st of November each year to elect the central committee, hear appeals from decisions of county councils or central executive, and consider any important questions with reference to the working of the association.
6. ***Meetings:*** That the central executive shall hold quarterly meetings in the first weeks of January, April, July and October each year.
7. ***Powers of Executive:*** That the executive shall have power to disqualify clubs or individuals for breaches of the rules of the association and shall also have power to reinstate clubs or individuals when they see just cause for it.
8. ***Championships:*** That the association shall hold hurling, football and athletic championship meetings each year at times and places to

be arranged by the central executive. These championships to be the only meeting worked by the association proper.

9. **County Committees:** That committees consisting of a chairman, secretary and five other members be elected in each county to decide on questions of affiliations of clubs in their respective counties and arrange preliminary matches for hurling, handball and football championships, five to form a quorum; one delegate from each affiliated club in the county to have power to vote at the election of county committees.

10. **Expelling:** That should any member of a club be guilty of conduct liable to bring discredit on the association, he shall be expelled from the club to which he belongs and may not afterwards become a member of any branch of the association.

11. **Clubs:** That clubs may be formed in every parish and that only one club can be in any parish without the consent of the county committee; a club must have 21 members before it can be affiliated; and shall be governed by a committee of management to consist of a president, vice-president and secretary; other members of clubs to be elected annually, five to form a quorum.

12. **Exclusions:** That any member of a club in Ireland hurling, playing handball or football under other rules than those of the GAA cannot be a member of any club affiliated to the association and that members of any other athletic club in Ireland cannot be members of the GAA.

13. **Finance:** That should the affiliation fees of clubs, entrance fees of competitors and moneys taken at the gate in championship meetings not be sufficient to meet the working expenses of the association, the treasurer and secretaries be empowered to receive subscriptions for the purpose.

14. **Changing Rules**: That no new rule shall be introduced, nor any of the foregoing altered, except at a meeting of the general committee called for that purpose. At such meetings two-thirds of the affiliated clubs must be represented and three-fourths of those present at the meeting must agree on the question; a fortnight's notice of motion must be given to the hon. secs. who shall notify it to the clubs at least one week before the meeting.

15. **No Politics:** That the GAA shall not be used in any way to oppose any national movement which has the confidence and support of the leaders of the Irish people.

Recommendations: All dress material and other articles required in the games to be as far as possible, of Irish manufacture.

Regarding rule 11, that only one club can be in any parish it was argued that the rule was too restrictive but Davin was well aware that under the political circumstances of the time there was the possibility of two clubs being formed in a parish, each sustained under the influence of rival political groups. Such a situation developed in Athenry in 1886. A branch of the GAA under the captaincy of the IRB man, P.C. Kelly, was flourishing in the town, when the supporters of the National League applied to affiliate a second branch and their case was taken up by William Duffy. In a letter to Duffy on 4 May, Michael Cusack wrote:

> I have neither power nor authority to recognise it (the new branch). Mr Davin's opinion is that my colleague and myself should write to the captain of the branch that took the field first and ask him whether it is desirable that another branch should be established in the one parish. If he answers yes, the executive will gladly recognise the new branch and accept the affiliation fee which I have received. Should he express himself satisfied that our movement is in a sufficiently flourishing condition in Athenry and that it does not stand in need of another, the matter should be allowed to drop for the present.

(This writer was shown the letter by William Duffy's son in Loughrea in 1970 and copied it. The final sentence urged the recipient not to neglect to do his best in promoting the Irish language.)

Davin was anxious to avoid a situation where a breakaway group that had some grievance would form a rival club and cause a split in a parish to the general detriment of the association. Whenever such a problem arose he advised the parties to go home and settle their differences amongst themselves. However the rule did leave an opening for more than one club, for example in a city or large town, if the county committee considered that a single club was not capable of meeting the needs of all the population.

The constitution was Maurice Davin's testament for the association and he offered it to the convention of delegates for their approval. It was adopted unanimously and became the official constitution of the GAA, demanding the allegiance of all its members. It was a simple uncomplicated document and it has survived the test of years. As the association expanded, it became necessary to introduce qualifications, refinements and one major addition to the structure – the provincial councils – but the essential fabric of Davin's constitution has remained intact. The initiation of inter-club and inter-county championships was an inspired move that proved to be a major influence on the growing popularity of Gaelic Games.

The revised rules on hurling, handball and football drafted by Davin were adopted. He had made minor changes in the dimensions of a playing pitch and the goal area. Point posts were introduced for the first time and the laws specified how goals and points were scored. No number of points could equal a goal. A free puck could be awarded in certain cases and the method of taking it was laid down. If a player suffered an injury due to foul play and could not continue the game, a substitute could take his place. For a serious breach of the rules the referee was empowered to order a player off the pitch for part or all of the remainder of the game. Control of a game was entrusted to the referee and two umpires and in case of disagreement the referee's decision would be final. An umpire at each goal was to decide when a goal or point was scored. The sliotar, made of cork and woollen thread covered with leather, should be not less than 4½ inches or more than 5 inches in diameter and should weigh not less than 7 ounces or more than 10 ounces.

The rules for football were somewhat similar, in cases where they could be applied to both games. The football pitch could be smaller than in the case of hurling and wrestling was abolished. As a safety measure, nails and iron tips could not be worn on boots, but strips of leather were allowed on the soles. Slight changes were made on the dimensions of a handball court and the handball was not to be lighter than 1¾ ounces nor heavier than 2 ounces.

Rules for the hurling and football championships were framed. Entries were to be submitted before 1 January, with an entrance fee of 2s 6d per team. The county championships were to be played between the 1st February and the first week in May so that the champion team would be ready for the All-Ireland series.

Davin's expectation that the county committees could be formed before the end of the year turned out to be too ambitious. Davin was in favour of a motion to increase the number of vice-presidents to seven, and there were good reasons for the change. The growing number of clubs demanded attention and the officers were not in a position to answer all the calls on their time and advice. Wyse Power sponsored the motion, but Bracken strenuously opposed it, either because he feared that his own status might be minimised or that the way could be opened for the election of National League supporters. The result was a disappointment for Davin as the motion was lost by 160 votes to 57.

The IRB assume control

Not all counties responded eagerly to the constitution and before the end of the year 1886 only six county committees were formed. Wexford led the way, followed by Dublin, Cork, Tipperary, Wicklow and Waterford, but early in the new year Limerick Louth, Kilkenny, Meath, Galway and Clare had organised.[4] Only those twelve counties were included when the draws were made in February for the first hurling and football All-Ireland championships. To an undiscerning observer the association was a united movement advancing confidently to achieve its objectives, but in reality a bitter struggle was unfolding in its councils between the physical force IRB supporters and the constitutional National League for control of its affairs.

Other counties were targeted by the Brotherhood and a strong foothold established in at least six of them. Vice-president E. Kennedy presided at the Cork convention and Alderman Horgan was elected chairman. At the Limerick convention in January Anthony Mackey presided and P. O'Brien became chairman. The principal officials elected in Kilkenny were P.J. O'Keeffe and S.J. Dunleavy and Galway's chairman and secretary were P.C. Kelly of Athenry and P.J. Kelly, Killeenedema, later to be elected GAA president. All were prominent IRB men.

P.N. Fitzgerald, a native of Ballinacurra near Midleton in county Cork, was an ardent believer in physical force as the means of gaining national freedom and establishing a republic. He was one of the leading organisers for the IRB. In his employment as an agent for Daly's, Wine and Spirit Merchants, Cork, he travelled through many counties, using the opportunity to keep in contact with local IRB leaders such as P. Hassett and Anthony Mackey in Limerick, P.J. O'Keeffe and S.J. Dunleavy, in Kilkenny, J.K. Bracken in Templemore and J.B. O'Reilly in Dublin.

P.J. Hoctor, native of Newport in county Tipperary was committed to the Fenian tradition and he actively promoted the revolutionary idea as he travelled around the country in the double capacity of taking orders for a Tea and Spirit Company and organiser for the IRB. He and P.N. Fitzgerald were under regular surveillance by the RIC and their movements throughout the country are recorded in the reports of the Crime Special Branch.[5]

Hoctor accepted the office of vice-president of the GAA at the second annual convention in November 1886 but Fitzgerald declined to accept any position on the officer board of the Association, yet it was he who planned and directed the IRB moves to take control of the GAA.

In the months preceding the 1886 Convention leading IRB men were particularly active in organising the support of the club representatives. Hoctor was busy in County Clare and F.B. Dineen travelled through County Cavan. The National League or constitutional party either could not match the intensity and eagerness of the IRB campaign, or else they failed to realise the strength of the opposition with which they had to contend.

The IRB were honest in their conviction that nothing worthwhile could be achieved through the Parliament in Westminster and the defeat of the Home Rule Bill in 1886 strengthened that belief. As a secret society, they aimed to achieve their ideal of freedom through armed insurrection, and so they were placed in opposition to the popular constitutional Home Rule movement – the National League. Although officers of the GAA regularly protested that the association was non-political, from the beginning it had the patronage of the leaders of the Home Rule movement. Following the elections at the second annual convention the executive was almost totally in the hands of the IRB.

To comply with rule nine of Davin's new constitution, each county was to arrange a convention of clubs to elect a county committee. The way was now open to the rival political groups to gain control of the new committees by having their men elected to them. The IRB grasped the opportunity and some of their leading members secured official positions in their counties – Bracken and Moloney, two vice-presidents of the GAA, organised the Tipperary convention in Nenagh; Bracken was appointed chairman, Moloney treasurer and E.M. Walsh of Nenagh secretary. Clubs in the south and west of the county were aggrieved because they had not been notified of the convention. Ten clubs in the Clanwilliam area objected to the 'hole and corner' proceedings in Nenagh and entered a protest to the central executive. Their letter was rejected, their action condemned and the Nenagh convention was pronounced to be 'thoroughly representative'.[6]

The high-handed action of the county committee did not go unchallenged and opposition to their authority grew as the year advanced. Further protest meetings were held in Clonmel and Tipperary town where Bracken and Moloney were highly unpopular. They did not help their cause by their mismanagement of the county championships. The Fethard club received notice on a Saturday evening that they were to play Templemore on the following day in the football final. They refused to travel at such short notice and the match was awarded to Templemore. Moycarkey hurlers suffered a similar fate. They refused to play a championship game because they did not get word of the match until the night before. Their opponents, the North Tipperary Club, were awarded the match. These decisions left the officials open to charges of favouritism. Moycarkey's captain Tom O'Grady commented that 'all the trouble was brought about by a couple of gentlemen who wanted to ride to distinction on the backs of the North Tipps. and though he would call them ignorant he would not call them dishonest.'[7]

A strong IRB delegation, including P.N. Fitzgerald, T. O'Riordan and Anthony Mackey, attended the Clare convention and Edmond Bennett an 1867 man and a future president, was elected chairman. The Louth convention in January elected James Moore as chairman.[8]

Captain O'Grady's charge of ignorance on the part of IRB activists within the GAA is supported by their failure to realise, or to take into consideration, the harmful effect they were having on a movement that had for its aim the realisation of a cultural ideal. In their concern to gain control of the councils and committees, they spent time and energy that could have been devoted to the development of the association on the lines laid down by Cusack and Davin. In their relations with clubs they were provocatively dictatorial when what was needed was understanding and encouragement.

The constitution flouted

The new executive voted in at the Annual Convention held their first quarterly meeting in Wynn's Hotel on 27 February 1887.[9] Davin did not attend and Bracken presided over a Fenian dominated committee of J.E. Kennedy, Cork and P.T. Hoctor, Tipperary vice-presidents, P. Hassett, Limerick treasurer, J. Wyse Power, Dublin, J.B. O'Reilly, Dublin and T. O'Riordan, Cork, secretaries, Anthony Mackey, Limerick, P.C. Kelly, Galway, P.J. O'Keeffe, Kilkenny and F.B. Dinneen, Limerick, handicapper. Wyse Power tendered his resignation, leaving Bracken as the only one of the original founders taking an active role in the proceedings.

One can only surmise about the real reasons for the resignation of M'Kay, Wyse Power, O'Crowley and Clancy, all of them active officials up until the end of 1886. M'Kay had been an ardent worker for the association especially in Munster, and pressure of business as a journalist could be a valid reason for his resignation; Wyse Power was chairman of Dublin county committee and was also on the staff of the *Freeman's Journal*, a paper committed to the Home Rule party. It could not be far wide of the mark to suggest that the departure of these four officials was to some extent influenced by the turn of events which gave the physical force element a stranglehold on the executive. Moreover their resignation opened the way for the executive to replace them with members of the Brotherhood.

Without a dissenting voice, the meeting in Wynn's Hotel treated with contempt the constitution adopted a few months previously and proceeded to act as if the executive was the legislative body with the power to make whatever rules they wished. (1) Members of the RIC were to be debarred from membership of a GAA club and were not allowed to enter for any GAA sports or tournaments. It was an effort to curb the surveillance of IRB members by the RIC, but it ran counter to Cusack's persistancy in gaining entry for police and soldiers to compete at sports meetings. (2) Clubs were required to submit a copy of the programme and a list of the officials of any proposed athletics meeting, and the secretary of the executive was given power to prohibit any meeting if all the rules were not observed, thus nullifying the county committee's control of matters within the county. (3) But the executive went further to extend their sway over all the affairs in a county. In defiance of rules 3, 7, 9 and 14 of the constitution, the members of the executive were appointed *ex officio* members of each county committee with power to act and vote on all questions coming before such committees.

Effectively the executive was given the deciding voice on any issue within a county whenever they wished to exercise it. Their thirteen members could easily outvote the seven on the county committee and they could depend on the acquiescence of the IRB supporters who had been voted on to the county committees. No resolution critical of the executive or contrary to their wishes could be passed by a county committee. Hearing of any such intention the executive members could attend a meeting in sufficient strength to thwart the move. In one meeting, the democratic structure designed by Davin had been demolished and the IRB executive had assumed absolute control. In unconcealed irony they proclaimed that the Association was non-political and individual members were allowed perfect freedom of action in political matters.

Davin resigns

When Davin read the official report of the meeting he was appalled at the way the executive had assumed legislative powers to themselves and had disregarded entirely the constitution they had accepted a few months before. When he took the chair at Cruise's Hotel in Limerick[10] on 11 April he faced a hostile executive of the four vice-presidents, Hoctor, Bracken, Moloney and Kennedy, secretaries O'Reilly and O'Riordan, recording secretary Butler from Thurles, treasurer Hassett, handicapper Dineen along with Anthony Mackey and a newly appointed member R.J. Frewen of Aherlow.

Addressing the meeting, the president referred to the proceedings at Wynn's Hotel in February when he was unable to be present. He informed them of his astonishment when he read in the official report that they had adopted new rules and regulations in direct defiance of the laws of the constitution. He spent a considerable time pointing out that under Rule 14 of the constitution they had no power to make rules, and those they had passed were not binding on the clubs. He quoted Rule 14 which clearly stated that no new rule could be introduced nor any rule altered except at a meeting of the central committee, that is a convention of delegates, appointed for the purpose and a fortnight's notice of motion given to the honorary secretaries.[11]

He listed the rules they had presumed to adopt. He was not concerned so much with the nature of the rules in question; some he could support if properly put before a convention, others he would oppose. What he objected to was the violation of the constitution by the executive whose functions were set out in that document and they did not include legislative powers. He did not think that they could control the association unless they worked on the lines of the general rules adopted at the Thurles convention. He warned that they were leading the way for the introduction of dissensions in their ranks and a return to the old days when there was nothing but quarrelling and fighting.

In his response Hoctor evaded the main issue of the unconstitutionality of the actions taken by the executive. Instead he tried to minimise the effects of the *ex officio* rule they had adopted. He claimed it was merely a precautionary measure to be used only when a county committee was not doing its duty. The argument failed to impress Davin, but the executive refused to change the rules they had adopted. It was a rejection of their president and he felt it keenly. Never one to made a hasty decision he left the meeting before the close, conveying his disapproval of the negative response that he received. He would give some thought to the options that were open to him. He attended no more meetings of the executive during 1887 and he remained silent until he gave an interview to *the Freeman's Journal* in November.

Hoctor presided at the next meeting of the executive at Limerick Junction on Saturday 28 May.[12] Mackey, Frewen, Dineen, Hassett and O'Riordan were the only others to attend. Davin's letter of resignation was read and another from James Butler, the recording secretary, who apparently had decided to support the president's move. There is nothing to indicate whether the executive were taken by surprise by the resignations or whether they were expecting them perhaps angling for them. Yet the unanimous support for Frewen's proposal that Davin be asked to reconsider his position might be taken to mean that the members of the executive had not expected the president to resign. But Davin remained adamant.

For the rest of the year the IRB had full control of the executive, but their use of power was dictatorial and met with increasing opposition from the supporters of the National League who realised that they were losing their grip on the membership of the GAA. The activities of both sides were stepped up and the split in the association became more pronounced as the year advanced. Intensive surveillance of Fenian suspects was conducted by the RIC and the police files are an important source of information on IRB activities in the GAA at that period. The observations of policemen were augmented by inside information supplied by informers, some of them according to the RIC were high-ranking and trusted members of the Brotherhood. Police Inspector Waters reported to Dublin Castle, 'we now have some valuable informants in its ranks and we may hope for some good results from the animosities and jealousies which the split will occasion.'[13]

Some at least of those listed as advanced IRB men displayed a degree of ambivalence by their actions, seeming to support the IRB at one time and the National League at another. John Horgan and Timothy O'Riordan led a deputation to Swansea from Cork County executive of the GAA in June 1887 to make a presentation to the Liberal leader W.E. Gladstone, the proponent of Home Rule (see appendix 3). Robert Frewen was one of the leaders of the reception party to welcome Parnell to Tipperary in 1885.

Evidence of Frank Moloney's involvement with the IRB is rather thin, being confined to two entries in police lists of members. J.K. Bracken departed from the 1887 convention hall with the dissenting party, which was not consistent with his support for P.N. Fitzgerald and the IRB group. Vice-president, J.E. Kennedy also left the Courthouse and addressed the meeting at Hayes's Hotel declaring that he had resigned from the executive. Wyse Power and J.B. O'Reilly led a party from Dublin to the great tournament in honour of Parnell at his home in Avondale in November 1886.

Michael Cusack returned to the GAA stage in January 1887 when he launched a weekly paper *The Celtic Times* owned and edited by himself. He used the paper to promote the Irish language, culture and industry as well as to express his views on the origin and aims of the GAA. He made frequent attacks on the opponents of the association and his most bitter comments were aimed at members of the IRB executive. To counter the influence of *The Celtic Times*, the executive brought out what they termed the official organ of the association, *The Gael,* edited by Patrick Hoctor. Davin did not accept that it was the 'official organ' and when he questioned the executive about it at the meeting in Cruise's Hotel on Easter Monday 1887, he was assured by Hoctor and some others that it was a private venture with no financial input from the association's funds.

Only one issue of *The Gael* has survived, but it is clear from reactions to some of its comments that it took a strong aggressive line against its opponents, including *The Celtic Times,* the *National League* and *Freeman's Journal.* Davin subscribed to both weeklies as he was accustomed to do in regard to the national papers. He took numerous cuttings from The *Celtic Times* and preserved them, but no trace of anything from *The Gael* has been found among his papers. The tendency of the Hoctor paper to adopt an extreme line is indicated in a statement by Davin when interviewed by *the Freeman's Journal;* he said he had 'observed in two issues of *The Gael* paragraphs and a letter amounting to threats of personal violence to members who seem to differ from the present executive if they attended the convention.'[14] The cross-fire between the two papers enlivened the GAA scene, especially in the months preceding the convention of 1887, but it exacerbated the rift or political lines that was afflicting the association like a plague.

For much of 1887 controversies raged as the executive used their position to demonstrate their authority over all aspects of the association. Their main concentration was on athletic meetings and their rigid application of the rules led them into conflict with some athletic clubs that for bitterness rivalled the old controversies of 1885.

Handicapping controversy

In the summer of 1886 a major controversy erupted between the Hoctor executive and a number of clubs regarding the appointing of handicappers at athletic meetings. The Association had appointed its first official handicapper, J.F. O'Crowley of Cork, at the Thurles meeting on 17 January 1885 and he was to see that the GAA rules were observed at the important meetings under its control. Furthermore it was ruled: 'that no handicapper, starter, judge or official of any kind from outside the district where the sports was held could be elected without the consent of the central committee of the Association.'[15] Maurice Davin, in his letter of 11 February 1885, expressed reservations about the system of handicapping in vogue up to then and he was opposed to any handicapping in the field events. At a meeting of the executive in Thurles on 5 June 1886, at which Davin presided, Wyse Power proposed that three official handicappers be appointed because of the increase in the number of important meetings, but the president ruled that a decision could not be reached without the prescribed notice. However, a resolution was adopted appointing P.B. Kirwan as handicapper for the sports of the Grocers' Assistants' and of the Freeman's Journal Club.[16] Some opposition to Kirwan was expressed because he had been officiating under the rules of the AAA in the past. Davin was not present at a meeting of the Executive in Wynn's Hotel on 1 August 1886 and J.K. Bracken presided. A resolution in the names of Wyse Power and John M'Kay was adopted:

> Abuses having arisen in connection with the handicapping of athletic meetings held under the auspices of the GAA, the executive hereby announce that, as the rules at present stand, the official handicapper is J.F. O'Crowley of Cork and that no other handicapper will be recognised

without the special permission of the executive. Any violation of this rule will entail prohibition of the meeting at which such infringement is made.[17]

Handicapping was discussed at the Annual General Meeting on 15 November, 1886 when J. Nannetti of the Freeman's Journal club proposed: 'That any club when holding a meeting shall be at liberty to appoint any handicapper or other official they choose provided always that he be a member of the GAA.' After some debate Nannetti agreed to withdraw the resolution on the assurance being given that the spirit of the motion would be recommended to the executive.[18]

P. Hoctor presided at a meeting of the Executive at Limerick Junction on 8 May 1887 when Maurice Davin's letter of resignation was read. It was decided to proclaim an athletic meeting promoted by the Dublin Grocers' Assistants' Club on the ground that the club had appointed a handicapper of their own, J.B. Kirwan and did not avail of the official handicapper, F.B. Dineen. The club held they were entitled to appoint their own handicapper and they were supported by the Dublin County Committee. They went ahead with their sports despite posters being distributed by the Executive proclaiming: 'nationalists of Dublin: Down with dissension. Discountenance disunion. Support not the would-be wreckers of the GAA. Down with the men who would disgrace the GAA that has for its patrons tried, true and illustrious Irishmen, Archbishop Croke, C.S. Parnell, Michael Davitt and John O'Leary. Who are those men who try to prove that Irishmen are not worthy of self-government? – The Grocers' Assistants' Sports Committee. Do not by your presence at their meeting commit an act of treason to Ireland. God save Ireland.'[19]

When a number of Dublin clubs met in July 1887 strong voices were raised in condemnation of the action of the executive, but the chairman, Wyse Power, held that clubs should acknowledge the authority of the ruling body. However, he did not agree with the aggressive way the executive was trying to impose its will.

A few days later, on the 23 July P Hoctor presided at a meeting of the executive at Limerick Junction. Bracken, Kennedy, Moloney, Frewen, Dineen, Mackey and O'Riordan were present. It was specially convened to deal with the handicapping dispute and to make it clear that they were the ruling body in the association. An account of the meeting was communicated to the national press so that their message would get to the general public.[20]

In the course of a long address the chairman Wyse Power said that: 'the Grocers' Assistants' Club of Dublin had held their Sports recently in defiance of the Central Executive. They were there that day to decide whether or not they were determined to carry out the spirit of the constitution. While they occupied their present position it was their duty to put their foot down and put it down firmly on this insubordination that had lately exhibited itself. A second application was now made on behalf of the Freeman's Journal Club to appoint Mr Kirwan as handicapper of their forthcoming sports. The *Freeman's Journal* might think that it was a strong power in the country. It had professed that it was preparing the people for self-government but it had attacked the Association in a most unwarrantable manner. They had been attacked from many quarters but the unveiled monster had now come to the front and that was the *Freeman's Journal.*

Mr Wyse Power said he was glad to tell them that the youth and manhood of the country was on their side and they would not allow Mr Dineen to be struck down. They would let the clubs all over the country see that they were determined that the rules of the Association would be carried out in a fair and honourable spirit and they would protest in the strongest manner against the outrage and injury the *Freeman's Journal* had tried in inflict on the national feeling of the country.'

Bracken emphatically denied that he had given an assurance at the Annual Convention that the handicapping rule would not be rigidly enforced and Hoctor agreed with him. Those present adopted a united front in regard to the Grocers' Assistants and three resolutions were passed: (1) expelling the club from the association, (2) expelling also those members of the Dublin county committee who supported the Grocers, and (3) suspending for three months any athlete who competed at the sports.

J.P. Nannetti, who had proposed the amendment at the Convention in November 1886, responded to Bracken in a letter to the press,[21] re-affirming his account of Bracken's promise at the 1886 Convention. If Nannetti's account is correct and it has the ring of truth about it, the executive created a dispute on very shaky ground. Having taken a stand they persevered in pursuing the matter when it would have been of greater benefit to the Association to have adopted a more reasonable position.

The extreme penalties imposed by the executive broadened the controversy. On 24 July 1887, Archbishop Croke, when replying to addresses from a group of GAA clubs in the Charleville area[22] said:

> There is a danger with which we have been more than once confronted, a danger to which a leading Dublin journal has called public attention, and that is the desire recently shown by some members of the Executive literally to rule the roost, to carry everything with a high hand and to be

Deerpark House home to the Davin's, built 1884.

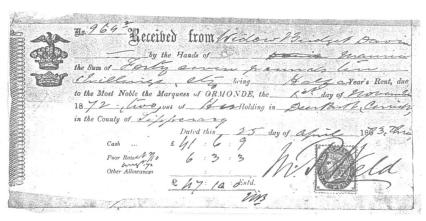

Rent receipt from marquis of Ormonde 1873.

Davin Family Tree

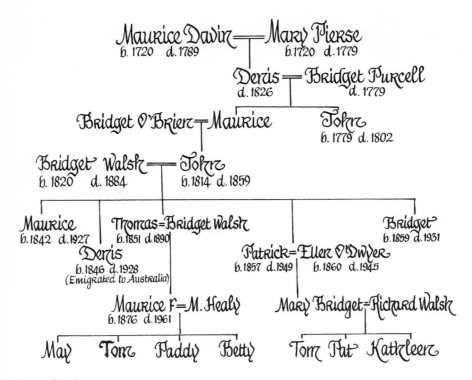

Maurice Davin —— Mary Pierse
b. 1720   d. 1789   b.1720   d.1779

Denis —— Bridget Purcell
d. 1826   d. 1779

Bridget O'Brien —— Maurice   John
b. 1779   d. 1802

Bridget Walsh —— John
b. 1820   d. 1884   b.1814 d. 1859

Maurice   Thomas = Bridget Walsh   Bridget
b.1842 d.1927   b.1851 d.1890   b.1859 d.1931

Denis   Patrick = Ellen O'Dwyer
b.1846 d.1928   b.1857 d.1949   b.1860 d.1945
(Emigrated to Australia)

Maurice F = M. Healy   Mary Bridget = Richard Walsh
b.1876 d.1961

May   Tom   Paddy   Betty   Tom Pat Kathleen

Davin family tree.

Athletic championship results recorded in Davin's notebook 1873.

Hints on training from Davin's notebook.

Sports at Clonmel 1882 – Pat Davin preparing to jump.

March 21.

Private

The Palace,
Thurles

My dear Mr Davin,

I have seen your letter in the days Freeman.

This unpleasant affair has already gone far enough, if not too far.

So, in the name of God, let it be forgotten.

Mr Cusack did not resign his undy sufficiently: but we all know he would not deliberately insult you.

Yrs faithfully

+ T. W. Croke.

Mr M Davin —

Archbishop Croke's letter to Davin, March 1886.

Archbishop Croke
"We have no reason whatever to be anything but Irish."

Committee Meeting Oct.ʳ 7th 1881.

Members present M Davin (in the chair) also present GW Bright M Meagher & F Nugent and J.J. Heard.

Mr Wm Crawley proposed by M Davin and seconded by M. Meagher.

Mr Rd Grey proposed by J F Nugent and seconded by M. Meagher. Mr Mc Power proposed by J & F Nugent and seconded by M. Meagher. To be balloted for Oct.ʳ 14th.

Proposed by M Davin and seconded by M Meagher that Messrs Noakes & Rickalls and J Cleary be paid for prizes supplied at last meeting.

Maurice Davin

Above: Extracts from minutes of Carrick-on-Suir AACFC, 1887.

Below: The local context of Deerpark House, the Davin homeplace.

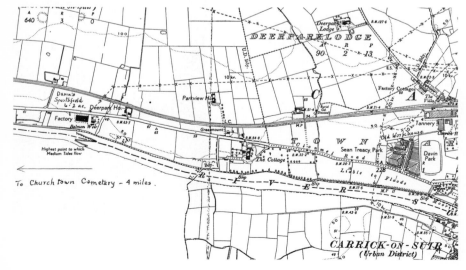

The new member of the G. A. A., otherwise known as the G. O. M., takes a hand in playing a game for Ireland. And that he will put the ball through the goal is a sure thing.

Cartoon from *The Dublin Weekly News*, 11 June 1887, on occasion of GAA presentation to Gladstone.

Central Council of GAA after reconstruction convention January, 1888.
Back row: J.J. O'Reilly, Dublin; Dr O'Connor, Kildare; Rev J. Concannon; John Cullinane, Tipperary; George F. Byrne, Meath.
Middle row: Rev C. Buckley, Cork; Alderman Mangan, Louth; Wm. Prendergast, Hon. Sec., Clonmel; James O'Connor, Wexford; Rev E. Sheehy, Limerick; J.J. Cullen, Dun Laoghaire, Record Sec.
Front row: R.J. Frewen, Treasurer, Aherlow; Maurice Davin, President; T. O'Riordan, Hon. Sec. of the Central Council, Cork.

The 'Invasion' team taken on steps of St Patrick's College, Thurles before departure for America in 1888. William Prendergast is on extreme right in front row. Maurice Davin is third from left (with hammer) in second row. Pat Davin is third from left in back row. The team captains, Tom O'Grady, Moycarkey, Tipperary and P. P. Sutton, Dublin are in the front row.

Another photograph of 'Invasion' team taken at an unknown location.

Sketches from *Boston Globe* relating to 'Invasion' team.

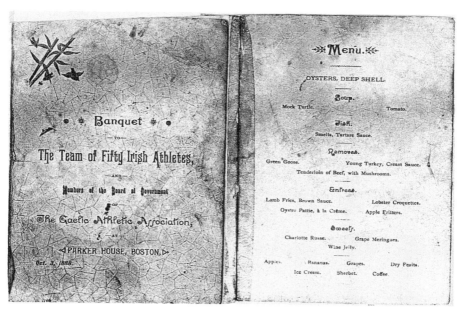

Menu from 'Invasion' banquet.

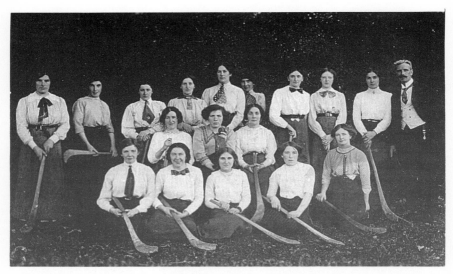

Carrick-on-Suir Camogie team, 1913. Player second from right on back row is Bridget Davin, daughter of Pat Davin and mother of Pat Walsh, Deerpark. The trainer is J.J. Healy.

Pat Davin, brother of Maurice, and his wife Ellen in 1944.

Maurice Davin, second from left, at Deerpark with his sister Bridget, third from left, Pat and Ellen Davin and their daughter, Mary Bridget, at left.

Davin headstone.

Joseph O'Ryan, one of the founders of GAA.
(See Appendix 2 p. 223).

Davin Memorial Park entrance, Carrick-on-Suir.

Davin's home with farm buildings.

Davin's grave at Churchtown overlooking the River Suir.

Group at opening of Davin Memorial Park in 1932. From left: D. Cleary, J. Keating, W. Clifford, Pat Davin, Fr John Meagher, Tom Kiely, Fr Lee, D. Dalton.

constantly at loggerheads with somebody. This regretful tendency cannot be sufficiently condemned. Everything savouring of dictation should be avoided and as long as the fundamental rules of the Association are complied with mere formalities should be left free, subject in the main to local partialities and influence, in so far at all events, as not to give rise to any unseemly squabbling and contention. We have progressed amazingly in a short time. Let us not prevent future progress by silly strife over trifles, or by irritating personalities. The object of the Association is to promote our national sports. If that object is kept steadily in view a good deal of latitude may be allowed as to the means of attaining it.

A week later representatives of thirty-six Dublin clubs came together to consider the decisions taken by the executive.[23] The chairman, Wyse Power, spoke of resigning because it seemed to him that by being a member of the GAA one had to face quarrels and squabbles that were no help to the association but rather injurious to its purpose.

Local supporters of the national executive, representing the Kickham and Grattan Esmond clubs, proposed that the county committee should resign but the majority countered with a vote of confidence and at length it was decided by fifty-six votes to six to refer the matter in dispute to arbitration by Dr Croke. A flood of letters to papers followed as each side took up entrenched positions.

Uncommitted observers who had watched the development of the association were impressed by its ideals and the influence for good that it was having on the youth of the country. Now they were dismayed as they witnessed its leading members splitting into two conflicting parties that threatened to destroy what they were committed to serve. T.W. Rolleston, poet and scholar, expressed public concern at the course being pursued in a letter to *the Freeman's Journal*.[24] He observed: 'that it would be nothing less than a national calamity and a disgrace if the dispute amongst the members of the Gaelic Athletic Association should break or even weaken that institution.' Referring to the handicapping rule, he felt that the Grocers' Assistants had some reason to believe that the executive would use their discretionary power in the case of their meeting.

On the other hand if the executive did not know how to vindicate their dignity and authority in the face of the defiance of that authority, Gaelic men would have reason to be ashamed of them. He made a suggestion which he thought would bring about a resolution of the problem and restore good relations between the parties. He revealed that the *The Gael,* the accredited organ of the executive, had published an unsolicited and honourable expression of regret for its own 'excesses in this line'. Accepting that the Grocers' Assistants were not deliberate enemies of lawful authority he asked could they not frankly admit their error.

Rolleston's intervention at this stage in an effort to heal the split is an indication of the status which the Association had achieved nationally and the impact it had made on public opinion. However, he failed to get a positive response. The Grocers' Assistants were no longer on their own as stronger forces were brought into play on their side.

P.B. Kirwan became the target of attacks by *The Gael* on the grounds that he had opposed the GAA in its early days. Kirwan replied that he had been secretary of the Freeman's Journal club before the GAA was founded, but he had 'fought the battle for the GAA' many a time since. *The Gael* refused to publish his letter.[25]

Although the GAA and the IAAA had mutually removed restrictive rules early in 1886, it is clear that the IRB dominated executive retained their hostility to anyone who had been associated with the IAAA in any capacity. They adopted a high patriotic stand and they were apt to regard those who criticised them as traitors or West Britons.

Replying to the invitation from the Grocers' Assistants to arbitrate in the dispute, Dr Croke remarked that if it were true that Mr Bracken undertook authoritatively to recommend the practical adoption of the amendment in the matter of handicapping proposed at the Thurles convention, there was little room for arbitration and none if the present executive was illegally constituted. Nevertheless, if he was to arbitrate, he wished to have his brother patron, Mr Davitt, with him. A few days later the executive met in Moloney's Castle Hotel in Nenagh.[26] Hoctor was in the chair and the others present were Bracken, Kennedy, Moloney and Mackey. They suspended the John Mitchel Club in Glasthule and the Dunleary club for breaches of the rules at their sports meetings, it being alleged that betting was allowed and that suspended athletes were permitted to compete. Sensing growing opposition to their authority, the executive issued a general warning that they 'would expel from the association any club that violated the rules.'

No compromise

The Freeman's Journal Club appointed their own handicapper for their sports fixed for September. This seemed to be a direct challenge to the executive. *The Freeman* gave strong support to the National League and Parnell's Home Rule movement and it took a definite stand against 'the men of violence.' The executive responded immediately by imposing a ban on the sports and threatening to suspend any athletes who competed there. The club ignored the ban and went ahead with preparations for their Sports. They also renewed the appeal to Archbishop Croke to arbitrate on the handicapping issue. Hoctor's reply to this offer was a flat refusal to accept arbitration by the Archbishop or any other patron. In his statement published in *The Gael* he stated:

> To cut the matter short, we do not want one or all of the patrons as judges. We wish them to remain in their high and dignified position of honour from which they should only descend to countenance, support or protect us, but certainly not to judge and sentence us. We further can only recognise as judges in this, as in all other matters belonging to the Gaelic Athletic Association, the Central Executive of that body, with of course, the inevitable annual reference of all matters in dispute to the convention as the final and supreme court of appeal.[27]

It was a calculated snub to Dr Croke and the other patrons, far removed from the reference to them as 'the tried and true patrons' a few months previously. But it was probably aimed also at the *Freeman's Journal* because of the strong line taken by that paper against the IRB and in favour of the National League and the Parliamentary Party. In attempting to read the mind of the executive during these turbulent months, one faces a distinct disadvantage in that no file of the issues of *The Gael* is available. *The Freeman* and its companion paper *Sport* gave extensive reports and comments on the course of events, but they could be classed as opposed to the executive while Cusack's *Celtic Times* was positively hostile in its comments. It is difficult to understand why the executive choose the course they followed in regard to the minor issue of the handicapping rule, which to say the least of it, was open to misinterpretation.

The Archbishop made one last attempt to reach a solution to the dispute between the Freeman club and the executive. His proposal that the official handicapper and the club's appointee should act together at the meeting received the backing of Davitt and Parnell; a final settlement could be deferred until the annual convention. However, the executive refused to accept any offer of compromise. The Freeman club went ahead with their sports and suspensions were imposed on the club and anyone involved in the meeting.

The firm and steadfast decisions taken by the executive were applauded by their supporters. Their nationalist physical force philosophy made an appeal to idealistic youth. Although they were a minority, their number was not inconsiderable and they were well organised. They made no concessions to those who did not agree with them and so they failed to gain widespread support.

The disenchantment of the south Tipperary clubs with Bracken and Moloney was extended to the national executive who were backing the two vice-presidents in their self-assertive control of the county

Tipperary committee. In July, John Cullinane presided at a meeting of south Tipperary clubs in Clonmel that was called to express their opposition to the county committee. They asked for the return of Davin, the father of the association and the rudder by which the GAA could be guided to victory.[28]

Delegates from clubs in west Tipperary and parts of Limerick gathered in Tipperary Town on 9 October and adopted a resolution to oppose the re-election of J.K. Bracken and F.R. Moloney at the coming convention because 'they could not be useful members of the central executive.' A fortnight later a large attendance of delegates from south Tipperary and parts of Kilkenny convened at Clonmel[29] and unanimously called for the return of Maurice Davin to lead the association.

Davin breaks his silence

Two days later, on 25 October 1887 Maurice Davin broke his silence on GAA affairs and in a letter to the editor of the *Celtic Times* he made a number of important suggestions and comments.[30]

> Deerpark
> Carrick-on-Suir
> Oct. 25th, 1887

Dear Sir,
Now that the time appointed for the Annual General Meeting of the Gaelic Athletic Association is approaching I wish to offer a few suggestions for the consideration of its members.

The Annual Convention of the GAA should be held at Thurles on the first of November next. According to the Constitution of the Association this Convention would consist of two members from each affiliated club. The business of the meeting would be to elect the Executive for the coming year, hear appeals from decisions of County Councils and the Executive and consider any important question with reference to the working of the Association. With the great number of clubs affiliated, the Convention should be very large, provided all were properly represented.

Large meetings were necessary in the earlier days of the Association, so as to find out what code of rules for the games would suit all districts. It is necessary to show some of our present friends how much the people were in favour of the movement before they came to our side.

Now, from my experience of some of the past general meetings and also taking into account the bitterness which appears to exist between some of the members, I feel certain the business cannot be properly transacted at a large convention. I believe it would be better for the interests of the Association to hold a convention of members representing counties – say, two from each county having thirty clubs or over, and one from each county having fourteen clubs or over. I would not have more than two members from any one county.

It would be the business of this convention to revise the Constitution and decide how the Executive should be formed in future. When this is done the Executive may be elected by the convention, or by the county clubs if it be thought proper to have county representation fairly divided on the executive and I believe the latter will be found the best system.

I see the executive have postponed the Annual Meeting to the 9th of November. If they had power to do that they have power to postpone it for another month so as to allow all to be prepared. If the course I have suggested be agreed to, the County Councils could proceed at once to organise County Conventions and elect members to represent them at the Annual Meeting. The county committees for the coming year might be elected at the same time, as I believe there will be no need to change the rule on that head.

County elections could be held on 21st of November and the Annual Meeting on 12th of December. All elections to be held by ballot if possible.

It is a pity that men who have worked so hard before this for the benefit of the Association should now disagree so much about the manner of governing it. Ill-feeling has spread, and bad motives have been attributed in many cases where there is only misunderstanding of the rules or of the position of some of the parties. All bickering should cease. They have done no good.

In conclusion I would say to the hurlers, football players and athletes generally: one of the objects of the founders of the GAA was to put down factions and make you be friends with one another. Do not allow your Association to be split up in parties by anyone. There is no reason why you should. Union amongst Irishmen was never more wanted than at the present time.

Yours truly,
Maurice Davin.

It may be said that Davin was naive in expecting a positive response to his appeal from parties divided by two distinct and separate ideologies. In his view, he said what needed to be said if the GAA was to be saved from destroying itself. Since he resigned the presidency in May, he had remained aloof from the bitter dispute that was raging. It was entirely against his nature and principles to engage in quarrelling and abusing his fellow members.

This is not to say that he took no part in activities outside the council rooms. He organised hurling and football matches, acted as referee and attended sports meetings. He was listed as judge for the weight events at the official tournament in Tralee in conjunction with the national championships in August, but it is doubtful if he attended. Yet it shows that the executive recognised his standing among the members and probably made use of the occasion to make a friendly gesture to him.

Cusack in the *Celtic Times* gave a warm welcome to Davin's letter 'although long delayed,' and unreservedly recommended the scheme he proposed for the convention. Davin had sound reasons for delaying any public expression of his views – (1) the annual convention was the proper place to deal with problems, (2) he was waiting for the time when his voice would gain the maximum attention, and (3) the executive should be given time to show whether they were competent to lead the Association. However, by not speaking out earlier he left very little time to bring about the changes he desired before the Convention. He had correctly foretold the chaotic conditions that would obtain at the convention if every club had direct representation there. His attempt to gain more time by a postponement for a few more weeks did not impress the executive who saw that their advantage lay in going ahead on the date they had fixed. His proposals were backed by the *Freeman's Journal* and *Sport* as well as by Cusack's paper, but the reaction of the executive can only be surmised because *The Gael* is not available.

His message acted as an inspiration in a number of counties where a change of leadership was desired.[31] At the Wexford convention on the last day of October, Davin's 'well-considered proposals' were unanimously approved and his return was welcomed. The following day in Waterford, several speakers called for the election of Davin as the one man above all others who could make the Association what it ought to be.

The Wicklow convention decided to endorse the views of Maurice Davin. Thirty-two clubs were represented at the Galway convention on 23 October. Peter Kelly, who was later to be elected president of the GAA, was in the chair and he appealed to all clubs to be present at the annual convention in Thurles, but there is no mention of any support for Davin's proposals. P.C. Kelly of Athenry warned that a fierce attack would be made on the executive by persons who in the earlier days would not look at them. He was expressing his support for the executive, but his reference to the earlier days, while true in regard to the *Freeman's Journal,* could have no validity in the case of many who were firmly committed to the principles of the GAA, but were strong in their opposition to the executive.

Davin interviewed

On 2 November, the *Freeman's Journal* published an interview with Maurice Davin in which he gave his views on a wide range of issues concerning the Association: Asked about his reasons for withdrawing from the Executive Davin replied:

It is rather a long story but I will make it as brief as I can. Early in the present year a meeting of the executive was held in Wynn's Hotel, Dublin. I was unable to be present and when the official report of the proceedings reached me I was astonished to find that the executive had adopted new rules and regulations in direct defiance of the laws of the Association. Rule 14 of the constitution lays down very clearly that 'No new law shall be introduced, nor any of the foregoing altered except at a meeting of the general committee called for the purpose. At such meetings two-thirds of the affiliated clubs must be represented and three-fourths of those present at the meeting must agree on the question. A fortnight's notice of motion to be given to the hon. sec. who shall notify it to the affiliated clubs at least one week before the meeting.'

I may remark, for the explanation of the public, that the phrase 'meeting of the general committee' means a convention of delegates. But what do we find the executive doing in face of that clear and distinct rule?. They passed a rule that no tournament of any kind under GAA rules would be permitted in any county without the sanction of the county committee. They passed a rule disqualifying members of the constabulary from competing at sports and tournaments. They passed a rule that every club about to hold sports should forward a copy of the programme and list of officers fourteen days previous to the holding of the Sports to the executive Hon. secretary of the province, who had power to suppress such Sports if not in accordance with the rules. And finally they passed a rule appointing themselves ex officio members of the county committees with power to act and vote on all questions coming before such committees.

I may remark here that I am not at all concerned now with the necessity for the rules thus adopted. Some of them I would support and others I would not support and I may add that with regard to a few of them, rules quite as effective were already in existence, though the executive, strange to say, appear to have been ignorant of the fact. It is to the violation of the Constitution by the Executive that I object.

I decided to await the next meeting of the Executive before making any formal protest. The meeting was held in Limerick on Easter Monday. I, as President of the Association, occupied the chair and for a considerable time I discussed with the other members of the Executive then present their action at the Dublin meeting. I pointed out to them that under the Constitution they had no power to make laws and told them plainly the rules they had adopted at Wynne's Hotel were not binding on the clubs. I said I did not think they could control the Association except they worked on the lines of the general laws and rules adopted by the Convention at Thurles and warned them they were leading the way for the introduction of dissensions and factions into the ranks; that they were bringing us back to the old times when there was nothing but quarrelling and fighting.

The Executive, however, were determined to stick to their new rules. There were two courses now open to me. One was to call a convention of delegates to consider the action of the Executive, and the other was to resign, and see how things went on under the new management. I thought the first course would result in arousing excitement among the clubs and lead to disputes and perhaps to a division in the national ranks; and so I determined on the latter course, being consoled by the thought that no matter what the Executive did, the fine old Irish games of hurling, football, weight-throwing and jumping would go on increasing in popularity.

On the 18th of April I wrote to Mr. O'Riordan, Hon. Sec. Cork: 'As I find that I cannot agree with the other members of the Executive in the present system of managing the Association, I have decided to resign the presidency'.

Asked if the Executive included their new rules in the Constitution, Mr. Davin replied: 'Yes, I find them printed in the book of rules. The Executive published them without sending me proofs, though as president I was, in a way, responsible for them. The wording of a few of the old rules was altered and even some rules were omitted. The omitted rules were those that enacted that one-third of the items on the programme of every sports shall be weight-throwing and jumping; that where records are claimed the ground must be proved level, or the performance done both ways, and that in weight-throwing contests the weights shall be properly tested. They also left out newspaper articles from national organs, which many considered had made the Association.'

When asked for his opinion on the ex officio rule he replied: 'I strongly disapprove of it and I told the Executive in Limerick what I thought about it. One of many principal objections is that under it no resolution adverse to the Executive could be passed by any County Committee. If the Executive got wind of the intention to move a resolution hostile to them they could come down in all their strength to swamp the County Committee. Freedom of action under such a rule could not exist.

Mr Davin said he would favour a rule under which every county would be represented on the Executive. 'I think it would be very satisfactory to the clubs', he said. 'An executive elected under such a rule would be more in touch with the clubs and would be better acquainted with the feelings of each county, in the matter, for instance, of the arrangements for championship meetings.'

Regarding the dispute between the Executive and the Grocers' Assistants and other Dublin clubs, Mr Davin said:

I must say there is a law obliging promoters of large meetings under GAA rules to engage the services of the official handicapper. I do not altogether approve of this rule and I would like to see it amended, as it affords many opportunities for disputes. It certainly was never intended to be used on hard and fast lines and was to apply solely to large meetings. At the last Convention in Thurles a delegate from Dublin moved to have the rule amended and after some discussion he withdrew his motion on the assurance that its spirit would be recommended to the Executive, or that the Executive would give any application from clubs to appoint their own handicapper their favourable consideration. In one instance the promoters of a large meeting in Dublin the previous year were allowed to appoint their own handicapper. Of course he was a member of the Association. The Executive allowed other rules to be infringed in other instances and they might have strained a point in the case you mention for the sake of harmony.

When questioned if it was wise of the executive to reject arbitration by the Archbishop of Cashel and Mr Davitt, Mr Davin said: 'Most certainly not. No one could doubt the justice and fairness of a decision from two such eminent Irishmen who have the cause of the Association so deeply at heart.'

In answer to a question whether *The Gael* was the official organ of the Association, Mr Davin replied:

Resolutions in favour of such an organ were passed by several county committees and the executive at their famous meeting in Wynne's Hotel decided to take the necessary steps for the purpose of inaugurating such a journal at the earliest possible date. The first number of the journal appeared before the meeting of the executive at Limerick on Easter Monday at which I presided and I asked the very question you have just put to me. Mr Hoctor and some others assured me that the Association would not be put to one penny expense in the matter; that it was altogether a private enterprise and that the funds of the Association would not be affected one way or the other.

Regarding the steps that ought to be taken to ensure order at the coming Convention Mr Davin gave his opinion:

I think it will be impossible to transact business fairly and impartially at the coming Convention if the existing rule which allows two delegates from each branch is followed. Under that rule there will be at least one thousand delegates at the Convention and from my experience of some of the past meetings and also taking into account the bitterness that seems to exist between some of the members, I feel certain that business cannot be properly transacted at so large a gathering. I believe that it would be better for the interests of the Association to hold a convention of members representing counties, say two delegates from each county having thirty clubs or more, and one delegate from each county having fourteen clubs or over. I would not have more than two members from any one county.

The Executive ought, in my opinion, further postpone the Convention and direct the county branches to follow some course such as I have suggested. As an illustration of how high the feeling runs I may mention I observed in two issues of *The Gael* paragraphs and a letter amounting to threats of personal violence to members who seem to differ from the present Executive if they attended the Convention. I am convinced that the spirit of fair play among Irishmen generally would not for a moment tolerate conduct of that kind. I hope no delegate will forget it is his duty to the Association to preserve order and not give our enemies in the Press an opportunity for spicy writing. Some slight changes may be necessary in the hurling and football rules but I think matters of the kind should not be discussed at the coming convention. Everyone should concentrate his attention on our election of a proper Executive and the amendment of the constitution. This will give the Convention quite enough to do.

The Freeman in an editorial on the same day explained that the views of Maurice Davin had been sought because he was recognised as the head of athletics in Ireland and during the heat of the recent discussion no one had ventured a word of disparagement against him, so great was the respect for him. The paper warned that the association was heading for destruction if left in the hands of those who had grievously mismanaged it.

Davin was not unscathed by verbal abuse. At a convention of Cork delegates from twenty-four clubs[32] in November 1887 with Alderman Horgan presiding, the meeting unanimously adopted a resolution condemning the way William O'Brien was being barbarously treated in prison. The chairman pointed out that while the association was non-political, it was entirely national and they were expressing their sympathy with a man who had given every assistance possible to the GAA when it was most wanted.

Mr Forrest proposed a resolution asking Maurice Davin to resume the presidency of the association he had piloted with untiring zeal. He believed that if Mr Davin had been at the head of the organisation during the past year, the bickerings would not have arisen. Mr Donnelly proposed a direct negative and referred to Davin as a renegade for allying himself with the *Freeman's Journal, Sport* and the *Celtic Times,* but when the chairman put the resolution to the meeting it was carried.

Mr Deering (a future president of the GAA) claimed that the meeting was not representative, and P.N. Fitzgerald thought that a poll should be taken, but Mr Donnelly declined to avail of that procedure. A motion in support of Dr Croke was also passed, but the chairman ruled that resolutions passed at the meeting need not be supported by the delegates at the convention.

The abuse levelled at Davin was entirely undeserved. He had stood firmly and consistently by the principles on which the GAA had been established and the only means available to him to get his message to the public was through the media mentioned. The antipathy of the executive to those journals was no excuse for the attacks on Davin's integrity. No doubt Cusack had been unrestrained and provocative in his language when referring to the executive as 'a junta of knaves and fools' and 'a miserable, mischievous and traitorous gang.'[33]

In the weeks leading up to the convention, antagonism between the opposing parties reached a stage where abusive language took the place of reasoned argument. A bitter and even violent confrontation at the convention appeared to be unavoidable.

Progress in games

Even though the GAA was racked by dissension, it also enjoyed some exceptional developments during the year.[34] The inauguration of the All Ireland championships in hurling and football created a new interest for the public. Only twelve counties entered for the championships and on an open draw system six first round ties were fixed to be played on dates in July.

Only one of the games was played as arranged. Galway (Meelick) defeated Wexford (Castlebridge) at Elm Park before an attendance estimated at ten thousand. Wicklow considered it unfair to be asked to make the long journey to Athlone and the match was awarded to Clare. Dublin sought a postponement which was refused and Tipperary were given a walk-over. Waterford and Louth failed to take part. Cork and Limerick were unable to resolve internal difficulties between rival claims as to what teams should represent the counties and Kilkenny were granted a walk-over in each case. Tipperary (Thurles) beat Clare (Smith O'Briens) at Nenagh and qualified for the semi-final against Kilkenny (Tullaroan) at Clonmel. Due to some confusion about the venue, the game was refixed for Urlingford and the victory was won by Tipperary. The final was not played until 1888.

The football championship fared better. Nine counties participated as against five in the hurling. Clare (Newmarket), Tipperary (Templemore) and Wexford (Castlebridge) met no opposition from Wicklow, Dublin and Galway. Limerick (Commercials) beat Meath (Dowdstown), Louth (Dundalk Young Irelands) beat Waterford (Ballyduff Lower) and Kilkenny (Kilmacow) beat Cork (Lees). In the second round Tipperary beat Clare in Nenagh and after beating Limerick the result was negatived on an objection and Limerick won the replay. In the semi-finals, Louth beat Wexford and Limerick beat Kilkenny, but the final was left over until 1888.

The absence of Davin and Cusack from the scene was keenly felt, especially in the area of games organisation. No member of the Executive could match the authoritative stature of Davin and his expert knowledge of the games; furthermore J.B. O'Reilly possessed neither Cusack's organisational skills nor his dynamic personality. Uncertainty, confusion and lack of central control marked the championships, but they were saved from complete failure by the determined pursuit of honour and fame by the clubs involved.

On the other hand, the number of affiliated clubs increased dramatically during the year due to an active campaign by P.N. Fitzgerald, P. Hoctor and F.B. Dineen in particular. It was a top priority in their policy to establish new clubs and they were remarkably successful especially in counties Limerick, Clare, Cork, Galway and Louth and a firm foothold was secured in a number of counties in Ulster.

Hurling and football games continued to thrive mainly through the efforts of individual clubs. Large tournaments were a common feature in Munster counties with up to twenty teams taking part in some of them that lasted a few weeks.

Encouraged by an active county committee, Galway clubs promoted numerous tournaments that attracted widespread support from the public. Reports from Louth and Dublin testify to similar activity on the playing fields. Fourteen teams were hosted by Birr club for a great hurling tournament in July and similar events were organised in Kilkenny, Callan, Wexford and Monasterevan. Amongst the foremost clubs in arranging matches were those in Tipperary and Dublin that had been suspended by the executive. There was no falling off in the number of athletic meetings and they continued to enjoy popularity with the public. The third annual athletic championships were held in Tralee during the Whit weekend and were distinguished for notable performances in the high jump and the hop, step and jump events and a clean sweep by Jim Mitchel in the weights. F.B. Dineen was in charge of arrangements, the two-day programme was completed efficiently and the secretaries reported that it was financially successful.

References
1.   O'Sullivan, T.F., op. cit., pp 27-40.
2.   Ibid., p. 37.
3.   *Freeman's Journal*, 2/11/1886.
4.   O'Sullivan, T.F., op. cit., p. 40.
5.   *C.B.S.*, 126/S, 12844/5, 120W/6765. N.A.
6.   *Sport,* 26/2/1887.
7.   Ibid., 27/8/1887.

8.   O'Sullivan, T.F., op. cit. p. 42.
9.   Ibid., p. 43.
10.   Ibid., pp 43-4; *Sport,* 16/4/1887.
11.   *Sport,* 16/4/1887.
12.   O'Sullivan, T.F., op. cit., pp 43-4.
13.   *C.B.S.,* 126/S, N.A.
14.   *Freeman's Journal,* 2/11/1887.
15.   O'Sullivan, T.F., op. cit., p. 11.
16.   *Sport,* 12/6/1886.
17.   O'Sullivan, T.F., op. cit., p. 34.
18.   *Freeman's Journal,* 16/11/1886.
19.   O'Sullivan, T.F., op. cit., p. 44.
20.   *Sport,* 30/7/1887.
21.   Ibid.
22.   Ibid.
23.   Ibid., 6/8/1887.
24.   *Freeman's Journal,* 29/7/1887.
25.   Ibid., 30/7/1887.
26.   O'Sullivan, T.F., op. cit., p. 44.
27.   Ibid., pp 45-46.
28.   *Sport,* 2/7/1887.
29.   *Freeman's Journal,* 23/10/1887.
30.   *Celtic Times,* 29/10/1887.
31.   *Freeman's Journal,* 31/10/1887, 1/11/1887, 2/11/1887.
32.   Ibid., 7/11/1997; *Celtic Times,* 12/11/1887.
33.   *Celtic Times,* 15/10/1887.
34.   O'Sullivan, T.F., op. cit., pp 56-57; Ó Laoi, P., op. cit., pp 41-50; Ryall, T., *Kilkenny: the GAA story 1984,* pp 13-14; Ó Ceallaigh, S., *History of Limerick G.A.A,* pp 42-45; Fogarty, Canon P., op. cit., pp 31-32.

Chapter 9

A new cohesion

A mini invasion of delegates from all over the country converged on Thurles for the Annual Convention on Wednesday 9 November 1887. Some arrived the day before and it was generally estimated that the total attendance lay somewhere between eight hundred and a thousand. Ostensibly their business was to review the proceedings of the Association during the past year and to plan for its future welfare but what concerned them more than anything else was the contest for control of the GAA between two politically motivated groups and the delegates made little or no attempt to disguise where their allegiance lay. A small minority held to the middle ground, their interest being solely concerned with the stated aims of the Association.

Apart from the appointed delegates, the crowd in the Square was swollen by other interested parties, including press reporters and spectators who were attracted there out of curiosity. A force of RIC men and plain clothes detectives, as well as police informers, mingled through the crowd observing the movements of the prominent officials. Neither Davin nor Cusack was present. Michael Cusack arrived in the town on Tuesday and when he appeared in Hayes' Hotel he was treated in a truculent manner by two members of the outgoing executive. Cusack gave his own account of the incident in the *Celtic Times:*[1]

> I reached Hayes's Hotel and found it cramped. While declining the proposed hospitality of friends, Hoctor, O'Reilly and a few others shifted around and a section of the gang held a consultation in a corner of the space outside the bar of the Hotel. One jerked alongside and gruffly asked why I had been looking at his party. Mr Butler's protestations against violation of the sacred laws of hospitality was answered by J.B. O'Reilly's pistol shot. The ladies in charge of the house at once closed up the bar. Mr Butler talked over the situation with me and I decided to return to town.

As the delegates arrived in the town they were closely scrutinised by the Special Branch men. John Murphy reported to DICS William Jacques: 'I observed the following leading suspects most of whom were well-known to me: J.K. Bracken, Templemore; P.J. Hoctor and

F.J. Allen, Dublin; J.E. Kennedy, Cork; T. O'Riordan, Cork; S.J. Dunleavy, Dublin; James Lynam, Eyrecourt; J.B. O'Reilly, Dublin; P.J. White, Clara; P.N. Fitzgerald, Cork; W.G. Fisher, Waterford; F.B. Dineen, Ballylanders; C. McCarthy-Teeling, Dublin; Leo Keegan, Enniscorthy.

The most active amongst them were F.J. Allen, P.J. Hoctor, J.E. Kennedy, S.J. Dunleavy, F.B. Dineen and J.B. O'Reilly. They kept constantly moving amongst the delegates who attended on the streets before the Convention sat, but I cannot say how they conducted themselves inside the Courthouse, except that I have been informed by a delegate who was present, that Hoctor spoke more strongly and at greater length on political matters than what has been reported in the *Freeman's Journal*.[2]

Maurice Davin had anticipated that the Convention would prove to be a disorderly affair, but his efforts to gain a postponement of the date and a reduction in the number of delegates from the counties failed to get support from the executive. He realised that the course being followed could not lead to a reconciliation of the parties, but would make matters worse. Consequently he decided there was nothing to be gained by attending.

Hayes's Hotel had no hope of accommodating the huge crowd of delegates and the meeting was transferred to the courthouse but even that was overcrowded.[3] Twenty-four representatives from Dublin and Moycarkey clubs were refused admission on the grounds that they were under suspension. The executive, determined to remain in control, laid their plans carefully beforehand to ensure they would command a majority of the votes. Their main spokesmen were P.N. Fitzgerald, P. Hoctor and J.B. O'Reilly. Leading the opposition were Fr Scanlan of Nenagh and a group of priests from north Tipperary, who were equally determined to prevent the IRB from using the association against the National League.

Immediately the meeting opened at half past one, Alderman Horgan of Cork proposed P.N. Fitzgerald as chairman and T. O'Riordan as secretary. The proposal was seconded by P. Hoctor. Fr Scanlan proposed Major O'Kelly of Moycarkey for the chair. Although no vote had been taken, Fitzgerald assumed the position of chairman and ruled that he could not accept Fr Scanlan's proposal because Major O'Kelly was expelled from the Association. For about an hour a running confrontation followed between the chairman and Fr Scanlan, but abusive interruptions, cheers and hisses from both sides made it impossible for either to be heard at times above the din.

The priest declared that Fitzgerald was not a suitable person to be chairman and he persisted in claiming there was no chairman. Fitzgerald repeatedly called for order, but without success and when he offered a show of hands or a poll on the issue of the chair, it was turned down by the priest. As the commotion increased, Fr Scanlan and a few other priests approached the bench and in a scuffle the desk was trampled on and the priests were handled roughly, but no blows were struck. Voices could be heard above the noise shouting 'we will have none but nationalists.' Eventually Fr Scanlan, claiming that he was being denied a proper hearing, left the room accompanied by the other priests and a crowd of two hundred, according to the estimate by the press, but put at forty by the supporters of the executive.

It appears that the stiff opposition to the chairmanship of P.N. Fitzgerald led to a change of plan by the IRB leaders, and E.M. Bennett of Ennis was proposed for president by Hoctor. Edward M. Bennett, a farmer from Newmarket-on-Fergus, Co. Clare was an old Fenian of 1867. He had an interest in athletics and he was elected the first Chairman of Clare County Committee of the GAA He was an active member of Parnell's National League. After Parnell's death he supported Redmond's Home Rule party.[4] W.P. O'Keeffe of Carrick-on-Suir proposed Maurice Davin and W.G. Fisher of Waterford seconded. J. Cullinane of Bansha complained that the Convention had ceased to be representative because a number of unauthorised people had come through the doors and the broken windows, so he withdrew from the room in protest. Amid a lot of confusion, a show of hands was taken, but it was inconclusive. A division was taken by counting the opposing voters as they passed through different doors and the tellers announced the count as 210 for Davin and 316 for Bennett.

The press estimate that two hundred left with Fr Scanlan could not be far off the mark seeing that only five hundred and twenty-six remained to vote out of a possible eight hundred. It has been suggested that the result of the vote might have been reversed had they all stayed in the Courtroom.

Secretaries J.B. O'Reilly and T.O'Riordan in their Annual Report stated:

> The first serious difficulty which the executive had to face was the almost hopeless state of chaos in which they found the Association when its care and management was handed over to them. This was principally owing to the gross mismanagement of the ex-secretary of the executive who apparently considered it no part of his duty to inform the members of the Association of his knowledge of its financial condition when he went out of office. There can be little doubt but that the individual referred to has still in his possession a considerable sum belonging to the Association.
>
> The debts now owing are exceedingly small compared to what they were at the close of September 1886. This is the first occasion since the

Association was founded in which a Balance Sheet has been submitted to the delegates assembled at any of the Annual Conventions. It will be seen from the Balance Sheet that the entire receipts during the past fourteen months amounted to 448.8s.6d, while the expenditure amounts to 413.4s.9d.

When the executive was elected over twelve months ago the number of affiliated branches was comparatively small. The report listed the number of affiliations in 1887:

Tipperary 130, Limerick 90, Galway 76, Cork 70, Clare 60, Louth 55, Meath 40, Kilkenny 40, Dublin 40, Wexford 38, Waterford 30, Connacht apart from Galway 10.

Precise figures were not given for other counties.

Although the income and expenditure figures were included in the published report no details of the Balance Sheet were included.

The following officers were elected without opposition:

Vice-Presidents:	P. Hoctor
	Alderman Horgan
	P. O'Brien, Nenagh
	W. Troy, Fermoy
Secretaries:	T. O'Riordan
	J.B. O'Reilly
	James Moore, Dundalk
Treasurer:	Anthony Mackey, Castleconnell
Recording Secretary:	J. Bradley, Cork Examiner
Handicappers:	F.B. Dineen, Ballylanders
	P. O'Shea, Dublin
Four Committee Members:	R. Frewen
	P.J. O'Keeffe, Kilkenny
	Dr Nally, Mayo
	G. Keegan, Wexford

In returning thanks for his election, P. Hoctor condemned the way he had been attacked by the 'enemies of the association', but he was as hard as granite and he would not back-down. In spite of the attacks by the *Freeman's Journal* and the 'scoundrelism' of the *Celtic Times,* he would remain true to the service of the GAA.

The Convention rescinded the unpopular rule which gave the executive ex officio membership of county committees, but decided to retain another controversial rule that the official handicapper should be present at all large meetings. It was resolved that the association would be non-political and that no club as a body should take part in any political meeting.

The Gael was declared the official organ of the GAA and the suspended or expelled clubs could be reinstated provided they apologised in writing for breaking the rules of the association. Mr Edmond Cahill, Kilteely, moved a resolution of sympathy with William O'Brien M.P. He was the initiator of the Plan of Campaign against rack-renting landlords and was imprisoned in Tullamore gaol where he was the victim of inhumane treatment that aroused nation-wide sympathy for his sufferings. The chairman ruled the motion out of order on the grounds that it was a political matter. He was pressed to accept it, but he declared the Convention adjourned and vacated the chair. In an impromptu meeting in the yard outside, Fr Scanlan addressed the delegates who had left the courthouse with him and those who had been denied admission. He argued that the GAA was being turned into a Fenian organisation with the object of breaking up the National League. The group proceeded to Hayes' Hotel and held another meeting in the open air. The speakers ascended a brake to address the crowd and a number of resolutions were passed expressing sympathy with William O'Brien and requesting Archbishop Croke, the champion of Irish freedom, to remain as patron of the GAA. J.K. Bracken, in seconding the second motion, declared that he was at the birth of the association and he entered a solemn protest against the action of the men in the courthouse. J.E. Kennedy announced his resignation from the vice-presidency of the executive and M.J. O'Connor of Wexford criticised the executive for proclaiming meetings, adopting a stringent coercion scheme, disregarding the laws of the GAA and creating a centralised government. J.J. Kenny of the Metropolitan Hurling Club in Dublin called for Maurice Davin to return to the helm.

The Convention had consolidated the grip of the IRB on the executive, not because they enjoyed majority support in the country, but because of their ability to organise effectively the support that they had. Their way was made easy by the lack of vigilance on the part of the majority and they could claim that their men had been elected legally. It cannot be said that the priests acted legally, although they could contend that they were justified in disrupting a meeting that was rigged. In the face of great provocation, P.N. Fitzgerald in the chair displayed a high degree of patience and control in dealing with the priests. He acted with the assurance of one who was firmly committed to keeping alive the spirit of Fenian resistance.

Fr Scanlan's background in a home dedicated to Fenianism could have influenced him to stand side by side with Fitzgerald, but his experience and his reasoning attracted him to the Home Rule movement that offered a hope of achieving a measure of freedom. He claimed that he hurled before most of the delegates were born and he was president of the Nenagh GAA club, bearing testimony to his bona fide attachment to the association. Regarding the Fenians, he said: 'I have mentioned the men of 1867, and I ask you to give a cheer for their names.' I admire these men. Can I say the same for those who with the experience of that movement would lead the youth of Ireland into the way of ruin and restore again the golden age of the informer.'[5]

The informers were close to the leaders of the IRB even at the Convention. When the meeting was over, 'Bendigo', a police informer, reported that he walked to the post office with Hoctor and saw him send a telegram to John Torley in Glasgow with the message 'Victory all along the line.'[6] However, Fitzgerald was taken by surprise by the strength of the protest by the priests and he was expecting further opposition in the coming days.

Reactions to the Convention
Reactions to the conduct and decisions of the convention came swiftly and decisively. On the following day, Thursday 10 November, Archbishop Croke, wrote to the *Freeman's Journal:*

> My dear Sir,
> In persuance of an engagement made more than a week ago I had to be absent from Thurles yesterday and only returned home to-day at one o'clock. I then heard with deep regret and afterwards read with pain and humiliation, an account of the proceedings of the Gaelic Convention held here on that day.
>
> Though not quite unprepared for a troubled, if not turbulent meeting, and for certain unpleasant revelations with which my ears had been rendered familiar for some time, I could not at all have believed that the elements of mischief were so painfully present in the organisation as they now appear to be and that evidence of the fact would have been so soon and so unmistakably given.
>
> Nothing therefore remains for me but to dissociate myself, as I now publicly do, from that branch of the Gaelic Athletic Association which exercised such a sinister influence over yesterday's proceedings.
>
> I remain, my dear sir,
> Your very faithful servant,
> T.W. Croke, Archbishop of Cashel.

While not going so far as to tender his resignation completely from the Association, he made it clear that he could not give any support to the Fenian element that was responsible for the disturbance.

In a letter to Archbishop Walsh of Dublin, he gave his reason for 'breaking with the Gaelics.' 'Their meeting here was disgraceful. It was packed to the throat with Fenian leaders and emissaries. The Killaloe priests made a bold but not a very effective stand.'[7]

Simultaneously and independently of the Archbishop, six north Tipperary priests issued a letter to the press in explanation of their actions at the Convention stating they had attended the Convention with the set purpose of opposing the re-election of the outgoing executive who were not competent to manage the Association. Their main argument was that the members of the executive were advanced men of one particular character who aimed (a) to smash the National League, and (b) to attract the youth of Ireland to the physical force movement.

One of the six priests, Fr. Moloney, Toomevara, wrote privately to Davin on Friday 11 November and on receipt of a reply he requested the *Freeman's Journal* to publish it:

Toomevara
November 14th, 1887

Dear Sir,
Please publish in next issue of *Freeman's Journal* copy of a letter of Mr Davin in reply to a note from me at the suggestion of the Gaels of North Tipperary requesting him to become again President of the Gaelic Athletic Association. If it were better known about the Convention Maurice Davin would have been elected even in the Courthouse.
Yours truly
John C. Moloney

Davin takes the initiative

Maurice Davin's response to Fr Moloney's letter:[8]

Deerpark
Carrick-on-Suir
Nov. 12th. 1887

Reverend Sir,
In obedience to the call contained in your letter of the 11th inst. I will rejoin the GAA and give whatever assistance I can in its reconstruction. I feel greatly honoured in being allowed to do so, more especially as I find the Archbishop of Cashel has not withdrawn altogether from the Association.

I have taken the liberty of appointing yourself, Messrs Hugh Ryan, Thurles, William Prendergast, Clonmel, T. Harrington, Johnstown, P. Shelly, jnr. Callan, Thos. Nolan, Ballyduff Lr.., Waterford, Dan Fraher, Dungarvan and John Wyse Power of the *Freeman* as a provisional committee to issue instructions to clubs and appoint dates and places for county conventions.

You will want to hold your first meeting at an early date. You can fix the time and place. I have asked Mr Power to act as secretary and communicate with you at once. He knows the addresses of the other members. Of course you have power to add as many as you like to the number. On the other page are all the instructions needed by clubs at present.

With the political or non-political aspect of the Association I do not feel able to deal. The Archbishop's instructions on this point must be our guide. I may state that no person had any authority to propose me as president at the meeting in Thurles Courthouse. I would have nothing to do with business conducted by those people.

Yours sincerely
Maurice Davin.

He issued a number of instructions for clubs to be acted on immediately:

1. Clubs intending to join should hold meetings at once and appoint their officers for the coming year.
2. County conventions should be held in about a month's time, when delegates must be elected to a convention in Thurles on January 3rd. Any county with two clubs to send one delegate; a county with five or more clubs to send two delegates. No county to send more than two.
3. This convention to have power to revise the constitution and to transact all business in connection with the association.
4. Should any question be brought forward on which the delegates may not think themselves empowered to vote, it can be adjourned until they have an opportunity of consulting their constituents.
5. At the county convention mentioned above, county committees (confined to 15 members or less) may be elected provisionally; they may be continued in office for the coming year if approved at the Thurles meeting on January 3rd.

Davin took the initiative and acted independently with a confident sense of authority, assuming the role of leader as if he were the recognised president. He went over the heads of the elected executive and county committees and made a direct appeal to the clubs where the real power resided. He pinned his faith on the ordinary members, believing they would respond favourably to his message.

The committee he selected were all people well-known to him as being genuinely interested in promoting the aims of the GAA, apart from whatever political views they might hold; he was aware that D.H. Ryan and Wyse Power were connected with the IRB. His main objective was to preserve the integrity of the association and to that end he adopted a neutral position, distancing himself from any connection with either political party.

Wyse Power acknowledged that it was an honour to be asked to co-operate with Davin and the other gentlemen, but he declined the invitation; in explanation he said his connection with the committee might be misinterpreted, probably because he was on the staff of the *Freeman's Journal* which had taken a strong line against the IRB influence. However, he joined the committee later.[9]

Davin received the following letter from Dr Fennelly, Administrator, Thurles:[10]

> The Presbytery
> Thurles
> 11th November
>
> My dear Mr Davin,
> You will have seen by this time what a fiasco was the convention of Wednesday.
> What is to become is the question on every tongue?. My own idea is that you and you alone, can remedy matters. Without any difficulty, I imagine that with your assistance we can get up a county association in Tipperary complete in itself. If you will kindly undertake to do this, or do anything in common with this view, I can promise you the fullest co-operation of the Archbishop and priests of Cashel. In any event something will have to be done to withdraw our young men from the evil influence of the association as it stands.
>
> I am, my dear Mr Davin,
> Yours faithfully,
> Thomas Fennelly, Adm.

The probability is that Davin had drafted his own extensive plan for reconstruction before he received Dr Fennelly's letter and it is doubtful if he was impressed by the modest proposal for a county association. However, he welcomed the assurance of Dr Croke's co-operation in whatever course he decided to follow.

He wrote to Dr Fennelly informing him that he was ready to reconstruct the association and on Tuesday November 15th he issued a statement to the press outlining his plan. He emphasised that it was only a framework subject to any alterations that may be deemed necessary by the convention in January and he made it clear that representatives at the convention should be allowed perfect freedom to vote according to their convictions, after hearing each point fully debated.[11]

In the case of clubs and county committees, his draft proposals kept more or less to the lines of his 1886 constitution:

1. The formation and management of clubs to remain the same as under the previous rules, with exceptions to the parish rule in cities and towns of more than one parish.

2. County committees to consist of a chairman, vice-chairman, secretary and treasurer. He proposed that the number of ordinary members be increased to eleven. They were to have absolute control of affiliations of clubs and the management of county championships in hurling, handball and football. They were given power to suspend, disqualify or expel clubs or individuals for breaches of the

rules of the GAA. Suspensions in any county to be binding in the others. To get rid of any suggestion of ambiguity regarding handicapping, power was given to a county committee to appoint a handicapper for the county, but clubs were given the option of having the handicapping done by one of their own members.

3. He proposed an innovation, a foreshadow of the present Games Administration Committee, to manage the inter-county championships in hurling, handball and football and the athletic championship meeting. This championship committee was to consist of a chairman, vice-chairman, secretary and twelve other members, all to be elected at the Annual Convention from nominations submitted by the county committees. They were also empowered to award an association medal to any athlete who achieved a record performance.

4. A general assembly or parliament was to meet once or twice a year with power to make, alter or expunge the rules of the games; it was to be given control of the finances, and the right to decide on the number, value and design of championship cups and medals; it would decide matters of dispute not provided for in the rules; all elections were to be by ballot.

Davin insisted that the document was but an outline of a constitution intended for examination and discussion. Yet it had some salient features that were meant to cope with the weaknesses that he perceived, with hindsight of experience, in his original constitution.

It was his intention to abolish the Central Executive since it had exercised almost complete control over the Association; it had usurped the legislative power of the Annual Convention and attempted to dominate the county committees. The powers of the county committees within their own area were to be restored and representation on the general assembly was to be regulated in proportion to the number of affiliated clubs in a county. The vexed question of financial control was to be exercised by the assembly.

Within a few days more than fifty clubs came out against the executive, calling for the return of Dr Croke and Maurice Davin and before the week was out the number exceeded two hundred including clubs of all counties of Leinster; all of Munster except Kerry; Galway and Roscommon from Connacht and Armagh, Cavan and Monaghan from Ulster. The greatest response came from counties Louth, Meath, Tipperary, Dublin and Limerick, with Wicklow, Kilkenny, Cork, Clare, Waterford and Wexford not far behind. Realising that their backs were to the wall, the executive issued statements to the press justifying their actions and trying to retrieve lost ground. E. Bennett repudiated the alleged objectionable remarks about the priests and the National League. He stated that he was and still remained a member of the

National League and the GAA and he was in no way hostile to it. John O'Leary accused Fr Scanlan of 'felon setting' by mentioning the names of Fenians in public. J.B. O'Reilly repudiated any suggestion that the GAA was politically motivated.[12]

Meanwhile some important developments took place. On Tuesday the 15th November, the day that Davin released his draft constitution, Dr Fennelly wrote again to Davin:

> The Presbytery
> Thurles
> Nov. 15th
>
> My Dear Mr Davin,
> I am delighted to hear from you that you are ready to reconstruct the GAA. Under the circumstances the best thing you can do is to visit His Grace, the Archbishop of Cashel on Saturday or Monday next.
>   If you will drop a line to say when we may expect you, you will much oblige.
>
> > Yours faithfully,
> > Thomas Fennelly, Adm.

Dr Fennelly wrote on the Monday advising of changes:

> The Presbytery
> Thurles
> Monday 21st
>
> My Dear Mr Davin,
> I find that Mr Davitt cannot spare Wednesday from his work, he will be here on tomorrow. You will be here to meet him and you will dine with Mr and Mrs Davitt at the Palace at 5 o'c. This arrangement will make it necessary for you to stay with us overnight, but I hope this will not put you to any serious inconvenience. I will secure you a comfortable bed for the night.
>
> > I am, my dear Mr Davin
> > Very faithfully yours
> > Thomas Fennelly.

Davin, Dr. Croke and Davitt met in conference on 22 November. By what appears to have been a previous arrangement P.N. Fitzgerald was in Thurles that day and Davitt conveyed to him the outcome of the conference. The following day the executive met at Limerick Junction to consider their position in the changed circumstances. E.M. Bennett presided and the others present were P. Hoctor and Alderman Horgan, vice-presidents; A. Mackey, treasurer; J.B. O'Reilly and T. O'Riordan secretaries and P. Kelly, W. Troy and R.J. Frewen.

A manifesto prepared by Bennett was issued for publication defending the executive's actions at the Convention. The clergy he stated, had been treated with forbearance in spite of provocation by them and they had tried to obstruct all the business until their demands were met. He suggested that the malcontents should either secede openly from the association or return to their allegiance and submit to the authority of the lawful officers.

Resolutions were passed –

1. Regretting the withdrawal of Dr Croke and hoping for his return.

2. Expressing contempt for the *Freeman's Journal* in calling for the arrest of members of the Association.

3. Disclaiming all hostility to the National League.[13]

P.N. Fitzgerald did not attend the meeting, but he submitted a letter to justify his own position to the public. His principal points were:

1. The *Freeman's Journal* was working against the executive in felon setting.

2. He was not hostile to the National League, to Dr Croke or to any of the clergy.

3. He knew nothing of the existence of a clique at the Convention.

4. He never paraded his political opinions and he was partly responsible for the non-political resolution that was adopted.

5. He would respectfully ask Archbishop Croke to consult with the other patrons to see if an amicable understanding could be reached; the GAA should be open to all; an Irish nation should include all sections of Irishmen.

6. He suggested that the political resolution should be expunged so that a resolution of sympathy with the prisoners could be passed.

The members of the executive had realised that they had over-played their hand and they were attempting to recover lost ground in regard to their attitude to the clergy, the National League and William O'Brien, without losing face with their own supporters. They were pinning their faith on Michael Davitt and John O'Leary, that in consultation with the archbishop some compromise might be achieved.

A police informer 'Nero', who was very close to the members of the executive, if not one of them, reported that a leading IRB man stated 'it would be fruitless for us to fight it out with the National League and the clergy, but we have decided not to "cry peccavi." On the contrary, by the aid of Davitt we have every hope of coming out successfully.' But later on he confessed that a complete smash was made of the arrangements, 'Croke would not budge an inch, but was intent on furthering Davin's crowd.'[14]

Dr Fennelly wrote another letter to Davin:

My Dear Mr Davin,

The Archbishop's views have not changed since your visit here, he thinks you are in a position to start your Association and he is prepared to approve your action and lend a helping hand to the movement. By all means see Fr Moloney here and I will do what I can to assist your efforts. In my view there should be no compromise, neither should there be any unecessary recriminations.

With best wishes,

I am dear Mr Davin,

Very faithfully yours,

Thomas Fennelly.

Arrangements for a second meeting on Nov. 30th and further assurance of the Archbishop's support was contained in another letter:

The Presbytery,

Thurles.

Nov. 28th.

My Dear Mr Davin,

If you can come on Wednesday you will be able to see the Archbishop at mid-day or any other hour at your convenience. I hope Fr Scanlan will be with you. The Archbishop will not be at home on Thursday owing to the death of the Dean of Cashel.

With best wishes,

I am my dear Mr Davin,

Very faithfully yours,

Thos. Fennelly.

P.S. The Archbishop is altogether in favour of your movement.

Because of rumours and different reports about what had been decided at the Conference in Thurles on November 22nd Dr Croke cleared the air in a long letter to the press:

Thurles

November 28th.

Dear Sir,

So many and such varied accounts have been published both in and out of Ireland as to what was decided on here on Tuesday evening last when Mr Michael Davitt, Mr Maurice Davin and myself had an interview in reference to recent events connected with the GAA that I deem it highly opportune, if not absolutely necessary, to make a short statement to the public on the situation all round.

In the first place, then, it is only fair that I should acquit, as I do, the Central Executive of the GAA, whether past or present, of any and every deliberate attempt to annoy or insult me. I am bound to say however, in this connection that it is greatly to be regretted and has given rise to a good deal of unfavourable comment, that some of the more influential and guiding members of the association did not call on me before the convention on Wednesday the 9th inst., as was done on all previous occasions and consult with me, one of their patrons, on the actual 'look out' of the organisation and the steps that should be taken to restore and maintain harmony amongst its members.

Coming now to business. I may safely assume, without in any way overstating the case, that our Gaelic clubs throughout the country have by this time expressed themselves in a manner not to be mistaken as to the proceedings at the Thurles convention. The all but universal feeling appears to be that the association has not of late especially, been judiciously handled; that it has gradually, but notoriously, drifted away from its original design; that they who had somehow secured the management of it were far more solicitous about individual supremacy and sectional tactics than about the success and development of our national sports. One thing at all events, is demonstratively certain, that as it has grown in numerical strength it has not proportionately advanced in stability, and in the confidence of thoughtful people.

When the Convention met here the other day, it was not apparently to remedy the past or judiciously to provide for the future, but to secure individual ascendency and a party triumph, thereby placing fully fifty thousand young and enthusiastic Irishmen under the irresponsible control of not less than a dozen men of whom, without meaning the slightest disparagement, the very best and most charitable thing that can be said is, that they are either wholly unknown, or not favourably known, to the country.

Any such result as that would, in the long run, be plainly most disastrous and steps should now be taken to guard against the possibility of its realisation in the near or distant future. With that in view Mr Maurice Davin (Ireland's greatest athlete) and others have undertaken the task of reorganising the association in strict accordance with the opinions expressed by the Gaelic clubs in the columns of the daily press. In this way it is thought that the stability and usefulness of the association will be abundantly secured. I should earnestly hope indeed to see all our Gaelic clubs without exception organised in due course on these lines. I dread and deprecate disunion amongst Irishmen.

Strictly speaking I am no party man. So long as one loves and labours for Ireland, according to his lights, and within limits of prudence and righteousness he may count me as his friend and fellow labourer. Ireland needs all our energy today. Let us not foolishly expend it in squabbling with and thus weakening each other.

I remain, my dear Sir,
Your very faithful servant,
T.W. Croke, Archbishop of Cashel.[15]

Peace Conference

Davin had a second conference with Dr Croke and Frs. Scanlan and

Moloney in the Archbishop's house on Wednesday 30 November. Final preparations were made for a meeting with members of the executive on the following Friday 2 January. On Friday, Bennett, Hoctor, Mackey, Frewen, P.A. Kelly (Dysart) and O'Riordan arrived at Hayes' Hotel where they were joined by John O'Leary.[16] After discussing Dr Croke's letter that appeared in the newspapers of the previous weeks it was agreed: That the members present wait on the Archbishop for the purpose of laying their views on the present situation before him and ascertaining his opinion with the object, if possible, of coming to some agreement. After a meeting lasting a few hours, all except O'Leary went to meet the Archbishop. In a conference lasting over an hour it seems that the executive members accepted the reconstruction plan. They returned to the hotel and discussed the situation with O'Leary. Some of them called to Hugh Ryan and Andy Callanan in the town while O'Riordan went to the post office to send telegrams, probably to P.N. Fitzgerald and O'Reilly. O'Leary and Frewen left the town by a late train, the others stayed overnight in the hotel.

Davin arrived by train at one o'clock the next day and was met at the station by Dr Fennelly who filled him in on what had transpired the previous day and escorted him to the Archbishop's house. Frs Scanlan and Cunningham arrived by car and went straight to the hotel where they met the members of the executive who had remained overnight and then went to confer with Dr Croke and Davin. Davin remained with the Archbishop until eight o'clock, then went to the hotel to meet the executive members there, and final arrangements were made for a meeting of representatives from the two sides at Limerick Junction on the following Monday 5 December.

Davin and Bennett walked together to the station and left by the 11.15 train. It appeared that the split had been healed.[17] A statement issued to the press read: 'The negotiations between the Archbishop of Cashel and the Executive of the GAA for the settlement of the existing dispute were continued today, Mr Maurice Davin being present. A thorough understanding was come to on the entire situation and will no doubt lead to durable results. All misunderstandings have been thoroughly cleared up and the foolish anticipations of those who so anxiously looked forward to the disruption of the Association have been signally frustrated. It was arranged that a provisional committee of four, representing both the supporters of the Executive and of Mr Davin should meet at Limerick Junction on Monday next for the settlement of matters of detail in connection with the calling of county committees, two delegates from each club; and that the representation at the General Convention should be in the proportion of one delegate to every ten clubs, or any fraction of that number up to and exceeding five clubs. Counties not having ten clubs to be entitled to send one delegate.' (The proceedings as on the preceding day were of a private character.)

Davin and Wyse Power on one side, O'Riordan and Frewen on the other met on Monday and issued a manifesto to the Gaels of the country signed by the four of them.[18] It announced that a General convention would be held on Wednesday 4 January to reconstruct the Association and directing that county conventions should be held before 27 December to elect county committees on the lines laid down by Davin, and to appoint representatives to the general convention on the following basis: One representative for every ten clubs or fraction of ten, not less than five; counties with less than ten clubs to send one representative.

The leading IRB man, P.N. Fitzgerald, did not take a direct part in the discussions, remaining aloof from them and he was not a party to any agreement that was made. At the convention he made it clear that although his side might be beaten then, perhaps in twelve months or two years they might rise again. It was a fairly accurate forecast.

The four-man reconciliation committee had some worries that misunderstandings existed about the reconstruction plans and to eliminate any such notions gaining currency they issued another statement that 'there is to be no Central Executive in the new organisation, whether in fact on in name.[19]

Before the end of December, fifteen counties had met in convention, elected their officers and committees and appointed their representatives to the general convention. Signs of lingering dissension appeared in counties Limerick, Kilkenny and Waterford; in each of the three counties, two opposing meetings were held on the same day and rival delegations claimed to represent the county at the general convention. The provisional committee, after consulting with Dr Croke, agreed that the delegates appointed at the Kilmacthomas meeting should represent Waterford. A decision regarding the other two counties was left over to the convention. The delegations from Galway and Cork were heavily weighted in favour of the IRB, but most other counties were represented by supporters of Croke and Davin and at least six counties included a priest on their delegation. E. Bennett, the president, failed to be elected in Clare, probably because of his refusal to take a motion of sympathy with William O'Brien at the November convention.[20]

Reconstruction Convention
Eighty-three delegates representing nineteen counties assembled in the hall of the Young Men's Society in Thurles on 4 January 1888 for the

reconstruction convention.[21] Amongst the press representatives present were Michael Cusack of the *Celtic Times* and Pat Hoctor of *The Gael;* the two papers were to cease publication within a few weeks. Davin's unanimous appointment to chair the meeting was greeted with applause and Wyse Power and O'Riordan were appointed secretaries.

The proceedings were conducted with a degree of dignity and respect for order that had been absent in the November convention. It was obvious to all that the majority was in favour of the reconstruction plan and that it fairly represented the national opinion. The members of the old executive who were present, realising the weakness of their position, accepted the decisions of the convention and made no attempt to disrupt the business. It is fair to say that they co-operated in bringing about a reconciliation that saved the GAA from breaking up into factions.

There can be no doubt that a letter from Dr Croke to the convention had a beneficent influence on the assembly. He complimented all sides on the brotherly feeling that manifested itself so conspicuously at the county conventions. He did not wish to interfere with their deliberations, but he offered a few practical suggestions which he hoped they would put into effect soon:

1. That alcoholic drink should not be on sale at or near where GAA matches are held and that no prizes should be accepted from publicans.
2. That matches should be fixed for a time that would not interfere with attendance at mass.

The reading of the letter was enthusiastically applauded.

Opening the convention, Maurice Davin said that he did not intend dealing with recent events. They had come together to reconstruct the GAA on the lines laid down by Archbishop Croke. Accordingly he was putting before them a constitution he had prepared, the details of which were open to amendment. First they had to decide which of the conventions held in Kilkenny and in Limerick should be recognised. P.N. Fitzgerald spoke in favour of a group of IRB supporters who had met at the Workingmen's Club in Kilkenny, but when he learned that the meeting in The Tholsel had been officially convened he said he had not been aware of the facts and he generously apologised to the chairman. In Limerick's case, after heated exchanges between the rival leaders, P. O'Brien of the IRB and Fr Sheehy supporting the National League, it was agreed to allow six delegates from O'Brien's group and three from Fr Sheehy's, an odd compromise to say the least.

The new draft constitution prepared by Davin was debated and adopted. In discussing the playing rules a few changes were made.

Forfeit points were abolished and instead a forty yards free was to be awarded against a defending team if one of them was the last to play the ball before it crossed the end line. The minimum dimensions of a pitch were fixed at 140 yards by 84 yards and the maximum 196 yards by 140 yards. Additional powers were given to a referee in dealing with foul play. The new playing rules submitted by Davin were adopted unanimously.

As six o'clock approached, demands were made to proceed with the elections as delegates from distant places were anxious to begin the journey home. P.N. Fitzgerald and P. O'Brien sought to delay the elections, calculating that it would be to their better advantage if some delegates left the meeting. They argued that decisions had yet to be made about unfinished championships and there were rules still to be agreed. However, when the chairman put the question to a vote the majority favoured proceeding with the elections.

P. O'Connor of Wexford proposed Maurice Davin for president and the seconder was P.J. Maguire of Clare. J. Crowe, Limerick put forward the name of E. Bennett, the president elected in November. Realising that Bennett could not hope to command much support considering that he had failed to be elected in County Clare, Alderman Horgan proposed John Mandeville, a nephew of John O'Mahony the Fenian chief, and he was supported by W. Troy. With William O'Brien, Mandeville had promoted the Plan of Campaign against landlords and both were imprisoned in Tullamore jail under Balfour's Crimes Act. Having suffered brutal treatment in prison he was recently released and was popularly regarded as a martyr for the cause.

For the IRB group to propose him for the presidency was not only surprising, but an example of political expediency. When a direct question was put to Horgan if he was proposing John Mandeville in opposition to Maurice Davin, he replied: 'I am not running him against Mr Davin, I will withdraw him if it is not unanimous.' Davin interjected: 'There would be very little opposition between John Mandeville and me if John Mandeville were here.' Mandeville and Bennett were withdrawn by the proposers and Davin was unanimously elected president.

A number of names were proposed for the position of general secretary, but following withdrawals a vote between T. O'Riordan and W. Prendergast resulted in the election of Prendergast by forty votes to twenty-eight. The election for the relatively minor post of recording secretary was marked by angry wrangling. The immediate cause of the unseemly behaviour was a ridiculous proposal from James Lynam (Galway) for the appointment of Arthur James Balfour, the Irish Chief Secretary, known as 'Bloody Balfour' on account of his harsh laws, but the underlying reason for it was the disappointment of the supporters of the old executive in losing the two major positions.

Wyse Power protested at the attempt to discredit the convention, and P.N. Fitzgerald deplored the unseemly conduct of the priests, claiming that the convention was rigged, nevertheless he was prepared to accept whatever decisions were made. When Fr Buckley defended the role of the priests and criticised the line of argument taken by Fitzgerald, the latter declared that no one had greater respect than he had for the general body of clerics. When tempers cooled, J.J. Cullen, Dunleary [Dun Laoghaire] was elected to the position of recording secretary.

No opposition was voiced to the election of T. O'Riordan as secretary of the Central Council and R.J. Frewen as treasurer, decisions which gave a proportional representation on the officer board to the IRB side. However, the great majority of the twenty county representatives elected to the Central Council were supporters of the National League and included four priests, but a balance was struck when Alderman Horgan and Fr. Buckley were appointed auditors of the accounts of the late executive.

United opposition to the activities of the RIC was expressed in a motion in the names of F.B. Dineen and Fr Clancy 'That no member of the constabulary, including the Dublin Metropolitan Police, be eligible for membership of any affiliated club or be allowed to compete at any Gaelic sports.'

This was followed by a unanimous vote of sympathy with the Lord Mayor of Dublin T.D. Sullivan, Alderman J. Hooper, Fr Matt Ryan and Mr David Sheehy, MP, who were in prison under the government's coercion act and congratulations to John Mandeville on his release. Fr Clancy moved and J. Forde seconded a motion which received unanimous approval requesting Wm. O'Brien to become a patron of the GAA There was a vote of thanks to Archbishop Croke and to the provisional committee, Maurice Davin, J. Wyse Power, R. Frewen and T. O'Riordan for bringing about the reconstruction of the Association.

Symbolic of the reconciliation of the parties, a cordial vote of thanks to Maurice Davin was adopted on the proposal of Alderman Horgan. To outward view a united front was presented and the officer board, drawn from two erstwhile opposing sides, were about to work together in promoting the aims of the GAA. The future seemed to be assured, but there were indications of what Cusack termed 'breakers ahead', in the warning of P.N. Fitzgerald that although beaten they would be back in a year or two.

Davin, restored to the presidency, took immediate steps to take control of the Association and to counter the changes made by the IRB executive during its time in office. He visited the office of *Sport* and authorised the editor to print the new constitution and rules on slips and to offer them free to the public. He withdrew the rule books that had been put on sale by the late executive as being unauthorised, inaccurate and incomplete.

The first All-Ireland finals

The most pressing problem facing the new officers was the completion of the All-Ireland championships in hurling and football that had been held over from 1887. Thurles (Tipperary) and Meelick (Galway) had qualified for the hurling final and Birr was chosen as the most convenient venue for the two teams, and Easter Sunday, 1 April 1888, as the most suitable date. The Birr club took charge of the arrangements and the referee was Patrick White, a native of Blakefield, Toomevara, who had a business in Birr.

The two teams dressed out in Cunningham's Hotel and marched to the field in military formation. A huge crowd travelled to witness the first All-Ireland final; they arrived by train, by horse-drawn cars and on foot. It was a low scoring game won by Tipperary by one goal and one point to no score. One Thurles player had to leave the field due to injury and a substitute was not allowed by rule. A Meelick player was sent off by the referee for tripping.

The football final between Commercials (Limerick) and Dundalk Young Irelands (Louth) was played in Clonskeagh (Dublin) on the 29 April 1888. The referee was John Cullinane (Bansha) who had served a term of imprisonment for his anti-landlord activities. According to reports the game was played in a fine manly spirit without any unpleasant incident. Victory was won by the Limerick team by one goal and four points to three points for Louth.

The successful completion of the first All-Ireland championships was a history-making achievement that inspired confidence in the organisational ability of the newly-constructed Association.

No doubt it was with justifiable pride that the new Central Council met for the first time in the Freeman's Journal club the day after the All-Ireland football final. All the officers and eleven county representatives attended. Because of the long list of matters to be considered, two days were needed to complete the business – the first day in the Freeman's Journal club and the second day in the Mansion House. They were pleased when the secretary, Wm Prendergast, read a letter from William O'Brien accepting the invitation to be a patron.[22]

To: William Prendergast, Esq. Hon. Sec. GAA

Dublin,
April 5th, 1888.

My dear Sir,
You are right in assuming that your communication must have been lost

in the very large number of letters which I was utterly unable to acknowledge after my release from prison. I take the opportunity now of acknowledging very gratefully the resolution of the Thurles Gaelic Athletic Convention. Of their sympathy with the struggle against coercion I never entertained a moment's doubt, although I am unwilling to increase the prominence which undoubtably [sic] the exigencies of the struggle have forced upon me for the moment, I cannot resist the voice of the young Gaelic athletes that they should add my name to those of their well-wishers in any capacity they may choose.

Sincerely yours,
William O'Brien.

Much of the time of the meetings was taken up with investigating disputes concerning matches. No sooner was a game finished than the losers sought a basis for an objection; the most common complaints were that the winners had included players from another club; that the referee erred regarding the time played; that spectators interfered with the play and scores were disputed.

Dundalk Young Irelands objected to the awarding of the All-Ireland football final to Commercials, contending that W. Spain was not eligible, but the objection was not sustained. Bray Emmets appealed against their suspension by the Wicklow county committee for 'showing antagonism to the National League', but the suspension was confirmed by the council.

J.F. O'Crowley attended the meeting to explain the delay in presenting the 1887 championship medals was because they were being produced in Ireland and the dyes had not been ready. He criticised clubs that failed to support goods of Irish manufacture when purchasing trophies or club equipment and a resolution in these terms was unanimously adopted.

The council had adequate evidence of protracted divisions on political lines in some counties. They were faced with a serious problem in Limerick where the two rival boards had their separate championships and each of the two winners claimed to be county champions. The council recommended a play-off between the rival claimants in hurling and football and the county titles should be awarded to the winners. They also decided to summon all the affiliated clubs in the county to a general convention to be supervised by W. Prendergast, T. O'Riordan, R. Frewen, Fr Buckley and J. Cullinane. Athenry Dr Crokes club appealed against the decision of the Galway county committee in refusing their affiliation and advising that they should join P.C. Kelly's club in the town. The council upheld the appeal.

When it came to making arrangements for the 1888 championships in hurling and football, it was decided to abandon the open draw that had been used the previous year and instead to base the draw on the four provinces and the provincial winners would meet in the semi-finals.

The president placed before the meeting a draft of the book of Rules and Constitution which was intended for publication. It included the revised constitution adopted at the recent convention and all the rules that had been sanctioned by a general convention. A place was found for a number of articles of special significance for the association including:

Cusacks's article 'A word about Irish athletics' that appeared in *United Ireland* in 1884;

Davins's letter in reply;

The letters of acceptance from Dr Croke, Parnell, Davitt and O'Leary;

Articles from *United Ireland* and the *Irishman* approving the establishment of the GAA;

Letters from Cusack and Davin defending the association against early attacks,

and 'Hints on training' for athletes.

Arising from a decision of the council, the secretaries convened a meeting of the affiliated clubs in County Limerick on 11 June in an attempt to restore unity there. R. Frewen presided and in a contest for the chair the IRB nominee P. O'Brien defeated Fr Dunworth by 123 votes to 86. Fr Eugene Sheehy protested that the convention was unconstitutional and led the dissenting group from the meeting. Their appeal to the central council was turned down and their secretary was directed to hand over to D. Liddy, the legally appointed secretary, whatever affiliation fees he had received.[23]

The new council gained in popular esteem as it was perceived to be going about its business with confident efficiency. Interest in the games was whetted, clubs and counties were organised with renewed energy and a remarkable upsurge of activity was seen on the playing fields during the months of summer and autumn. *Sport* making up for its early neglect of the association, gave extensive publicity every week to the games and athletic meetings and invited clubs to supply reports of their activities. Many of the provincial papers kept the public informed of what was happening at club level, adding to the interest in the Association's affairs.

O'Sullivan acknowledges that his list of fifty tournaments for the year is far from complete. It included only one from Galway although in that county inter-club hurling and football matches were regular features of every Sunday in the months of March, April and May.[24]

Eight and even ten teams participated in some of the tournaments such as those at Clonskeagh, Thurles and Birr. Athletic meetings maintained their popularity especially in the counties where the number of affiliated clubs was low and hurling and football had not yet gained a strong foothold. In the county championships, inter club rivalry created the greatest interest locally. In Tipperary twenty-two teams contested the football title and fifteen teams the hurling, but only Boherlahan, Two-Mile-Borris, Thurles and Clonmel took part in both.

The inter-county games were beset with many problems. It was common for clubs to include a few players from a neighbouring club in spite of stern warnings from the central council that such illegalities would incur severe punishments. Objections and appeals resulted, causing long delays and consequent disruption of the championships. In some instances county champions did not contest the provincial title because their players were not in a position to meet the considerable demands in time and expense that were involved in travelling to a far distant venue. The Leinster championships were completed and Kilkenny won both, the hurling title by Mooncoin and the football by Kilmacow. Bohercrowe (Tipperary) won the football championship of Munster, but the hurling was undecided.

References.
1. *Celtic Times*, 12/11/1887.
2. *C.B.S.*, 126/S, 120W/6765, N.A.
3. *Freeman's Journal*, 10/11/1887; O'Sullivan, T.F., op. cit., pp 48-52; *Sport*, 12/11/1887.
4. Enright, F., 'Edward Bennett' in *Dal gCais*, no. 6, 1982.
5. *Tipperary Advocate*, 26/11/1887; *Freeman's Journal*, 21/11/1887.
6. *C.B.S.*, 126/S, N.A.
7. Larkin, E., *The Roman Catholic Church and the Plan of Campaign*, Cork, 1878, p. 141; Tierney, M. Croke of Cashel. p. 203.
8. *Freeman's Journal*, 16/11/1887.
9. Ibid.
10. Dr Fennelly's letters in Maurice Davin's papers in Deerpark.
11. *Freeman's Journal*, 17/11/1887.
12. Ibid., 22/11/1887.
13. Ibid., 14/11/1887; O'Sullivan, T.F., op. cit., pp 53-54.
14. *C.B.S.*, 126/S, N.A.
15. *Freeman's Journal*, 29/11/1887.
16. *C.B.S.*, 126/S, N.A.
17. Ibid.
18. *Freeman's Journal*, 6/12/1887.
19. Ibid., 14/12/1887.
20. O'Sullivan, T.F., op. cit., p. 55; Ó Laoi, P., op. cit., p. 55; Ó Ceallaigh, S., op. cit., p. 45; Ryall, T., op. cit., p. 15.
21. *Freeman's Journal*, 5/1/1888.
22. O'Sullivan, T.F., op. cit., p. 55.
23. Ibid., p. 73; Ó Ceallaigh, S., op. cit., p. 48.
24. Ó Laoi, P., op. cit., pp 41-44.

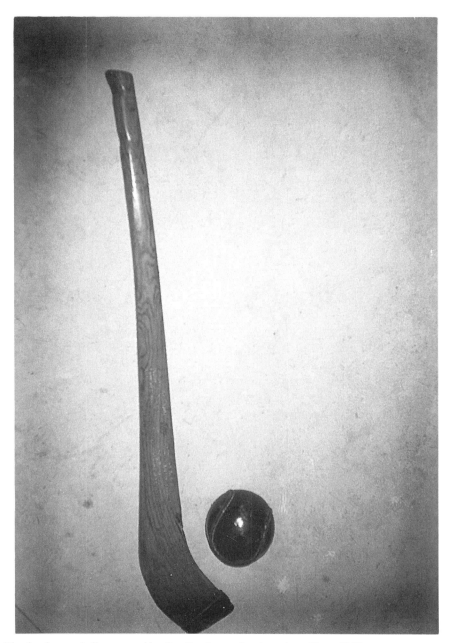

The hurley and sliotar used by Pat Davin on the American Tour 1888.

Chapter 10

Davin and the 'Invaders'

Davin, at a meeting of the Central Council in the Mansion House[1] on 1 May 1888 made it known to the members that for some time he had been considering the idea of sending a body of representative Gaels to America to compete against the best athletes there. He thought that two hurling teams should accompany the party to afford an opportunity to the American public of seeing the old Irish pastime of hurling played under proper rules. He considered that the best time would be in August when the weather would be most suitable for outdoor games.

Some members of the Council did not share Davin's enthusiasm for the venture and they hesitated to give their approval. They anticipated some difficulty in raising the finance necessary to pay for the fares and other expenses for a party of about fifty.

Davin, strengthened by the memory of the massive support he got from clubs a few months previously calling on him to return and lead the Association, was confident they would now respond to his appeal for contributions. It seemed to be a reasonable assumption at the time, but later experience was to prove otherwise. After discussing the pros and cons, the Council gave a conditional approval, but witheld a definite decision until they would meet again in July. In the meantime they would gauge the reaction of the public to the appeal.

The idea of taking a group of athletes to America was not entirely new. Michael Davitt writing from London on 30 October 1884, expressing regret that he could not attend the Thurles meeting on 1 November continued:[2]

> Why should we not have our athletic festival like other peoples? ... why not make an effort for a revival of the Tailtean Games? A grand National Festival could be organised to come off at some historic spot at which prizes could be awarded for merit not only in the various athletic sports peculiar to the Celtic people (and in this expression I would include the Scotch, Welsh and Manx), but also in music, poetry, oratory and other kindred accomplishments.

It was accepted that the cost of organising and producing such an event would be in the region of £1,000 and it would take time to raise that sum, but Davitt was confident that half that money could be raised from the Irish in America. The idea of a National Festival faded into the background as the work of establishing the Association absorbed the time and energies of the leaders.

However, contact with America presented an attractive possibility to Irish athletes that was exploited by Frank Gallagher the editor of *Sport*. He took a party of nine athletes on a tour of cities in the United States and Canada in the autumn of 1885. Drawn mainly from clubs affiliated to the Dublin-based IAAA which was at loggerheads with the GAA, they did not represent the best performers in the country and were not very successful in competition with the Americans.

A letter signed by of some prominent Irish-Americans was published in a New York paper *Irish World* in the first week of October 1885, referring to Gallagher's team of 'athletes at present in the country posing as Irishmen, composed entirely of what constituted the British garrison in Ireland, there being nothing Irish about them except the accident of their birth'. The comment could hardly be applied to at least some of the athletes.

In the next issue of *Irish World* a leading article entitled 'A Suggestion to the Gaelic Athletes' proposed that the Gaelic Athletic Association should send out to America a team thoroughly representative of Irish athletes. They would be welcomed by every Irishman by birth or descent in America and a team of hurlers could show the Irish-American youth how their fathers played the game.[3]

The Association at that time was not in a position to make a positive response to the proposal, so the matter was left over for consideration at a more convenient time. The idea was given a slight airing again in 1887, but nothing came of it.

The arrival in Ireland of a team of athletes from Manhattan and New York clubs in the summer of 1888 created a lot of excitement. An international athletics contest was arranged between the New York visitors and an Irish team in Ballsbridge on 7 and 9 July. The Irish winners were Dr J.C. Daly in slinging the 56 pound weight; Pat Davin in the 120 yards hurdles and T.P. Conneff in the mile. J.S. Mitchel, J.P. O'Sullivan and J. McCarthy did not take part in the contest. In the first individual all-round athletic championship held in Ireland Pat Davin's victory over George Gray of New York and D. Bolger, Dublin was highly popular with the spectators and focussed interest on the possibility of an American tour. The final total points for each contestant were: Pat Davin 30 points, George Gray 25 points and D. Bolger 19 points.[4]

The Association was enjoying its most fruitful year following the reconciliation convention and the buoyant atmosphere created by the sense of achievement was favourable to the invasion idea. The press was confidently predicting that before the end of the year two hurling teams would travel to America to give exhibitions there and that even Davitt's great Gaelic festival might be realised.

It is doubtful if anyone at the time realised the magnitude of the enterprise. It is equally doubtful if any commentator has given due credit to Davin and those who followed his lead for initiating the project and carrying it out with little resources except their courage and their belief in what they were doing.

Davin took up the challenge with enthusiasm and he promoted the tour at every opportunity in line with his conviction that Irishmen could match the best in the world in the events that were traditional to them. In his years competing he had accepted that his personal responsibility was to prove by his own efforts the high standards that Irishmen were capable of reaching.

America offered a daring prospect that Maurice Davin could not turn his back on, although his own days of active competition were over. His objectives were (1) to demonstrate to the people in America that the GAA was restoring the ancient games and pastimes of the country, (2) to establish the Association in America especially among the exiles there, (3) to initiate international competition between the two countries, and (4) to strengthen the finances of the Association. A number of Ireland's top athletes, including T.P. Conneff and W. Barry, had already emigrated to New York and they, as well as other exiles, encouraged the undertaking and gave assurance that it would be crowned with success. The proposal was warmly welcomed by the nationalist press and letters to the papers called on all Gaels to support Maurice Davin 'our worthy president, who had so eminently led us to such a high standard', and 'a man of unrivalled knowledge, calm deliberation and determination'.[5]

It was stated that the scheme was receiving universal approval and in order to get the message to the public Davin gave an interview to Sport.[6] He outlined the plans and expressed his confidence in its success. They planned firstly, to take two teams of hurlers to play exhibitions in the major cities of America; secondly, to take a number of athletes to compete in international contests:(a) the Gaelic athletes against American athletes; (b) the invaders against a team drawn from all foreign residents in the United States; (c) the invaders against a team from all American residents; (d) the invaders against a team of Irish-Americans.

They hoped to leave in August and return in October. The expenses could be met if each of the seven or eight hundred affiliated clubs gave a small subscription to the fund. George Byrne, the Meath representative on the Central Council, called on all Gaels to support the initiative and he expressed optimism that the expedition would prove to be a gigantic success. Clubs were requested to pass resolutions in favour of the tour.

Before a final decision could be reached, Davin considered it wise that the financial position of the Association should be examined and a statement of accounts presented to the Central Council. Unfortunately the Association had no proper system of control over financial affairs. No treasurer was elected until some time in 1886, when John Clancy, sub-sheriff of Dublin, was appointed. Patrick Hassett, Limerick was elected treasurer at the 1886 Convention, but apparently none was elected at the famous Convention in 1887. R.J. Frewen was chosen as treasurer in January 1888.

The responsibilities of the treasurer are nowhere clarified but the indications are that he did not transact any financial business and that his position was merely nominal. It appears that the affiliation fees were sent to the secretary and that he was made responsible for all financial matters, but no statement of accounts or balance sheet was presented to the Convention at the end of the year until T. O'Riordan and J.B. O'Reilly gave an account of the income and expenditure for the year at the 1887 Convention.

When Davin, with Fr Buckley and Alderman Horgan as auditors, examined all the tickets and vouchers that were available, they were unable to get a clear picture of the financial position.[7] When the Central Council met at Limerick Junction on 6 July, Davin submitted the auditor's report as far as they could ascertain from their examination. Debts remaining due since 1884 amounted to £211; the championship prizes for 1887 would cost £280, leaving a total indebtedness of £491. To meet this deficit Davin estimated that 100 would come from the athletic championships and £200 from the hurling and football finals. About £200 was due for club affiliation fees as required by rule and if these were paid it would enable the council to clear all its debts.

Commenting on the report, Davin criticised the clubs and county committees for not living up to their commitments in regard to fees. This remained a strong point with him and it was one of the causes of dissension later. He emphasised to the Council that J.B. O'Reilly, T. O'Riordan, J. Wyse Power and John M'Kay, who had been secretaries during the period under review, had each fully accounted for all monies received by them. The report was a fair estimate of the position as it appeared to the auditors, but some old debts, that they were not aware of, came to light later and were another cause of a major upset in the Association.

Since it appeared to everyone and especially to Davin, that the projected income would clear all the debts, unanimous approval was granted by the Council and preparations for the tour were immediately put in train. The Council resolved itself into a special committee to take charge of the entire project and a circular was distributed calling on clubs to support the project with subscriptions.

The Central Council of the GAA at a meeting held on 5 July 1888 at Limerick Junction formed themselves into a committee 'for the purpose of sending two teams of hurlers and athletes to America;

> to show our exiled countrymen beyond the Atlantic the enormous progress made in reviving the grand old Irish pastimes and that the old country, despite the numerous disadvantages under which it labours can yet produce bone and muscle second to none in the world.
>
> The council are confident that the grand project will tend to more closely cement the bonds of affection and sympathy already existing between the Irish at home and in America and prove to the world that the Celts though sea-divided are still united. As the carrying out of this grand project will require funds it is expected that the clubs belonging to the GAA will show their sympathy in a practical manner by subscribing the greater part of the amount required which will be about £1,000 before 6 August when the Central Council will meet at the championship sports in Limerick to make final arrangements.
>
> If the sum then subscribed is insufficient all money will have to be returned and the project postponed. The funds proper to the Association will not be encroached upon but if a surplus remains ... it will be converted into a fund for the purpose of carrying out the noble ideas of Michael Davitt by holding the monster national festival.
>
> The teams will be chosen by the Central Council and all counties having hurling clubs affiliated will be represented. It is intended that the invaders will leave about the end of August and as that time is now approaching you are requested to convene a meeting of your club and at your earliest convenience forward your subscription for the purpose of the fund to: Robert Frewen, Treasurer; T.O'Riordan, Cork Herald, Secretary; William Prendergast, Clonmel, Secretary; or the Freeman's Journal.

If it became necessary to postpone the date of departure the tour would run into deteriorating weather conditions in the States which would surely have an adverse effect on the attendances, so there was an urgent need to get in the subscriptions. The *New York World* on 1 July 1888 assured the visitors would be welcome in America:

> There is no question that the visitors will receive a hearty welcome on their arrival. Among the Gaels here the greatest enthusiasm has been aroused by the proposed trip and already several Irish societies are making arrangements for the reception of the visitors.

Doubts expressed

The national press put its weight behind the appeal for funds, and friends in America were sending optimistic messages, promising large attendances at the games and giving hope that at the end of the day surplus funds would be substantial. However, despite all the appeals, the response from the clubs was disappointing. The majority of people showed a surprising indifference to the scheme, either because they were not sufficiently informed about what was expected of them, or there was no effective system within the counties for collecting subscriptions.

There were other factors which did not help. Priests who had been extremely vocal in their support of the reconstruction plan were strangely silent, apart from the notable exceptions of Fr Buckley of Buttevant and Fr Concannon of Tullamore. It appears that the reconciliation reached with the IRB was not pleasing to some of the clergy who would have preferred that the extremists were excluded from any place on the Central Council. Furthermore many priests severed any connection they had with those who supported the Plan of Campaign, including GAA clubs, following Pope Leo's decree declaring it unlawful.[8]

The IRB, smarting under the defeat suffered at the recent Convention, reorganised to regain lost ground. Leading members employed as company representatives, including P.N. Fitzgerald, P. Hoctor, P.R. Clery, travelled over wide areas of the country and keeping in regular contact with sympathisers, they won many clubs to their support. The counties of Cork and Limerick, in each of which two rival county committees operated and Galway where the IRB influence was strongest, displayed no sympathy with the American tour plan and offered no assistance.

The tour fund received a moral boost when Dr Croke and Michael Davitt publicly conveyed their support for the scheme. The Archbishop, although heavily involved with Rome concerning the Plan of Campaign and the land agitation, took time to write to William Prendergast:

> Dear Sir,
> The project of sending a couple of teams to America appears to be popular and I shall gladly subscribe £5 towards the fund required for the purpose.
>
> Very sincerely yours,
> TW Croke, Archbishop of Cashel.

On 20 August the *Freeman's Journal* published a long letter from Michael Davitt conveying his warm support for the 'invasion' project:

> 'The contemplated "Invasion" is but a means to an end – the end being a

projected international festival here in Ireland in 1889. It has been proposed that an effort on a national scale should be made next year to establish the old Tailtean Games. We have yet to show that, concurrently with our assertion of our natural and national rights, we can, under even the most adverse circumstances, exhibit our claims to a universal recognition of our country's nationhood. In a word, the festival should be made an occasion on which all that would tend to develop the physique, the mind and the material well-being of our country might be honoured and stimulated by national recognition and reward.

Mr Maurice Davin's project of invading America and Canada with a force of fifty picked athletes of the GAA is the second practical step towards the inauguration of international Celtic festivals; the foundation of the GAA was the first.'

Mr Davitt asserted that the 'gates' made in America would go far towards providing prizes for the projected festival, which would cost approximately £1,000 and he had no doubt that the enthusiasm it would call forth would produce that amount within twelve months. He concluded:

'Those who sympathise with Mr Davin's great project ought to come forward and help him in an enterprise that is certain to bring credit and renown to this country. The fifty athletes will be dressed in Irish manufacture solely and will in every way be an honour to Ireland. An immense reception awaits them in America and they are certain to uphold the athletic fame of their country in their contests with competitors on the other side of the Atlantic'.[9]

At last subscriptions began to arrive from individual enthusiasts. J. Barry, M.P. Wexford, sent £5 and stated that it would be a national disgrace if the required target was not reached. Others to subscribe were T. Harrington, Johnstown, D.H. Ryan, Thurles and P.J. Maher, Clonmel. Bray O'Byrne's Club sent in two guineas and a good response came from Offaly due to the efforts of Fr Concannon and Patrick White. As these examples were taken up by others, the doubts were dispelled and the Council proceeded with renewed confidence to make the final arrangements.

Selecting the Party
Selection of the individuals to make up the tour party was entrusted to the organising committee and they were to be chosen from amongst those who had proved their worth at championship events. Davin as leader was given a deciding role and he insisted that those chosen should be of stainless character, should be highly skilled performers and should be free to take time off for the period of the tour. Counties where properly constituted boards were operating were asked to

nominate a number of skilful hurlers in proportion to the number of affiliation fees forwarded to the Central Council. Each player's record was to be fully scrutinised before a final selection was made. The numbers of nominations allowed to the counties were: Dublin – 4; Kilkenny – 3; Kildare – 1; Offaly – 4; Laois – 2; Waterford – 1; Clare – 2; Galway – 1. Tipperary, being All-Ireland hurling champions, was treated as a special case. The county was allowed to nominate three hurlers and Thurles, having won the All-Ireland title for 1887, was permitted to nominate one player. Clonoulty, then county champions, was granted one nomination making a total of five for the county.

Limerick was ruled out because the two rival county committees, one supporting the National League, the other controlled by the IRB could not agree. In Cork there were two committees opposing each other on political lines, each claiming to be the authority and before the end of the year a third, the O'Brien committee, was formed in north Cork. However, the Tower Street club, which was recognised as the champions of the county, was allowed one nomination.

Galway county, which was among the most active and best organised in the country did not nominate any hurler for the tour. The county committee was in conflict with the Central Council on a number of issues. A strong IRB element held the power on the committee and did not favour the reconstruction plan; they had a difference with the Council about the portion of the affiliation fees to be paid over to the Council, and they opposed the invasion plan from the beginning.[10] The Tower Street team in Cork failed to nominate any player.

The players selected to travel were:

Tipperary: T. O'Grady, Moycarkey; J.O'Brien, Moycarkey; J. Stapleton, Thurles; T. Ryan, Clonoulty and W. Prendergast, Clonmel.
Dublin: P.P. Sutton, Metropolitan Hurling Club; G. Burgess, Dunleary; T. Furlong, Davitts; J. Hayes, Faughs and F. Coughlan, Kickhams.
Wexford: J. Royce, Oulart Hill.
Laois: P.J. Molohan, Monasterevin; P. Ryan, Rathdowney and J. McEvoy, Knockaroo.
Kilkenny: P. Fox, Mooncoin; M. Curran, Castlecomer and J. Grace, Tullaroan.
Offaly: J. Dunne, Rahan; J. Nolan Dunkerrin; J. Cordial, Kinnitty and P. Meleady, Birr.
Waterford: M. Hickey, Carrickbeg.
Clare: J. Rourke, Kilbane; J. Fitzgibbon, Ogonnoloe and P. Minogue, Tulla.

Although Cork and Limerick were ruled out, J. Coughlan Buttevant was included, probably through the influence of Fr C. Buckley who was an ardent supporter of the scheme. D. Godfrey of Murroe in

Limerick was also added to the party. To make up two teams of twenty-one, some of the athletes who were excellent hurlers were called into service.

President Davin and Treasurer Frewen attended the All-Ireland athletic championships in Limerick in August, supervising the events and noting the individual performances. The selection of the eighteen athletes to travel on the tour was straightforward. All were championship winners or runners-up, while Pat Davin and J.C. Daly had established an international reputation. Dan Fraher, Dungarvan and J.P. O'Sullivan, Killorglin were considered but were unable to travel. The county representation was – six from Cork, five from Limerick, four from Tipperary, two from Waterford and one from Kerry.

The athletes selected for the tour were:

> Pat Davin, the all-round champion who had won seventeen Irish titles in different events and two British championships.
> J.S. Mitchell of Emly, aged 24, a champion weight-thrower and record breaker.
> Dan Shanahan, Kilfinnane, aged 20, hop, step and jump champion.
> Pat T. Keoghan, Dungarvan, aged 24, champion at standing jumps.
> T.M. O'Connor, Ballyclough, aged 25, champion high jumper.
> William Phibbs, Glenville, aged 26, champion half miler.
> Mike Connery, Staker Wallace Club, Limerick, aged 26, excellent high jumper.
> J. Connery, Staker Wallace Club, pole vault champion.
> Pat Looney, Macroom, an all-round athlete, a specialist at hop, step and jump.
> T. O'Mahoney, the 'Rosscarbery Steam engine', quarter mile champion.
> William McCarthy, Macroom, aged 19, the mile champion.
> Dr J.C. Daly, Borrisokance, aged 35, a giant of a man, a former champion at the weights.
> William Real, Pallasgreen, aged 28, another champion weight thrower.
> P. O'Donnell, Carrick-on-Suir, excelled at the hammer and weights.
> J. McCarthy, Staker Wallace Club, aged 21, weight thrower and sprinter.
> T. Barry Dungarvan, a champion at standing jumps.
> D. Power, Shanballymore, Cork, a hurdles champion and long jumper.
> J. Mooney, Ballyhea, Cork, champion sprinter.

Davin was anxious to include an athlete from one of the northern counties and he organised a special mile race in Dundalk for runners from the north and the counties of east Leinster. The winner was to receive a special medal prize and he could earn a place on the invasion party if his standard of performance merited it. Davin travelled to Dundalk to supervise the event, but the plan was upset when the race was won easily by J.B. Curran of Dublin.[11]

As August drew near the Central Council anxiously examined the details of the fund and discovered that despite all the appeals, the amount collected fell far short of the target. No list of subscribers has been published nor is there any account available to indicate the total amount subscribed to the fund. From scattered references in *Sport* and *Freeman's Journal* the following list has been compiled:

Archbishop Croke £5.	Michael Davitt amount not known
Dublin Co. Committee £5.	J. Barry M.P. Wexford £5.
Bray O'Byrnes £2.2s.	D.H. Ryan, Thurles 10s.
P.J. Maher, Clonmel 10s.	T. Harrington, Callan £1.
W. Prendergast, Clonmel £10.	(from a fine imposed on a member).
Offaly Co. Committee £20.	(made up of subs. from clubs per P. White and Fr Concannon).
Cork County Board £15.	(subscribed after the return of the invaders).

Sport and *Freeman's Journal* subscribed unknown amounts. The above merely indicates the scale of the contributions made.

The preparations had gone so far that they could not contemplate turning back and they were faced with no alternative but to postpone the date of departure and to intensify the fund-raising campaign. When they met at Limerick Junction in August, they announced the new departure date would be 16 September and they finalised the travel arrangements.

Maurice Davin, Robert Frewen, William Prendergast and J.J. Cullen were to travel as the officials in charge and Fr Concannon was appointed as chaplain in recognition of his efforts in support of the project. As advance agent, John Cullinane of Bansha was to sail to America before the main party to make arrangements about accommodation, venues and publicity.

Independently of the official party, Thomas Harrington, Johnstown, an enthusiastic supporter of the venture and Joseph Whelan, a journalist with the *Freeman's Journal* accompanied the group. Because some lingering doubts remained about reaching the financial target, Davin decided to bring the entire party to Dublin a week before embarking for the States and to hold a number of exhibition games in order to boost the fund. He envisaged a whirlwind campaign at a number of venues where most support could be expected. Davin drew up an itinerary for the exhibitions:

Sunday 9 September 1888	Donnybrook, Dublin 11 am
	Dun Laoghaire 4 pm
Monday 10 September	Wexford
Tuesday 11 September	Dundalk

Wednesday 12 September	Tullamore
Thursday 13 September	Kilkenny
Friday 14 September	Thurles
Saturday 15 September	Cork
Sunday 16 September	Embark in Cobh.

He thought it advisable to go to Cork beforehand because of the dissension that existed there between the two boards. He met Alderman Horgan to discuss the arrangements for the reception of the tour party and for the proposed exhibition if a suitable venue could be got.

When the 'invasion' party assembled outside the Angel Hotel at Inns Quay in Dublin on Saturday 8 September, they received an enthusiastic welcome from a large crowd that had gathered there for the unique occasion and the scene was enlivened by two city bands playing Irish airs.[12] That evening the hurlers came together and nominated Thomas O'Grady and P.P. Sutton as captains and they chose the following teams:

> **P.P. Sutton's Team:** P.P. Sutton, J. Royce, W. Fox, F. Coughlan, D. Godfrey, P. Molohan, J. McEvoy, J. O'Rourke, J. Nolan, P. Minogue, J. Grace, T. Ryan, J. Hayes, P.J. O'Donnell, J.J. Cullen, J. Mooney, J. Connery, D. Power, D. Shanahan and W. Real.

> **Thomas O'Grady's Team:** T. O'Grady, J. Furlong, J. O'Brien, J. Stapleton, J. Dunne, J. Cordial, J. Fitzgibbon, M. Hickey, P. Meleady, M.J. Curran, P. Ryan, J. McCarthy, J. Coughlan, W. Prendergast, P. Davin, M. Connery, W. Phibbs, T.M. O'Connor, T.J. O'Mahoney and J.S. Mitchel.

The teams were neatly presented in distinctive attire, one set manufactured by Merne of Cork and the other by a Clonmel clothing firm. Sutton's team wore jerseys with deep orange and yellow stripes, caps of the same colours with an uncrowned harp on the frontpiece, brown corduroy knee breeches, brown stockings and blue leather shoes with rubber soles. O'Grady's side were dressed in bright green jerseys and caps, drab knee breeches, black stockings and russet leather shoes with rubber soles. Both teams had the letters GAA woven on their jerseys and their attractive dress presented a pleasing appearance that caused much favourable comment from the onlookers and reflected the care taken by the officials in preparing for the trip.

The weight of responsibility for the success of the exhibitions fell on Davin and he worked day and night, rushing from town to town, rousing local leaders to enthusiasm and making the necessary arrangements for the displays and accommodation. It was an over-ambitious programme involving a lot of travel within the constraints of the time – over 650 miles inside a week – and placing a strain on the stamina of the participants. Davin himself, then forty-six years old, set the pace with boyish enthusiasm. He was full of confidence, inspired as one in charge of a historic mission, a life's wish fulfilled. He was not dismayed even by the news from Cork that co-operation there was doubtful owing to disagreement with the arrangements and friction between rival boards.

D. Walsh, the secretary of the IRB dominated board in Cork, wrote a sharp letter to Davin:

Cork County Board GAA
6th September, 1888.

Dear Sir,

At a meeting of the County Board held on Tuesday, Chairman Alderman Horgan brought before the meeting a conversation he had with you a few days ago. I am directed to write to you for particulars. What time will the WISCONSIN arrive on Sunday?. When will the team arrive in Cork? When do you intend to leave for Queenstown? What do you expect the County Board to do? Are the steamers chartered for the conveyance of the team to transatlantic liner? Will she anchor in the harbour or outside? The reason I ask is that the Citizen's River Steamers will do if she anchors in the harbour, otherwise one of the harbour steam tugs will have to be chartered as the steamers are not chartered to go further than the line between the forts. Let me have any particulars that you have in answer and I will see to give the invaders a big send off.

Yours truly,
D. Walsh, Hon. Sec.

Are the Gaels to represent Cork County selected yet and if they are who are they? The sooner the Board receives a direct and immediate reply the better for the success of the undertaking.

D.W.

Davin replied by return of post on 7 September 1888.

Dear Sir,

In reply to yours of the 6th inst., the Wisconsin will arrive at 10 o'clock on Sunday 16th. I don't know where it will anchor. The teams will arrive in Cork on Friday evening. I was under the impression there was no ground in Cork in which the teams could give an exhibition. When in Cork Mr Forrest showed me the race course and it appeared to me that an exhibition could be given there if no objection. I found that the Corn Market is not available on week days for an athletic meeting. I cannot ask the County Board to do anything as the Invasion is outside the regular business of the Association. If they wish to have an exhibition hurling match in the Park I should be glad to make arrangements for it.

We have not chartered steamers and we intend to leave Queenstown by tender in the usual way.[13]

Yours truly,
Maurice Davin.

It cannot be denied that there was insidious opposition to the tour in some counties, especially by opponents of the new constitution and by others who were aggrieved because they were left out of the plans. Such opposition was muted and expressed more in non co-operation than in outright criticism, but later when the 'invaders' returned, it was given full rein in bitter terms.

The series of exhibitions commenced on Sunday 9 September. During the week beforehand the national press kept the public informed of the times, dates and venues of the performances so that large crowds were expected to turn up to cheer on the 'invaders', as they became known.

Fund-raising exhibitions

The leaders were greatly encouraged when the exhibitions at Donnybrook and Dunleary attracted crowds of 4,000 and 3,000 respectively. The following day they took the train to Wexford where they were cheered by an attendance of 6,000 in the park and the entire party was entertained to a meal in the Imperial Hotel.

They returned to Dublin by the evening train and set out for Dundalk early the next morning. Again they were given a rousing reception and the local committee had planned a full programme of athletic events as well as the hurling exhibition. When they arrived in Tullamore on Wednesday, a huge crowd had gathered to welcome them at the railway station under the direction of Fr Concannon. Led by a local band, the players were escorted in a parade to the sports field.

Next day the reception in Kilkenny was equally enthusiastic. The Castlecomer Gaels presented the team with hurleys and Martin Butler made a presentation of handballs to Davin. Their journey from one venue to the next resembled a victory parade as crowds gathered at the railway stations to greet them and wish them 'God speed.' From Kilkenny they drove to Thurles in horse-drawn coaches. The exhibition was performed in the ground of St Patrick's College and a photograph of the party was taken by Thomas Gray of Templemore. Davin was disappointed that Archbishop Croke could not be there to greet them. He had departed for Europe to take a rest a short while before.[14]

At Buttevant station, on the way to Cork on Friday evening, the group was greeted by a crowd and Fr Buckley read an address of welcome. On arrival in Cork station, a number of people displayed hostility to the president and the other officials. Cork, it was alleged was not fairly represented on the hurling team and some claimed that twenty Corkmen could beat the twenty-two selected. More insidiously they threatened that the invaders would not be welcomed on the other side.[15] Davin ignored the taunts, pointing out that they were going to their friends in America and he made it clear that the place reserved for the Tower Street club was still open, but this was not acceptable to the Cork committee.

He expressed his thanks to E. Fitzgerald and J. Forrest for looking after their luggage and escorting them to O'Keeffe's Italian Hotel where they were accommodated until their departure on Sunday. Because of the strained feelings between the rival boards, it was decided not to hold an exhibition, in order to avoid the possibility of causing any disturbance.

When they arrived in Cobh on Sunday morning, their spirits were raised by the rousing reception they received from the local supporters. Two telegrams awaited them: One from Cullinane read: 'Inform Davin Gaelic team prospects good National championships October 8th exercise on board'; the other was from Michael Davitt: 'Only just arrived from England sorry can't see you off accept hearty wishes for successful tour and laurels galore'. As they boarded the WISCONSIN the crowd on the shore sang 'God save Ireland'. The baggage included two hundred hurleys bearing green labels inscribed 'Gaelic-American Invasion'.

Arrival in New York

After a nine-day voyage, the ship berthed in New York harbour on Tuesday 25 September 1888. They were accorded a tumultuous welcome by the representatives of the Irish societies who crowded the quayside, led by Colonel Kavanagh of the 69th regiment, E.J. Curry of the Home Rule Club, James O'Gorman, president of the Irish Municipal Council, Captain O'Meagher Condon who twenty-one years previously had been sentenced to death with Allen, Larkin and O'Brien but was later reprieved; Lieut. McLoughlin, assistant district attorney, Rev J. Doherty, Dr William O'Meagher, Rev J. Larkin, Dr J.E. Kelly, T. Conneff, J. Purcell, Officers of C.J. Kickham Club; the Gaelic Club and the Manhattan Athletic Club.

They were entertained to a banquet in their honour in the Park Avenue Hotel which had been built by an Irish emigrant millionaire A.T. Stewart. For the remainder of the week they trained in the Manhattan club grounds every day and in their spare time they went sight-seeing with their friends. The New York press was expansive in its praise of the impressive uniforms.[16] *The New York Herald* was impressed:

> It would prove a difficult task to bring together at short notice a more splendid assemblage of specimens of manhood than the half hundred clear-complexioned and clean-limbed, stalwart, bright-eyed muscular young fellows who were grouped together on the deck of the Wisconsin yesterday.

The Globe, Boston, reported:

> There has been a great deal of talk in Irish newspapers for the past two months of a Gaelic Invasion of America and on Tuesday last the 'Invaders' entered New York, by way of the Guion steamship, WISCONSIN. They were fifty-three strong, as stalwart and manly a lot of men as one could wish to see. They have taken the town by storm and have conquered the hearts of everyone.

In the ten days since his arrival in New York, John Cullinane had been active in making contact with societies and communities in about twelve cities and towns close to the east coast and he had been assured by them of full co-operation in making arrangements for the reception of the 'Invasion' party. However, he encountered some disappointments which disrupted the original plans, threatened to defeat the objectives of the tour and placed its financial success in jeopardy. He had originally hoped to extend the tour to Toronto, Detroit and Chicago, but he was persuaded to abandon that portion of his plan because of the severe weather conditions in those cities. He was confronted with a much more serious problem arising from a bitter dispute between the two rival athletic bodies, the National American Athletic Association based in New York and the Amateur Athletic Union which was more widely supported throughout the United States. Cullinane decided to take a neutral stand on the grounds that the visitors should not take sides in the dispute but should try to make independent arrangements for competition with both Associations. However, he failed to get agreement for this course from Otto Ruhl, the secretary of the AAU, who would only support the 'Invaders' if they agreed to denounce the rival body. Ruhl, interviewed by the *Sporting World* referring to the possibility of the 'Invaders' competing in the NAAA championships said:

> If they persist in participating on this occasion they will render themselves ineligible to compete in any of the full games of the Amateur Athletic Union clubs in America. I explained the situation to Mr Cullinane, the Irish team's representative, and made him an offer of support if he would renounce the NAAA but he has not deemed it advisable to accept it.

John Cullinane commented: 'We will compete at the NAAA games and if the AAU clubs won't compete against us we shall have to give exhibitions amongst ourselves'. Davin agreed with Cullinane's decision although it meant that the tour would lose much of its appeal for the public without the attraction of international contests between the Irish visitors and the best of the Americans.[17]

Manhattan Athletic Club, the principal club in the NAAA, had amongst its members many Irish athletes including T.P. Conneff, the mile record holder and M.J.M. Barry, a champion weight thrower, both recently arrived in New York, and it was supported by the Irish societies in the city. Cullinane could not turn his back on his own who had befriended him and assisted him in every way from the day he landed. His decision was fully supported by Davin.

Another cause of upset to the invaders and particularly to Davin, was a letter written by Michael Cusack on 1 September and published in the *Chicago Citizen* on the 19th before the invaders had arrived in New York, in which Cusack expressed extreme criticism of Davitt and Davin and the invasion in general:[18]

... You are threatened with a 'Gaelic' invasion. Favour me with space to say a few words about the invaders. There is a rule of the Gaelic Athletic Association that a club must have twenty-one playing members before it can be affiliated. Let me ask Maurice Davin how many 'playing' members in the bogus athletic club attached to the *Freeman's Journal* company limited? Did they ever hurl or play football? And if they never played a match against any Gaelic club why should the GAA be farmed out to them? Why should Maurice Davin persistently support those who organise athletic 'booms' under Gaelic rules and bring in constabulary and military bands that play 'God Save the Queen' to the exclusion of National bands that play national music. These things are not told to Dr Croke and I need not add that I am not going to tell his Grace after the experience of March 1886. But Michael Davitt knows them and marvellous to speak he approves of the invasion. He knows more. He knows that in athletic matters the Association is absolutely under the dominion of its hereditary Saxon foe. But Michael Davitt sees nothing wrong in this. Furthermore he has promised to rig out the invaders in home manufactured clothes. I hope they won't have the smell of the shop off them, for it is freely stated that the suits of Blarney tweed sold at Cork are made in England. Will Davitt and Davin pledge themselves publicly that they propose to encourage cottage industry by annually purchasing a quarter of a million pairs of long stockings for the hurlers and football players? Will they state publicly where the jerseys are woven? Will they state publicly that they will support National music by giving at least a portion of the gate money to the promoters of band contests? Will they promise to support the Irish language as heartily as

Davitt's quinquennial pronouncements would lead the casual listener to hope? Will the money raised in America be devoted to reviving the Tailtean Games or will it be spent in confectioners' shops after the manner of those Gaels who owe thirty-four pounds, three shillings and a penny to the comfit vendor of Nassau Street, Dublin? Will Davitt who has taken as peculiar an interest in athletes, who quite recently in the *Freeman* poopood [sic] the historical aspect of the Tailtean games, kindly tell the Irish in America has he ever seen a hurling match, although thousands of matches have been played in Ireland since he settled down at home? Will Davin and Davitt tell the Celts of America why the inter-county champion hurling matches are not yet played off? ....

Yours faithfully,

Michael Cusack. Founder of the Gaelic Athletic Association.

In the next issue of the *Citizen*, 26 September 1888, the editor John F. Finnerty said that Cusack's letter had been published without his knowledge or sanction and that it would have been suppressed had he been in the city when it was received. He added: 'The visiting delegation of the Gaelic Athletic Club to this country should be received by all Irish Americans with consideration and cordiality and any attempt by any man to perpetuate dissension between Irishmen because of honourable differences of opinion, should be sternly frowned on'.

Cusack's disappointment at losing his position in the Association that he had founded, perhaps his annoyance at being excluded from the invasion project that he had originally supported, because he was no longer an official, his anxiety to let the Irish at home and abroad realise how he had laboured without stint for the Association, as well as his eagerness to ensure that the GAA would pursue and adhere to its original purpose are all understandable. Yet, in giving full rein to his penchant for scathing criticism, he was unfairly attacking two men whose bona fides in relation to the Association were beyond question. They had responded eagerly to his call in 1884 and he had given an enthusiastic welcome to Davin's return to lead the Association. It cannot be said that the letter adversely affected the welcome given to the invaders, but it almost certainly was a cause of distress to Davin, so much so that he retained a copy of the letter amongst his papers.

The first official exhibitions were given at the Manhattan grounds on Saturday 29 September. The main interest was centred on the hurling match since the great majority of the spectators had never seen the game played. Although the crowd was wildly enthusiastic, it was not as large as had been expected.[19] The *New York Herald* reported:

By far the most interesting feature of the day was the Irish national game of hurling. When the stalwart Irish lads marched out with their hurleys on their shoulders the spectators gave them a big cheer. They formed in lines in the middle of the field, the ball was thrown up and the fun began. Such leaping, jumping, running, hitting and tumbling was never seen on these grounds. There was not a man on the field who was not ambidextrous. To the stranger it seemed dangerous, but the men from long practice, never hit a head.

The following Monday, in an exhibition given at Brooklyn, Jim Mitchel and Dr Daly were the heroes of the day when they broke the records in throwing the 56 pound weight in both Irish and American styles, but again the attendance was disappointing. On Wednesday they went by train to Boston and it proved to be the highlight of the tour. The strong Irish population in the city turned out in force and a cavalcade of cars, escorted by bands, conducted the invaders to the Parker House Hotel and later they were taken on an excursion on the river. That night Boston Irish societies entertained them to a banquet in the hotel.

On Thursday they were paraded through the principal streets of the city to Beacon Park where a crowd estimated at two thousand had assembled in anticipation of real contests. Through the exertions of John Cullinane, some prominent athletes from the New England area were to provide the opposition in defiance of the ban by the Amateur Union. Two days were needed to complete the comprehensive programme of events. The invaders were successful in the weights, jumps, hurdles and middle-distance running. On the second day the attendance was even bigger, which was pleasing to Frewen and Prendergast who had charge of the 'gate money'. Once again the hurling exhibition caused a lot of excitement and favourable comment.

Some of the athletes returned to New York for the athletic championships on Monday 9 October, while the remainder of the party visited towns in the State of Massachusetts that had a strong Irish element in the population. At Lawrence they were washed out with rain such as they had never seen in Ireland and the programme had to be curtailed. When they reached Lowell, the weather changed to severe cold and the players had difficulty in keeping a grip on their hurleys. Yet the spectators enjoyed the skill of the players and the *Lowell Daily News* commented: 'The skill shown in the men's work of picking the ball off the ground with their sticks and keeping it in the air was marvellous. They do not seem to rely so much on passing the ball but go in for long hard hits'. Conditions at Worcester were somewhat improved and about a thousand turned out to cheer them, but the day was spoiled by another downpour.

The Irish societies in all those towns entertained the invaders in the evening time and if they had cause for complaint that the days were wet, the nights were exceedingly dry since prohibition was in operation in the State. The weather was no less severe in Albany, the New York State capital and the small crowd that shivered in the cold and rain at Riverside Park were highly appreciative of the efforts of the athletes and hurlers who performed as if it was a bright sunny day and the crowd twice as big.

The town of Troy, close to Albany, had attracted many emigrants after the Famine and consequently had a sizeable Irish population who came out in large numbers on a fine sunny day to give a hearty welcome to the champions from the old country. After displaying their prowess, the party boarded a steamer and travelled down the Hudson to New York.

From New York they went south to Philadelphia and gave exhibitions of hurling, running, weight-throwing and jumping, and Maurice Davin gave a demonstration of throwing the wooden-handled hammer in the one-handed style. Public Ledger described the hurling display as 'an exhilarating sport, much more exciting than lacrosse, polo, shinny [shinty] or football'. In a stadium capable of accommodating 60,000 spectators, the attendance appeared to be very small.

On the return journey to New York, they stopped off at Yonkers where they were received by the newly-formed Wolfe Tone GAA club and the large Irish section of the population who took a keen interest in the hurling display. The *New York Morning Journal* reported: 'A sport worthy of a place among those which have been naturalised here is the ancient game of hurling. It calls for sound lungs, active muscles, a quick eye and a ready hand and foot. It tends to gracefulness of build and lightness of carriage.' The hurlers played another short game for the Irish in nearby Pattison before returning to New York.

They made their last public display in competition with some of the American champions at Manhattan ground on 29 October when the weight-throwers, especially Mitchell and Real, excelled. As usual the hurling match attracted most interest and the *Brooklyn Citizen* observed that it was played in most spirited style all through. Unfortunately the weather continued to act as a spoil sport and the second half had to be abandoned on account of a downpour. The American all-round champion, Malcolm Forde, and J. Jordan were present, but they showed no inclination to accept the challenge for a contest offered by Pat Davin, leaving the Irish champion a very disappointed man. The athletes had their most severe test in Boston, being opposed by some of the best athletes from both American Unions, in spite of the dispute between them. J. Mooney won the 220 yards sprint. T. O'Mahoney won the 440 yards and W. Phibbs won the mile. Pat Davin was first in the 120 yards hurdles and J.S. Mitchell won in the weights. Dr J.C. Daly created record throws in the 56 pound weight in both Irish and American style.

In the National Athletic Association championships in Madison Square Gardens in New York, J. O'Connor won the high jump at 5 ft 10 ins; T. O'Mahoney was first in the 440 yards and Mitchell won both the 56 pound weight and the hammer throw. In Philedelphia Mitchell threw the 56 pound weight a new distance of 36 ft 6 ins.

Davin and the other officials were disappointed when they came to examine their financial position in the last days of the tour. The returns from the exhibitions fell far short of what they had expected and did not come near to meeting their expenses in travel and accommodation.

The poor weather was a principal cause of the small attendances at many of the venues and that came about as a result of the need to postpone the departure from Ireland from August to September. Had the original arrangements stood, more favourable weather conditions in America would certainly have attracted greater crowds and higher gate receipts.

Attendances were also adversely affected by the counter attraction of the American presidential election which was in full swing in the lead-up to polling day in November. The Democrat President, Grover Cleveland, was facing a challenge from Republican Benjamin Harrison, in a campaign marked by the usual flamboyant displays associated with American elections and it commanded the attention of Irish-American societies that were deeply involved in American politics.

The dispute between the two rival athletic bodies in America imposed a damper on the tour. In some of the cities the Irish champions were confined to exhibitions amongst themselves because no opposition appeared to test them. It must also be said that the bright promises of support from the American side were not consistently fulfilled, although the American press gave widespread publicity before and after the tour and cannot be faulted.

Financial crisis

Davin and his fellow officials faced a financial crisis. An amount of £450 was needed to meet their hotel and transport expenses. Michael Davitt came to their aid, and through his intervention all the outstanding accounts were cleared.[20] Some years later, when Davitt was questioned in the bankruptcy court about the money he advanced to the Gaelic tour to America, he said that as a patron he felt bound to support the tour; Patrick Ford (editor of the *Irish World* had access to a Skirmishing Fund from which he sent about half a million dollars to Ireland for various national movements), communicated with him and advanced the £450 to pay hotel and other expenses at Philadelphia. The only people he communicated with were Maurice Davin and John Cullinane.

Dr Croke in a letter to F.B. Dineen on 30 September 1890, stated that there ought to be no difficulty in raising the sum required to pay off the outstanding debts incurred by the Association, either in Ireland or America and Mr Davitt should not be a penny out of pocket in view of the generous aid he afforded when it was sorely needed.[21] When a deputation from the Central Council approached Davitt about money, he informed them that the money used to pay the debts had been subscribed for national purposes and he considered that he had put the money to good use under the circumstances. Davin and Cullinane were obviously made aware of the source of the money and that it was not a personal loan from Michael Davitt.

At the adjourned Convention of the Association in 1903, T.F. O'Sullivan, one of the trustees, referred to the money paid by Mr Davitt in connection with the American invasion and on the suggestion of D. Fraher, Waterford, it was unanimously agreed to present a testimonial to him in recognition of what he had done.[22]

Maurice Davin in a letter to *Sport*, 12 July 1890 clarified the position, "As regards the Invasion Team the amount mentioned is quite distinct from the G.A.A. accounts; nothing of it is charged to the G.A.A. I am sure that those who are mainly concerned will be able to settle their affairs without issuing an appeal to the country'.[23]

Glowing tributes were paid to the invaders at a farewell banquet organised by the nationalists of New York in Tammany Hall, which was attended by about three thousand. Maurice Davin and John Cullinane on behalf of the group responded with thanks to their hosts for their kindness to the entire party during their stay in the city. Courtesy to their hosts would not permit them to suggest that if each of those present contributed a dollar, the tour would be rated an outstanding financial success and could possibly have altered the future course of the Association. On the eve of their departure for home, they were entertained to a concert and dance by the United Irish Societies at their rooms on West 28th Street.

On the last day of October 1888, twenty-four of the original party of fifty-one boarded the *City of New York* bound for home. Fr Concannon had departed earlier and eight or nine others would sail later after spending a while visiting relatives. Seventeen were to remain permanently in America and a few others would return later to take up residence in the States. Those who remained permanently in America were; J.S. Mitchell, Tipperary; P. O'Donnell, Tipperary; J. Connery and M. Connery, Limerick; J. McCarthy, Limerick; J. Furlong, Dublin; J.J. Cullen, Dublin; F. Coughlin, Dublin; J. Mooney, Cork; W. McCarthy, Cork; J. Dunne, Offaly; P. Meleady, Offaly; J. Royce, Wexford; J. McEvoy,

Laois; P. Molohan, Kildare; J. Rourke, Clare and P. Minogue, Clare.

While they were en voyage an address of welcome was being prepared for presentation to them on their return to Cork. The change of heart came about at the Annual Convention of the board on 18 October when E. Fitzgerald, a strong supporter of the tour, opposed E. Crean for the chair without success. However, he made his point, stating that it was a shame that no reception was given to the fine body of men, including a number of Corkmen, who went out to challenge America. O'Riordan reported that since the invaders had departed, a sum of £15 had been donated to their fund and would be presented to the treasurer when they returned. Fr Buckley proposed a reception committee of E. Crean, T. O'Riordan, M. Deering, J.F. O'Crowley and J. Russell to greet the invaders when they arrived back. Only three members disapproved.[24]

When they disembarked from the City of New York on 8 November the returning invaders were welcomed on the tender by the delegation from the Cork county board and an address was read by Michael Deering, congratulating them on the manner in which they sustained the honour of Ireland; they had proved to the American people that Ireland could still boast of men whose strong hands and gallant hearts are ready should she need them; they had shown that hurling deserved its reputation as the most inspiring pastime peculiar to any country in the world. No hint of political involvement appeared in the address presented by the Cobh Gaelic Club congratulating Maurice Davin and the party on bringing the tour to a successful and brilliant conclusion.

In returning thanks for the reception given to them, Maurice Davin expressed their appreciation of the flattering addresses presented by the county board and the local club. They had been well received in America and they were told that they had done a lot to elevate the Irish character there, although they had to contend with some unexpected problems that disrupted some of their plans. The positive effects of the tour in establishing the eminent status of the GAA at home and in America are inclined to be overlooked. That the failure was a financial one cannot be attributed to any lapse or lack of care on the part of Davin or the other officials, but to a set of adverse circumstances beyond their control. Such considerations were not taken into account when criticisms were being levelled at Davin in the weeks ahead by those who sought to overturn his position as head of the Association.

References
1.   *Sport*, 5/5/1888.
2.   O'Sullivan, T.F., op. cit., p. 8; *Sport*, 30/10/1884.
3.   Davin, P., op. cit., pp 22-3.

4. Ibid., pp 65-6.
5. *Sport*, 28/7/1888.
6. Ibid., 9/6/1888.
7. Ibid., 7/7/1888, 21/7/1888; O'Sullivan, T.F., op. cit., p. 67.
8. Tierney, M., op. cit., p. 222; Curtis, L.P., *Coercion & Conciliation*, London, 1963, p. 274.
9. *Sport*, 25/8/1888; O'Sullivan, T.F., op. cit., pp 68-9.
10. Ó Laoi, P., *Annals of the GAA in Galway*, 1983, pp 80-81.
11. *Sport*, 18/8/1888.
12. Ibid., September 1888.
13. *Cork Daily Herald*, 17/9/1888.
14. Tierney, M., op. cit., p. 225.
15. *Cork Daily Herald*, 17/9/1888.
16. Extracts from *The Morning Journal, New York Herald, Boston Globe* in Maurice Davin's papers.
17. *Sporting World*, New York, in Maurice Davin's papers.
18. *Chicago Citizen*, 19/9/1888, 26/9/1888 in Maurice Davin's papers.
19. Account of American tour from Pat Davin, *Recollections*, chapter iv; *Sport*; American papers in Maurice Davin's papers.
20. *Irish Independent GAA Golden Jubilee Supplement 1934*, article by Joseph Whelan, pp vii and viii; O'Brien, Wm. & Ryan, D., ed., *Devoy's Postbag*, Dublin, 1948, pp 184, 459-469.
21. O'Sullivan, T.F., op. cit., pp 90, 104.
22. Ibid., pp 149, 159; *Tipperary People*, 30/6/1893.
23. *Sport*, 12/7/1890.
24. *Cork Examiner*, 19/10/1888; *Cork Daily Herald*, 9/11/1888.

Chapter 11

Davin leaves the Presidency

As the train entered the valley of the Suir on its way to Carrick, Maurice Davin's mood changed. The American invasion and its problems vanished from his mind and a sense of elation gripped him as the familiar sights opened before him and he was back again amongst the people and in the life that he knew since childhood. He had been away for two months, the longest period he was ever absent from Deerpark and many changes could have happened in that time, the busiest season of the year. From the train his experienced eye viewed the fertile lands on both sides of the river, the stubbled fields left bare of corn, the stacks of hay and straw in the well-stocked haggards, the cattle grazing in the aftergrass, little groups of workers in the tillage getting out the potatoes and on the river, barges plying against the current, bearing wares to Clonmel. He was excited and a little anxious to learn how Deerpark had fared while he was away.

As he and Pat alighted from the train at the station, they were surrounded by welcoming friends who were full of questions. So seldom had anyone returned from the United States to give a first-hand account of what it was like in the New World that here was a unique opportunity, and although Maurice was eager to learn how the harvest had turned out, he had to wait for another time while he answered enquiries about relations and how they were doing in the big cities of New York, Boston and Philadelphia. Even in smaller places such as Troy, a town near Albany, many Irish had settled, including some from Carrick and there they had found congenial employment as river men, working barges down the Hudson to New York as their ancestors had done for years on the Suir.

The older people wanted to know if they had found any trace of Bob Kelly the old Fenian who had escaped to America after he had shot Talbot, the informer. Talbot was a notorious character who had been sent to Carrick by the police authorities in 1867, the year of the Fenian Rising. He was employed as a water bailiff by a local magistrate. He posed as an IRB organiser and having gained the confidence of young men in the locality he pretended to swear them into the organisation; then on his evidence they were convicted and sentenced to serve long periods in prison. He was viewed with intense enmity in Carrick for his perfidy and being traced to Dublin he was shot there by Kelly. The Davins were able to report that Kelly now old and lame was still living in New York.[1]

General disappointment was expressed when the people learned that despite all his efforts, Pat Davin was denied the chance of competition for the all-round championship of the world against the American champions; they had been confident that he would bring that title home to Carrick.

At home in Deerpark, Tom and Bridget reported to Maurice all the happenings on the farm while he was away. The harvest was in and stored, the yield was up to standard, and the farm stock had presented no problems. He was worried about the river trade on account of the strong opposition from the railway. Ten years previously, eight hundred were employed on the river between Waterford and Clonmel and Davins had five barges engaged in the trade. The signs were that the horsedrawn barge was being ousted by the faster transport of merchandise over land on the railways, and by steamboats on the river. The barges could not be profitable for many more years and adjustments would be necessary to meet a diminishing trade.

Within a few days Maurice was settled back to his customary life on the farm. He discussed with the herdsman the condition of the cattle and what animals would be ready for the December fair, and when they would commence housing the cows for the winter months. He viewed the horses in their stables and talked about sending some corn to the mill for grinding. He visited the quay side to watch the barges being loaded and he had a word with the haulers about the business. The peace and tranquillity of rural life stirred him as never before, especially in contrasting it with the rush and bustle of the life in the great cities he had visited.

Financial Problems

But the problems facing the GAA were never far from his mind, especially when the curiosity of the neighbours prompted them to enquire how the athletes and the hurlers were received on the American tour, and did huge crowds attend the exhibitions. Davin did not conceal his disappointment at the rather small numbers who turned up at most of the venues and where many thousands were reported to have attended the takings did not meet the expenses. He had been confident that the promise of financial profit on the tour would be realised, and that whatever debts had been accumulated over the years could be cancelled. He explained the problems they had to contend with, and although his hopes of returning profits were dashed he did not apportion the blame to anyone. The neighbours were disappointed but sympathetic because they could not believe that any undertaking by Davin would not be crowned with unqualified success.

The full extent of the Association's indebtedness gradually unfolded during the year 1888, but the precise nature of the debts was not clear owing to the haphazard and confusing way in which accounts were kept. There was no system and certainly no advance budgeting, so that the Association lived from day to day in the hope that income from their activities would meet the necessary expenditure.

During his twenty month period as Secretary, Michael Cusack had travelled extensively throughout the country, had managed the central office, had written copious letters and articles while his only resource was what he received in affiliation fees from clubs. Doubtless he suffered financial loss, not alone in making up deficiencies from his own pocket, but also in neglecting his private business when devoting more of his time to the Association. At the meeting on July 4th 1886, when it was insinuated that all money was not accounted for, Cusack defiantly produced whatever cash he had on hands and placed it on the table. On the same occasion, when Cusack and Bracken engaged in a heated exchange, the latter boasted that he had always paid his way to the meetings and that he had never cost the Association anything. This was equally true of the other members of the executive, but they did not feel that it was a matter for self-praise since they accepted it as part of their contribution to the movement.

It appears certain that only the secretaries and the official handicapper were allowed any expenses and when Davin and the other auditors examined the finances prior to the 'American Invasion,' they confirmed that the secretaries Wyse Power, M'Kay, O'Riordan and O'Reilly had fully accounted for all the money received by them. Furthermore, the meagre income of the early years was insufficient to meet the necessary expenditure, much less to warrant the payment of expenses to members of the executive.

On more than one occasion P.N. Fitzgerald referred to what it cost him in time and money to attend the Association's meetings. Financial concerns had a crucial influence on the events leading up to Davin's resignation in January 1889 and his attempt to clear the accumulated debts was used as one of the targets of attack by his opponents.

The financial report submitted by T. O'Riordan and J.B. O'Reilly to the 1887 Annual Convention on 9 November covered the fourteen months of the Hoctor executive.[2] Income was £448.8s.6d. and expenditure £413.4s.9d., leaving a credit surplus of £35.3s.4d but the reports of the Convention do not give any details. It was claimed that the expenditure included clearing off some debts incurred during the previous administration but their report did not mention debts arising from activities in 1887. They made unjustified charges against the ex-secretary, Michael Cusack, claiming that they found the finances in a state of chaos due to his mismanagement and that he had still in his possession a considerable sum which would be sufficient to clear the Association of all its liabilities. The main thrust of the report was to applaud the Hoctor executive and to denigrate what Cusack had achieved. At their first meeting of the Central Council on April 30th 1888, Davin estimated that the liabilities could be as high as £400.

Davin was shocked when he received a letter from the great American champion, W. Byrd Page, sharply criticising the GAA for not keeping their promise to send him the gold medal which he had been awarded for the High Jump at the championship meeting at Tralee on 1 August 1887. He had tied with P.J. Kelly for the title at 6ft 1⅜ins. and the officials had agreed to award a gold medal to both. The letter concluded: 'I hope that this will remind the Gaelic Athletic Association to discharge its just debts for I am led to believe that it either has forgotten all about the matter or else does not propose to give me the medal I have won. In either case the Gaelic people are in great fault and put forth poor inducement for American champions to visit or to compete with them. You will greatly oblige me by ordering the medal to be forwarded to me at once.[3]

Although Davin had nothing to do with the athletic championships in Tralee in 1887, Byrd Page directed his appeal to him as the one most likely to respond positively. No provision had been made for the athletic championship medals of 1887 and Davin had no direct responsibility for shortcomings of the previous administration. The medals for the 1888 athletic championships held in Limerick on 6 August, had been presented by him to the winners on board the *Wisconsin* on the way to New York, but owing to the large debts money was not available to purchase the 1887 medals and many years passed before Byrd Page received his.

The impression had been given that sufficient surplus funds remained over from 1887 to carry business in 1888, but this proved to be unfounded when the accounts were examined by the auditors on 6 July. On the other hand, it was found that almost £500 was needed to clear the debts remaining over from previous years, of which £200 was incurred in 1887. Furthermore, during the year Davin received several letters from creditors demanding payment of old accounts, and writs were served on him as president and on Wyse Power, secretary, and on John Clancy, the former treasurer in 1885-'86.[4]

The creditors were:

Cahill, Printers and Stationers	£39. 8s. 0d.
Hopkins & Hopkins Jewellers for trophies	£79. 12s. 6d.
Chancellor & Son	£11. 12s. 0d.
Unspecified creditor	£40. 0s. 0d.
Smaller items	£9. 2s. 6d.
Coyle Solicitor, Fee	£2. 2s. 3d.
Total	£181. 17s. 3d.

Wyse Power had apparently been singled out by the creditors, an execution was issued against him and the sheriff's men were about to possess his home and property. Wyse Power moved to protect his home. His solicitor called on Davin to ascertain the assets and liabilities of the GAA with a view to winding it up. But Davin's intervention brought about a stay. There is no evidence about the nature of Davin's assurance to the creditors nor was any further action taken by them. The Association was facing a financial crisis and drastic action was needed if its disintegration was to be avoided, but the greatest obstacle to a resolution of the problem was the lack of unity within the membership.

The experience of the first few years had shown clearly that the income from the sources available was not sufficient to meet the outgoings. First, the receipts from the national events, athletic and hurling and football championships frequently fell short of the cost of trophies, printing and incidental expenses. Secondly, it was a big disappointment that the club affiliation fees were failing to bring in the revenue expected from them. In 1887, when the total number of clubs stood at 850 and the executive was entitled to the full ten shillings fee per club, the amount collected was £220, when it ought to have been twice that figure. When Davin resumed the presidency in 1888, only £120 was received in fees in spite of repeated calls to clubs and county committees to meet their commitments.

Although on the surface the rift in the Association between the moderate nationalists and the revolutionary IRB elements appeared to have been resolved at the January Convention, it was considerably broadened during the year. Political influences were at play affecting the attitude of clubs and county committees towards whichever of the two parties was in power, so that neither during the Hoctor administration in 1887, nor under Davin's presidency in 1888, was there full co-operation forthcoming from the membership and the amount collected in fees failed to reflect the total strength of the clubs. The miserable return of £120 in 1888 could be explained by the lack of co-operation that Davin's leadership received from the Fenian motivated clubs.

The IRB were particularly active during the year 1888 and in their determination to recover the dominant position they held the previous year, they promoted new GAA clubs especially in the Ulster counties, in Connacht and in Kerry and Clare, and they were much more successful in securing the leading positions in clubs and counties than were the supporters of the National League and the clergy. A considerable number of the latter found reasons to distance themselves from the National League and even from the GAA. The papal rescript issued in April 1888 forbade the Catholic clergy to have anything to do with the Plan of Campaign, but Archbishop Croke defended the right of the tenants to take action against bad landlords.

Many priests came to look on the GAA as increasingly dominated by the Fenians, if not a Fenian organisation. Consequently the leadership influence of the clergy declined and they failed to offer an effective counter to the IRB. P.N. Fitzgerald's expressed promise that his side would rise again in a year or two was being realised. According to official police reports, the IRB was riddled with informers even amongst its higher ranks, and the RIC, being made aware of its activities, confidently predicted that it was well set to recover control of the GAA before the end of the year.[5]

Davin held the firm belief that no progress could be made until the debts were cleared and he set out to plan a financial strategy to that end. When the new Central Council at its first meeting on 30 April and 1 May 1888 considered the draft of the new rules, some doubts existed as to what the January Convention had decided about the share out of the affiliation fees; was the Central Council entitled to one half or one third of the ten shilling fee? After discussion, the Council agreed that one half should be paid to the national treasurer in view of the poor state of the finances and that decision was included in the new rule book under rule ten which read:

> The affiliation fee of clubs shall be ten shillings per year, due and payable on the first of October to qualify for voting at the annual county committee and if not paid before the first of January the club shall not be allowed to enter for the county championships. The fee must be paid to the honorary secretary of the county committee, who shall forward half the fee to the treasurer of the Central Council and half to the treasurer of the county committee.[6]

Davin presided at that meeting and the other officers present were; R.J. Frewen, treasurer; W. Prendergast and T. O'Riordan, secretaries and J.J. Cullen, recording secretary. Eleven counties were represented – Cork, Limerick, Meath, Cavan, Offaly, Dublin, Wexford, Wicklow, Kildare, Louth and Tipperary. No dissenting voice was raised against the adoption of rule 10, but later on, in the months leading up to the

Convention, it became a bone of contention that was fully exploited by the opponents of Davin's administration.

The optimistic projection made by Davin in July 1886, that the income for the year would be sufficient to meet the demands of the creditors, did not materialise and , as a consequence he imposed severe restrictions on any further expenditure in order to avoid adding to the debts. The medals for the hurling and football champions were not to be purchased until the debts were paid and money was available to pay for them.

The Annual Convention could not be held in the first week of November as laid down by rule, because the officers did not arrive back from the American tour until the 9th of that month. When Davin found time to examine the full implications of the grim financial position, he called a meeting of the Central Council in Limerick Junction on 20 December 1888 to inform them of the true state of the finances and to brief them on the course of action that he intended to follow to meet the crisis.[7] Present were Fr Sheehy, Limerick; Fr Buckley, Cork; G.Byrne, Meath; P.J.Kelly, Galway; J. Cullinane, Tipperary; R.J.Frewen, treasurer and W. Prendergast, secretary.

The small attendance may have been an indication of the incipient criticism of the administration that was to erupt into hostile expression during the ensuing month. The accounts for 1887 during the Hoctor administration as far as could be ascertained from the vouchers available were presented by Davin to Central Council meeting on Dec. 20th 1888:

Income:

Affiliation Fees	£220.
Receipts at Elm Park Gaelic Carnival	£92.
Receipts at Kilmainham Tournament	£30.
Receipts from Tralee Athletic Sports	£80.

Expenditure:

Printing, Stationery and Advertising	£216.
Secretaries Expenses O'Riordan & O'Reilly	£45.
Handicapper Expenses at Tralee & Advertising	£25.
Band at Tralee	£26.
Refreshments at Elm Park etc.	£25.

Plans to eliminate debts

The President commented on the accounts: (a) Some debts remained from 1886 and he was not aware of them until recently when he received letters from creditors demanding payment, (b) If all the clubs represented at the Convention of November 1887 had paid affiliation fees the income under that head would be doubled, (c) The amount of affiliation fees paid in 1888, some of it at the last moment and under pressure, was only £120. It was clear he said that some county committees were not observing the rules that had been adopted and printed in the book of rules; if the proper procedures were carried out and the fees were paid in advance at the appropriate time, the president was satisfied that all liabilities could in time be met.

For the coming year 1889, only 61 had been received by the council treasurer, but from the replies received it appeared that the rules of the Association had been broken in many instances; Conventions had been held and officers and delegates elected by clubs of the past year and not of the present one. Such Conventions were irregular and the elections thereat void.

Only eight counties had proceeded according to rule. They were – Longford, Roscommon, Kerry, Offaly, Carlow, Kildare, Derry and Fermanagh. Kildare had the highest number of clubs (28) followed by Offaly (26). Davin insisted that the lines of the constitution must be observed by all counties and after discussion of that point the following resolution was proposed by G.Byrne, Meath and seconded by Fr Sheehy, Limerick:

> In as much as several counties have not complied with rule ten of the Gaelic rules, which states that all affiliation fees are due and payable on or before 1 October to qualify for acting at the general county Convention and that half of same be payable to the Central Council treasurer, we declare that all county committees appointed in violation of this rule to be illegally constituted. We declare that for admission to the Convention at Thurles, delegates must be appointed according to the above rule; with a view to having these errors rectified we fix 6 January as the date on or before which all affiliation fees are due and payable in order to qualify for election of county officers and delegates; county Conventions, where void, to be held on 15 January and to be convoked and carried through by the county secretary and county representative on the Central Council.

The resolution was adopted, P.J.Kelly being the lone dissenting voice. The date for the general convention was fixed for 23 January.

The IRB challenge for control

Davin adopted a strong line in confronting a critical situation and he held the conviction that unless the constitution and the rules were accepted the Association would fall apart. The accumulated debts weighed heavily on him and he could see no way of clearing them except by insisting on the obligation set out in rule ten. As the elected President he was entitled to get support and although he knew that he could expect opposition he was ready to confront it. However, he could not have anticipated the violent reaction that ensued. There had been murmurings of discontent for some time, but the extent of the opposition to the Central Council's resolution and the vehemence with which it was expressed, came as a shock to him.

Within a few days of the Council meeting, the tone of the attack was set by P.J. Delaney of Dunmore in Galway.[8] He referred to the Council as 'self-constituted law-givers who had advertised themselves at the expense of the Association by sending out a team to America against the wishes, implied at least, of the general body'. The charge was unfair and untrue. The tour was financed by individual subscriptions and Davin had insisted that no money proper to the Association was to be spent on it. But the accusation had an in-built popular appeal, especially for the disgruntled ones who were omitted from the Invasion party and it was taken up by others.

The Chairman of the Dublin committee, J. Bolger, claimed that the resolution was arbitrary and unjust, but he spoke in a conciliatory spirit, while the Louth Secretary gave his view that when the new Council was elected the clubs ought to pay the fees. Writing from Ennis, S.J. Dunleavy stated that Davin was not entitled to speak for the Association since his term as president had expired in November and furthermore he should not have disclosed the present or past financial position; he made a wild accusation that the only ambition of the Council was to wreck the Association and he demanded that the Convention should get rid of them.

The Munster counties went so far as to convene a provincial meeting where they expressed their solidarity in opposition to the Central council, claiming that the resolution passed at Limerick Junction in December had no binding force since the Council had ceased to exist in November. They also claimed that the Conventions held in their counties were in accordance with the rules. Davin answered his critics and reiterated clearly and forcefully the points at issue in a letter to the *Freeman's Journal*:[9]

> Dear Sir,
> Since the last meeting of the Central Council of the Gaelic Athletic Association, some letters and reports of meetings condemnatory of the Council have appeared in your paper. I shall be prepared to justify the action of the Council at the General Convention, which is, I think, the proper place for an explanation.. I wish, however, to make it clear to the members of the Association that only those clubs that have paid their affiliation fees for the year ending 29 September 1889 are entitled to vote at the county Convention and only counties that have lodged their portion of fees for the year ending 29 September 1889 with the treasurer of the Association can be allowed representation at the General Convention.

The rules are simple enough and should be easily understood. A man should pay his subscription before claiming membership of a club. A club must pay its fee before it can be affiliated to the county committee and a county must pay fees in proportion to the number of affiliated clubs, before it can be admitted as part of the Association. Anyone in arrears ceases to be a member until such arrears are paid up. Parties who have not subscribed to a fund cannot expect to be allowed to control its disbursement. None of your correspondents, nor any of the speakers at the meetings reported in the Freeman have, as far as I know, touched on a very important part of the business. The Council elected on the 4 January 1888 found the claims at that date to be nearly £500. The system which some counties wished to adopt would result in having a considerable addition made to the debt. But business could not be carried out any longer in that way and debts will have to be settled, or in all probability there must be an end to the Association as at present constituted.

Maurice Davin.

Davin believed too many clubs and counties were reneging on their obligation to pay fees and he hinted that if this rule was not accepted he would not bear the responsibility of the office any further, for experience had shown that if the fees were not paid in advance, less than half would be paid at all.

Davin's reasoned plan of action failed to make any impact on the IRB section. They were assured of a majority of delegates at the Convention following their intensive campaign during 1888, especially in Munster and Connacht and they were determined to recover the leadership and control of the GAA to advance their cause.

The general convention

The hall of the Young Men's Society in Thurles was adequate to accommodate the attendance of seventy-seven at the Convention on 23 January 1889.[10] The four officers were present, Maurice Davin, president; T. O'Riordan and W. Prendergast, secretaries and R. Frewen, treasurer, but only five of the Central Council representatives appeared, Frs Buckley, and Sheehy, J. Cullinane, D. Fraher and J.F. Byrne. Among notable absentees were Fr Concannon, Offaly; John Meagher, Laois; P.A. McHugh, Sligo and J.J. Cantwell, Kilkenny. Sixteen counties sent delegates, the bulk of them (forty-seven) from the six Munster counties and Galway and only twenty-one altogether from the other nine counties. Michael Cusack was on the Dublin delegation and Kerry was represented (for the first time at a General Convention) by Maurice Moynihan (who served as secretary of the GAA 1890-1892), and

Thomas Slattery. When comparison is made between this Convention and the reconstruction one of twelve months beforehand, some similarities are found, but also a number of important differences.

When the representatives met in January 1888, eighty-three delegates representing nineteen counties attended, forty-six of them from five Munster counties and Galway and thirty-seven from the other thirteen counties. Five counties included priests on their delegations; Cork (1), Limerick (2), Louth (2), Clare (2) and Waterford (1), whereas in 1889, two priests were delegates from each of the rival boards in Cork and Limerick and Fr Clancy attended from Clare. Over the twelve months that elapsed between one Convention and the next, a most remarkable change occurred in the personnel of the delegations. Dublin brought a completely new team, as did Kilkenny, Laois and Kildare. Tipperary, Clare, Waterford, Offaly and Mayo retained only one of their former delegates. Galway changed all but three of their representatives and both Cork and Limerick changed all but four of theirs.

The greatest change was in the mood of the delegates. In 1888 they arrived in Thurles enthusiastically committed to Davin's reconstruction plan and to re-elect him to lead the Association. Twelve months later a greatly changed group of delegates came to the same venue, determined to undermine the authority of the president and committed to establishing Fenian domination of the Association.

The applause that greeted the president when he rose to address the Convention conveyed no hint of the recriminations that were to follow. He presented a detailed report on the management during 1888, showing a total income of £259 and an expenditure of £236. The gate from the athletic championships at Limerick was £35 and the expenses amounted to £30. Real, Mitchel, Shanahan and Looney were entitled to championship records. He agreed that the hurling and football championships were unsatisfactory, in that a small number of teams took part. He was referring to a hurling match arranged by Tralee Athletic Tournament and played in Limerick between Newmarket-on-Fergus, Clare and the Lee Club, Cork. Due to disturbances on the field of play the game was unfinished and it was alleged that the Clare team was set upon on their way home and beaten.

Replying to further questions he said that the rule books had been printed in Clonmel; the athletic medals had been presented to the winners; there was no money to purchase the hurling and football medals, and he had nothing to do with the 1887 athletic championships.

Resuming his account of the debts incurred since the beginning, as far as he could ascertain, he faced interruptions as Fitzgerald, Dineen, Mackey and Forde plied him with questions loaded with insinuations:

'You were in office when the debts were incurred'? (Fitzgerald). 'Was not the Association in debt when you resigned'? (Dineen). 'Would you inform us on how the debt was raised'? (Mackey). 'When the auditors examined the accounts in 1888, did they find them correct?' (Forde). Had you not to do with the disbursement of the money?' (Fitzgerald).

A noisy scene followed as many speakers tried to be heard at the same time. The president asked to be allowed to continue and having dealt with the debts accumulated during 1887 he went on to refer to the unsettled accounts in connection with the athletic Sports at the Abattoir Ground in June 1886 for which writs had been served. He could not account for the affiliation fees for that year as Mr Cusack had not handed over the books when he retired. Michael Cusack stated that was perfectly correct, but he had nothing to do with the Sports at the Abattoir Ground and he had nothing to do with the gate money while he was in the Association.

At this stage a question was raised as to who was entitled to be present and some slight disorder ensued. The president made another appeal to be heard. He said he was willing to proceed and he was just as willing to go outside. To bring home to the delegates the seriousness of the financial state he read the letter from Mr Coyle, Solicitor, on behalf of Wyse Power who had been singled out by the Association's creditors; none of them would like to be placed in that position; the debts would have to be paid in some way, he said.

Much was made by Fitzgerald of an item for a supper on the date of the Abattoir Sports in 1886 to which the president replied that no fuss was made a little while before for a similar item at another meeting, pointedly referring to 1887. Finding it impossible to continue, Davin warned that he might as well leave the meeting and retire. At this there was some confusion and a few delegates mounted the platform but were put down.

A.Mackey stated the Mr Davin was president in 1888, but he ceased to be in November because according to rule the Annual Convention should have been held on the 7th of that month. P.J.Kelly supported this view and he held that clubs should not be asked to pay fees twice in the same year. He opposed the resolution passed at the Council meeting at Limerick Junction. At this stage the delegates from the dissident clubs in Cork and Limerick left the meeting, accompanied by Frs Buckley, O'Connor and Sheehy.

Davin retires

It was clear to Davin that the meeting was dominated by the IRB members; that they rejected his plan for solving the financial problems and that he was isolated with no support. He made a final statement declaring that he had presented the Convention with a report of the accounts for his term of office. Eleven counties had accepted the Council's resolution and had paid the fees accordingly. He would see that the money was returned to them. He then withdrew from the Convention. He walked out with dignity, displaying no sign of emotion, although he must have had a tinge of sadness on departing from a scene of action to which he had committed much of his time and talents. Over seventy delegates from sixteen counties remained at the meeting. John Cullinane defended the actions of the Central Council saying that they had found last year that they must clear the debts, but they could not do so out of an income of £180.

P.N. Fitzgerald did not wish to repudiate the debts, but he thought that Mr Davin should have remained to take counsel on how they could be paid off. Fr Clancy, the only Killaloe priest at the Convention, gave his opinion that they had treated Mr Davin too severely; too many had been cross-examining him at the same time as if he were personally responsible for the Association's debts. He believed that the action taken by the Council at Limerick Junction was justified, although they may have been unreasonable in their attitude to the clubs.

The softening of attitude towards Davin after he had left the meeting was influenced to some extent by the manner of his leaving without a murmur of complaint, but more so by the universal respect for him as a leader, that swung opinion in his favour. Expressing the change of mood, F.B. Dineen called on Fr Clancy and E. Cahill to wait on Mr Davin and request him to return to the meeting, but extreme voices were raised against such a move. When P.J. Kelly was elected to take the chair, he proposed a short adjournment to explore the possibility of coming to an amicable arrangement with those who had left the meeting and accompanied by Messrs Bryan, Redmond, Mackey and Cahill they approached Mr Davin in an adjoining room. He would not hear the deputation and refused their request to return.

IRB return to power

In the circumstances his decision was not surprising, because he was not prepared to be a mere figurehead as president. His experiences in 1887 had shown the policy decisions would be made without reference to the president and he could not even consider such a demeaning position. When the deputation returned to the hall, P.J. Kelly informed the delegates that their mission had been fruitless and it was decided to proceed with the elections. The officers elected were:

> **president** – P.J. Kelly, Loughrea
> **treasurer** – A. Mackey, Castleconnell

secretary – P.B. Clery, Caherconlish
secretary to Central Council – S.J. Dunleavy, Clare
record secretary – C. Clinton, Dublin.

Of the seventeen Central Council representatives elected, only four of the previous Council were retained. They were – P.J. McHugh, Sligo; T. Slattery, Kerry; G.F. Byrne, Meath and Dr O'Connor, Kildare, but the last named refused to accept the position.

Dunleavy, who had been amongst those most critical of the outgoing council, resigned his position at the first meeting and was replaced by P.J. O'Keeffe of Kilkenny. A Dublin delegate proposed that they set up their own paper because Gaelic affairs did not receive a fair share of publicity form the *Freeman's Journal*, but A. Mackey disagreed saying he saw no reason why they should be antagonistic to the *Journal*. The proposal received no support so it was dropped. The experience with the shortlived *The Gael* did not encourage another venture into publication.

The Convention of January 1889 resulted in a more serious division than ever in the ranks of the GAA and full control was once more in the hands of the IRB. According to police reports, the president P.J. Kelly, the secretary, P.R. Clery, treasurer Anthony Mackey and the secretary to the Central Council P.J. O'Keeffe were all advanced IRB men and in addition they had secured for their members the principal officerships in up to fifteen county committees, although spirited opposition to them continued in counties such as Cork and Limerick.

The tactics used in forcing Davin out of the presidency were highly questionable. P.P Sutton, a staunch upholder of the GAA ideal, writing in *Sport* referred to the badgering, brow-beating style which some delegates assumed towards the president: 'It has come to a sad state of affairs when people are allowed to treat with so much intolerance and disrespect a man like Davin; a man who has made the Association what it is, who is the father of its rules and constitution, who when it was in throes of an internecine squabble came from his business at the almost unanimous call of the clubs and devoted his energies and his time to taking our grand Association out of the shoals and quicksands into which it had fallen, and placing it on a sound footing once more'.[11]

Led by the dissenting priests, less than thirty delegates who had departed from the Convention in protest at the IRB takeover, assembled in another room in the building to consider what action they should take.[12] They were joined by the Clare priest, Fr Clancy and a little later by Davin. Fr Sheehy occupied the Chair and a resolution in the following terms was proposed by Fr Carver, Cork and seconded by J. Ryan, Limerick and adopted: 'That in face of the disastrous condition of the GAA, as presented to us in a statement by our president, Mr Davin, and seeing the necessity of devising the best means to limit expense and stave off indebtedness in the future and observing that the growth of our debts hitherto come from maintaining a central governing body and from prizes connected with the inter-county and All-Ireland championships, desiring at the same time to continue our national pastimes and foster a true Gaelic spirit amongst our young men, we conclude that all this can be best done by witholding the central government and prizes for inter-county championships and by leaving each county separately to manage Gaelic matters under its several boards and according to the rules of the existing constitution, regulating matters in all particulars as hitherto, with the exception of the points indicated.'

The resolution highlighted the financial problems as the main source of the division between the parties and certainly the disputation at the Convention was concentrated on the debts, how and by whom they were incurred. Much deeper causes divided the contending sides on political lines, but these were not adverted to in the resolution, nor indeed were they brought out into the open in the Convention although they provided the motivation for all that took place there.

Although Davin was present at the Fr Sheehy meeting after the Convention, it is impossible to say with certainty that he took any part in its deliberations, or that he approved of the resolution that put aside much of the structure that he had built up. His vision of an Association, disciplined and controlled, was embodied in a constitution and rules that he had devised for that purpose and it is improbable that he would agree to abandon an essential element of his plan. The resolution did not, as sometimes suggested, call for an end to the GAA, but proposed that it should be completely decentralised and its fundamental objectives pursued at club and county level and that is what happened to an appreciable degree during the first half of the nineties decade. Many counties and clubs refused to recognise the new central authority, but continued to organise unofficial games and sports meetings locally.

In contrast to what had happened after the previous takeover by the IRB at the 1887 Convention, on this occasion the newly elected Central Council was not confronted by any serious and direct challenge to their authority. Not by the National League or the Home Rule party, not by Archbishop Croke or Michael Davitt, not even by the Priests, except in Cork and Limerick, was any move made to mobilise opposition to the IRB dominated body, even though if such a move were made it could be assured of the support of the majority of the members. It could be that it was felt that a widespread withdrawal of support would be more effective in weakening the council's position than any thing that could be achieved in an open confrontation with them. On the other hand, the situation was different to what it had been in 1887. The IRB was more firmly entrenched in clubs throughout the country than at any time previously and they would not be easily dislodged.

The strength of the IRB in the GAA rested on its organised campaign to capture the allegiance of dedicated young people to its policy of armed revolution. Its weakness lay in its determination to control the GAA and force out from an effective voice in its direction the majority who did not accept the IRB policy. That policy in relation to the GAA was enunciated by P.N. Fitzgerald who made it clear that he had never been an official of the GAA and never would be, but that he would do his best to advance its ideals. He asked that more toleration be practised; his aim was to kill faction and unite Irishmen in friendly rivalry, but he added that they would crush jarring elements amongst Irishmen.[13]

The ambiguity of the statement reveals his negative attitude to unity and reconciliation in the GAA. It also explains his anxiety to force Maurice Davin from the presidency. On the other hand Fitzgerald could claim that the Association was politically influenced by the nationalists from the start. In the circumstances of the time, it was inevitable that political influences would be at work in a national Association and it would find it difficult to maintain a non-political stance. In a reference to the Gaelic League, T.W. Rolleston held that to be non-political did not mean that the League was to have no political views in matters that directly concerned its existence and its work;[14] the GAA was in a similar position in regard to politics. But domination of the GAA by one political strand of the nationalist movement to the exclusion of others could not prove to be other than detrimental to the progress of the Association.

Of all those who held leading positions in the early years. few could claim to be less influenced by political concerns in his work for the GAA than Maurice Davin. His sole interest was in promoting the Association's objectives and he made it known that as far as politics were concerned they should take their lead from Archbishop Croke. It was a serious miscalculation on the part of the IRB to undermine his position, for no one among the leading members was as well fitted to assume the presidency as he; there was no one to command the general respect and authority which he enjoyed amongst the general membership.

The new regime failed to remedy the defects and shortcomings which they found in his administration. Instead of improving the financial position it became progressively worse; the appeal to clubs to pay their affiliation fees received a poor response; when secretary P.R. Clery wrote to the outgoing officers for the books of accounts, Davin replied that he held nothing that they were entitled to, and Prendergast stated that when he took office he did not receive the books from the previous secretary J.B. O'Reilly. An appeal to all clubs for a subscription of £1 to clear their debts failed to produce anything.[15]

Secretary Clery succeeded in completing the hurling and football championships for 1889 although in each case only seven counties participated and the number dropped to six in 1891. The number of counties represented at the Annual Convention fell from eight in 1889 to six in 1891. In those years the controlling body of the GAA could not claim to be representative of the nationalist population. They alienated the Catholic clergy who had played leading roles in organising parish clubs, but who now turned to advising the members against affiliating with the Central Council. A number of bishops condemned the Fenian element in the GAA as a demoralising influence, but Archbishop Croke refrained from uttering any word of criticism.

The nationalist Archbishop of Dublin, Dr Walsh, stated in an interview that he was aware of the efforts being made to engraft on the Gaelic Association a secret society of a political nature that was opposed to the national leaders and Parnell's constitutional movement.[16] Counties were divided in their allegiance. Wicklow added to the number of counties where rival boards existed. Wexford resolved that the Central Council appointed by a section of delegates at Thurles, not being representative of the GAA did not command their confidence. Dublin, Wexford, Wicklow and Louth refused to accept the right of the Central Council to appoint their county representatives.

In 1890, the county committees of Wexford, Kilkenny, Wicklow, Carlow, Kildare, Offaly, Meath, Waterford, Cavan and Louth did not affiliate and only 15 clubs affiliated from Tipperary, nor was the county represented at the annual Convention. All over the country many clubs ceased to exist, but a report by a Dublin Castle agent claimed that 851 clubs were functioning in 1890. Of that number 506 were affiliated to the Central Council, 196 were under clerical control, favouring the Home Rule movement, and 149 were unattached to either side.[17]

The G.A.A was to a large extent in disarray, but people became so attached to the games and athletics that activity on the playing fields was fairly widespread. Brave efforts were made by the officials to organise the county and All-Ireland championships, but with reduced participation by teams. The athletic championships continued to attract the finest athletes and support from the public. Unofficial events assumed a new popularity as local sides arranged challenge games and tournaments were organised for a variety of purposes, political and charitable, and the annual athletic parish sports meeting was not allowed to lapse.

The opposing parties may have reached a reconciliation in time, and there is some evidence that thoughts were turning to a revival of the Association as a purely national athletic body without political party influences. All such thoughts vanished under the shock of the Parnell split which tore the country apart and almost killed the GAA. Seeing Parnell as the victim of British intrigue and perceiving his statements as an endorsement of their physical force outlook, the Central Council placed their support unequivocally behind him. A special Convention assembled in the Rotunda in Dublin in July 1891, attended by about sixty clubs and with president P.J. Kelly in the Chair, decided to support the policy of independent opposition under the leadership of Mr Parnell.[18] This decision aligned the GAA with the Parnellites and exposed it to the full brunt of the anti-Parnellite opposition which had a disastrous influence on the fortunes of the Association for a few years.

Consideration of the decline during that period and of the efforts made to arrest it, are outside the scope of this study, but Secretary Patrick Tobin in his report to the Convention of January 1892 revealed some very disturbing facts: 'The athletic championship meeting in Tralee was a financial failure; in 1888 the GAA was in the heyday of its existence with close to 1,000 clubs; from all the information available, the total number of affiliated clubs in 1892 was down to 220.'[19]

References
1. Davin, P., op. cit., pp 33-4.
2. *Sport*, 12/11/1887.
3. Byrd Page's letter in Davin's papers.
4. O'Sullivan, T.F., op. cit., p. 74.
5. C.B.S., 126/S, N.A.
6. *Book of Constitution and Rules of the GAA*, 1888.
7. O'Sullivan, T.F., op. cit., p. 74; *Cork Examiner*, 22/12/1888.
8. *Freeman's Journal*, 8, 11, 15/1/1889.
9. Ibid., January 1889.
10. Account of Convention, *Cork Examiner* 24/1/1889; *Sport* 26/1/1889; O'Sullivan, T.F., op. cit., pp 75-8.
11. *Sport*, 26/1/1889.
12. *Cork Examiner*, 24/1/1889.
13. Ibid., 28/1/1889.
14. In letter to the *Freeman's Journal*.
15. O'Sullivan, T.F., op. cit., p. 78.
16. Ibid., p. 78; *Tipperary Advocate*, 10/8/1889.
17. *Irish Press*, 21/4/1967, article by M. Tierney, OSB.
18. O'Sullivan, T.F., op. cit., p. 93; *Freeman's Journal*, 22/7/1891.
19. O'Sullivan, T.F., op. cit., p. 98.

Maurice Davin.

Chapter 12

Epilogue

Maurice Davin's decision to leave the Convention was not taken hurriedly, nor without sufficient good reasons. Since the spring of 1887 when the constitution was set at naught by the Hoctor/Reilly executive, he had no confidence that the group they represented would direct the Association on the lines most conducive to its welfare. On that occasion he had resigned from the presidency in protest and finding himself in a similar position almost two years later he acted consistently with his principles.

Because nationalists in the nineteenth century were divided about the most effective means of achieving their aspirations, whether they should pin their faith on constitutional agitation or turn to the physical force ideal, every national movement was influenced to some extent by this division. It was the misfortune of the GAA that it was the arena where the opposing ideologies clashed. Davin's attempt to steer a middle course was met by the determination of the IRB to gain full control and he was perceived to be an obstacle in the way.

The attack on him, both before and at the Convention of January 1889, was couched in terms that were a deep reflection on his personal honour and was entirely unacceptable to him and he saw no other course to follow than the one he took.

His refusal to meet the deputation sent from the Convention was based on his belief that it was not a sincere effort to persuade him to return to the presidency, but was intended to present its members in a good light and to shift the blame for the debacle upon him. He had grounds for this belief. When the question of sending the deputation was raised at the Convention, a Dublin delegate, R. Cashman, said that if Davin did not comply with the suggestion they would know on whom to lay the blame.

The new president, P.J. Kelly, remarked that if there was any discord it was not the fault of the delegates present. They had done all in their power to bring about an amicable settlement to meet the other side half way, but if Mr Davin could not see his way to compromise, they could not help him.[1] The press reports of the Convention do not offer any evidence of an effort being made to bring about an amicable settlement. A few days after the Convention, P.N. Fitzgerald made no bones about his intention to oust Davin from the presidency.

In a letter to the press in justification of the course he had pursued, he wrote:

Under Mr Davin a sound financial scheme was never promulgated. Many Gaels like myself had no confidence in his constructive ability so we wanted change. Another cause of hostility was the Gaelic Invasion of America without consulting the Association and picking men on his own responsibility and hurting the feelings of every Gaelic county. These were the principal reasons for the attacks on Mr Davin at Thurles.[2]

The strenuous opposition mounted against Davin's scheme to raise finance to meet the running costs of the GAA rebounded on the next Central Council when they adopted a similar plan and got little or no return from it. The special care exercised by Davin in devising a method of selecting the members of the party for the American Invasion is described in chapter ten and if some counties declined to participate in the undertaking, or to support it, the fault could hardly be laid at Davin's door.

On his part Davin indulged in no recriminations against his opponents, although he could have fully justified his actions and policies. He was satisfied to leave the judgement to others. He blamed no one, he maintained a dignified silence. He had faith in the GAA and he held firmly to the ideals which first impelled him to take a leading role in its foundation and development. But he was no longer president and he lacked the power to influence the Association on a national scale.

Deerpark Sportsfield

He still had a part to play on a more confined stage in his own locality, as he had been accustomed to do, encouraging young talent and organising athletics and hurling and football matches. In particular he turned his attention to a project he had in mind for some time, to develop a hurling and football pitch and an athletic arena in one of the fields on his farm. It was a level piece of ground running parallel to the main Carrick/Clonmel road on one side and to the railway line on the other. It was there that Maurice and his brothers had trained and perfected the skills in which they earned international acclaim. A running path or track was prepared and special places set aside for jumping and weight-throwing. Within a few months, Maurice had all things in readiness and the first athletic sports at Deerpark grounds in 1889 attracted the best of local talent and much spectator interest.[3]

Pleased with the success of his first venture, he undertook other improvements to cater for the practical requirements of players and spectators and to control entry to the pitch. Some type of shelter where players could prepare for action was a priority, so a prototype dressing room or pavilion was constructed on larch poles with corrugated iron sheeting on the sides and roof. To modern eyes it would be seen as very primitive, but it served its purpose for many years and players were very glad to have it at a time when it was usual to tog out under the ditch. Years later when there was no further need for it, it was taken down and re-erected in the farmyard to serve as a shed for implements.

A wooden paling six to seven feet high was built to enclose the ground using timber from old river barges. A timber stand was erected at a vantage point on the sidelines to give seated accommodation for officials and anyone who was prepared to pay a little extra for the convenience. Such amenities were rare at any venue and on that account Deerpark became a popular centre for all types of Gaelic activity.[4]

Free from the cares of office that involved long travelling and equally long and contentious meetings, Davin had the time to give practical expression to his own ideas of what the GAA should be doing on the local scene. The sports he organised were a welcome respite at a period when communities were divided by the bitter Parnell controversy and people longed for a day of relaxation and enjoyment at Deerpark grounds where the spirit of carnival prevailed. The public was not slow to express the popular regard for the Davins. On the day of a hurling match, a hawker employed a subtle line in sales advertising when he shouted 'Up the Davins, even if I never sold an orange'.

It has been suggested that Davin had hopes of gaining support for a reorganisation of the GAA on much the same lines as had been done in 1888. Some support for this view is contained in a letter from William O'Brien to Archbishop Croke in August 1892 which has the following passage: 'It appears that Maurice Davin, Prendergast of Clonmel and other good fellows are thinking of giving the GAA a new start in the south independent of the influence that has dominated the Association for the past few years. They are certain they could bring all the old clubs of the counties of Cork, Tipperary and Limerick into line.'[5] No doubt the anti-Parnell Home Rule Party would welcome such a move, but their local leaders, both lay and clerical, were so engrossed in the political conflict and apathetic to the GAA at that time that a move in that direction lacked the force and commitment needed to make any headway and Prendergast, who would have supplied organisational ability, emigrated to America.

Dark days for GAA

The GAA experienced its darkest days in the first half of the nineties decade. Only 220 clubs affiliated to the Central Council in 1892. County organisation was negligible and county championships in hurling and football were rarely completed. Only three counties were represented at the Annual Convention in 1893 and of those Tipperary's J.K. Bracken was not officially appointed. In the All-Ireland championships, Cork in hurling and Wexford in football were required to play only two games to win their respective titles and the football final was unfinished. The position was only slightly improved the following year.[6]

Significant rule changes were made in those years. In 1892 the number of players on a hurling or football team was reduced to 17 and five points was declared equal to one goal. The ban that prohibited members of the police force from competing at GAA sports, or becoming members of an affiliated club, was abolished. Counties were allowed representation on the Central Council if they had at least five affiliated clubs, instead of ten under the old rule.[7] These two measures, together with a willingness on the part of the officials to co-operate with the IAAA for a common policy on athletic records, point to an admission that the Association had reached a turning point.

Hurling and football were languishing, apart from unofficial challenge games and tournaments, but athletics were thriving mainly due to the continued success of the local sports meetings organised by parish committees. New star performers arrived on the scene to follow in the footsteps of the Davins, Mitchel and Real. Tom Kiely of Ballyneale, a protégé of Maurice Davin, won seven events at the All-Ireland championships at Jones's Road in 1892 including the remarkable distance of 49 ft 7 ins in the Hop, Step and Jump. During a long and brilliant career he won fifty Irish titles, five English ones, eleven international wins, two American all-round championships as well as the four Irish ones he had competed in. J.M.Ryan, a young teacher from Tipperary, won the Irish High Jump championship and the English title in 1893. In August of that year he cleared 6 ft 3⅛ ins at Nenagh sports to create a new Irish record. His greatest feat was at Tipperary Sports in 1895 when he cleared the lath at 6 ft 4½ ins, a new world record. He died aged 23 in 1900.[8]

John Flanagan of Kilmallock came into prominence in 1885 as an all-round field athlete and the following year at Stamford Bridge he broke two hammer records. He emigrated to America a few months later and won three Olympic gold medals in the hammer events in 1900, 1904 and 1908. Denis Horgan of Banteer commenced as a high jumper in 1893 but changed to shot-putting which became his favourite event and after putting beyond the 48 ft mark on a few occasions in 1887 he eventually created a new Irish record of 48 ft 10 ins at Mallow in 1904.[9]

These first class athletes in the traditional Irish field events and others who competed against them, attracted huge crowds of spectators whenever they appeared at sports meetings. On the other hand the breakdown of the GAA organisation in many counties resulted in a marked falling off in the number of attractive hurling and football matches being played and enthusiasm for the games waned. For example, in the three years from 1891 to 1893, no GAA organisation existed in Tipperary and the county like many others was almost completely deprived of hurling and football activity.[10]

The situation was so serious that some ardent spirits issued a call for a closing of ranks with an invitation to a number of prominent Gaels to attend a meeting in Dobbyn's Hotel in Tipperary Town with a view to re-organising the Association in the county. Among those who met there on February 27th 1893 were Maurice Davin, Tom Kiely, Carrick-on-Suir; Bob Frewen, Aherlow; J.K. Bracken, Templemore; John Bourke, Tipperary; D.H. Ryan, Thurles; Tom O'Grady, Moycarkey; Joe Ryan, Bohercrowe and Michael Cusack.[11] A provisional committee, including Bracken, Joe Ryan, D.H. Ryan and John Bourke was set up to reorganise clubs and to arrange challenge games. Templemore played Bohercrowe in football, Thurles played North Tipperary in hurling and inter-county games were arranged in hurling and football with Kerry and Cork. These activities re-awakened interest in the games and as more clubs bestirred themselves they way was paved for the formation of a new county committee in 1894 when the officers elected were: D.H. Ryan, president, (Bracken was beaten by one vote), Hugh Ryan, treasurer, John Bourke, secretary. County championships were revived and while eleven football teams took part, only four hurling sides affiliated that year. The next year witnessed an upsurge in hurling and ushered in a new spring in the county.[12]

Those who came together in Dobbyn's Hotel could be said to be from different strands of the Association, but they were all deeply concerned for its welfare; they had witnessed the dire condition to which it had fallen and they realised the urgent need to check the decline. Three of the original founders were present to give their influential support for a renewal of spirit and it can be claimed that the meeting marked an upward turning point in the county. Enthusiasm was rekindled and the message spread to influence the national scene. Davin's association with this revival movement was not insignificant and it indicates his constant attachment to the objectives he expressed at the foundation meeting.

As a result Tipperary clubs successfully challenged the supremacy that had been established by Cork in the All-Ireland hurling championships and in the six-year period from 1895 to 1900, clubs from the county won the title on five occasions. Arravale Rovers made it a double for Tipperary when they won the football title in 1895 and for the first time Jones's Road was the venue for the two finals. As the baleful influence of the Parnell split was on the wane other counties re-organised. In 1894, Kerry in Munster, and Meath, Kildare and Offaly in Leinster made progress leading to a rise in a number of affiliations and more activity on the playing fields,[13] but few counties contested the All-Ireland Championships and none from Connacht or Ulster challenged for the titles.

Revivals

The advent of new officers was an important factor in bringing about an improvement in the fortunes of the GAA. P.J. Kelly resigned the presidency in 1895 and F.B. Dineen was appointed in his place. R.T. Blake of Meath became secretary and he introduced a measure of efficiency to the administration as well as changing the direction away from political influences. Up to seventy athletic sports were held under GAA rules during the year and for the first time the Association promoted the all-round championships in 1896, which up to then had been held under IAAA management. The event attracted a large crowd to Clonmel on 9 September 1895 to witness some of the finest athletes in the country competing for the top award. Maurice and Pat Davin were present with Tom Kiely, the holder of the title, who did not compete and the title was won by T.E. Wood, Inniskeane.[14]

In 1896 a difference arose between the Central Council and the Cork County Committee regarding the implementation of the rule debarring rugby players from membership of a club.[15] Secretary Blake maintained that the rule had been altered at the adjourned Convention, but Michael Deering, the Cork Chairman, held that the rule was still in force and to strengthen his hand he wrote to some of the patrons and some former officers. Bracken and Mackey replied favouring the retention of the rule and Michael Davitt considered it would be a mistake to depart from the principle involved in it. There is no mention of a reply from Archbishop Croke, but Maurice Davin retained his stand-off attitude to the Central Council and replied by letter that he did not think his views would carry much weight with the members of the Association of that day.[16]

President Dineen remarked that some of those consulted had left the Association at a trying time and he questioned their right to influence decisions; he agreed with the secretary that the rugby men could compete in Gaelic matches, but he thought the Council should give permission to the Cork County Committee to deal with the matter of the rule as they thought fit, which left the question unresolved.

One of the Vice-Presidents, Patrick Tobin, criticised the President for placing a slight on the former officers who had served the Association well in the past. Although Davin held aloof from the central body, his interest in the local scene had not diminished and he became involved in organising and supporting Gaelic activities in south Tipperary. He was a delegate to the Tipperary county Convention in 1897 representing Carrick-on-Suir with Tom Kiely, who was one of the Associations Vice-Presidents from 1896 to 1898.[17] He took special delight in organising and supervising the annual sports meeting at Deerpark. He looked forward eagerly to those occasions and he was in his element directing events and encouraging and advising the young competitors.

The event of August 1898 surpassed any other sports meeting in the country in the number of champion athletes who competed there and in the standard of their performances in the traditional Irish events. They were attracted to Deerpark, not by the quality of the awards on offer, because they were rather modest compared to the usual prizes at athletic sports; they came however out of respect for the old champion and to acknowledge their indebtedness to the inspiration they had received from his example. Assisting Davin in the judging were his brother Pat and his great friend Dan Fraher and at the end of the day he expressed his thanks to the athletes who had paid him a unique honour in establishing five new records during the day's sport.[18]

As the Tipperary county committee made progress with championships in hurling and football, the Deerpark grounds became a popular venue for the local games. One of the great attractions there was the county football final of 1900 between the Clonmel rivals Commercials and Shamrocks, won by the latter after a rousing contest. As the popularity of the venue increased, Davin opened its gates to the 1900 inter-provincial tests in hurling and football between Tipperary and Kilkenny that attracted a huge attendance. Tipperary went forward to win both the hurling and football All-Ireland finals.

Deerpark was again the venue for the 'All-Ireland' final of 1901 won by Cork over Wexford, but not played until June 1903. Deerpark was chosen as the venue for the 1903 county football final between neighbouring rivals Mullinahone (Poulacapple) and Grangemockler, and Maurice Davin contributed to the enjoyment of the game by his excellent refereeing. The year 1904 was the busiest for the venue. Tipperary and Waterford met there to decide their Munster championship ties in hurling and football; the county football semi-final games were played there and the 1904 All-Ireland hurling final was decided in Deerpark when Kilkenny scored a one point victory over Cork in a most exciting game which was not played until June 1906.

While the All-Ireland championships were completed for all years, although belatedly, it was a serious cause of concern that few counties were prepared to take part, reflecting the low state of organisation in most of the country. Under Blake's direction from 1895 to 1898, a marked increase in activity on the playing fields was evident, but even during his time as secretary many of the old problems persisted, especially the lack of finance which remained a constant worry and, ostensibly at least, was the cause of Blake's dismissal in 1898. His departure was followed by years of decline in organisational efficiency.

The time of the Central Council officers was taken up mainly with disputes and objections regarding venues for matches, referees' decisions and the application of rules, so that championships fell behind, usually by a few years. Davin viewed the confused state of the organisation with feelings of regret for what might have been. Amongst his papers are many cuttings of newspaper reports of incidents at games and if he considered something occurred that deserved censure he appended a short comment: 'Some of the new Gaels'. Whenever he was pressed for a comment on the state of the GAA, he usually replied that it would come right in time.[19]

When the morale of the GAA was at its lowest point, the annual Convention of 1900, with Michael Deering presiding, adopted a motion by Thomas Dooley, Cork, that provincial councils be set up. Although there was some opposition, the motion was carried on a vote and it appeared that it was inspired by the dire necessity to introduce some measure that would bring new life to the organisation. The absence of effective communication and the reluctance of people of independent mind to accept without question the dictates of a remote controlling body, had bedevilled the relationships between the Central Council and the people on the ground.

Setting up provincial councils meant that decision-making was localised and more acceptable to county representatives. This amendment to Davin's constitution was a major influence on the dramatic advances made during the first decade of the new century. Among other contributing factors were the Gaelic League, Sinn Féin and the founding of the Camogie Association in 1903. Cusack, Davin and others of the GAA founders had given their support to the League's forerunners and it was natural that they would back the Gaelic League when it was founded in 1893; Cusack gave it his active support in Dublin and Davin was among the attendance at the first meeting of the League in Carrick-on-Suir. Younger language enthusiasts attached themselves to GAA clubs, as did others who were inspired by Griffith's Sinn Féin philosophy, and women found an outlet to express their support in the Camogie Association.

From these sources the GAA gained an infusion of fresh blood that nourished the developing organisation. Dr Douglas Hyde, a founder of Conradh na Gaeilge, while acknowledging the national importance of the GAA, made a strong appeal to its members to support the language movement: 'No good Irishman would wish to see the old Irish nation classed as an English county. This was close to happening. The establishment of the GAA was an enormous step in the direction of Irish nationhood, the marks of which are the national games, sports, music, plays, dances and above all the language of the country.' Hyde had joined the GAA shortly after its foundation, but he was mildly critical of its members for not doing more for the language: 'The players', he wrote, 'never think of any other aspect of the Association than that of the match. The idea that they are contributing to the revival of Irish nationality has never occurred to thousands of them'.[20]

Yet a measure of co-operation between the GAA and the Gaelic League was beneficial to both movements. When urban clubs organised Irish language classes, the League supplied the teachers, and some of the League branches formed their own hurling and football teams. Urged by the prompting of the League's 'bicycle itinerant teachers', many rural clubs arranged Irish classes for the winter months and the sessions were enlivened by the introduction of rince fóirne.

Reports coming from America in the nineties telling of the dramatic progress of Gaelic games in the New York area brought some solace to Davin. The *New York Sun,* commenting on the fifteen clubs affiliated, as well as five associated ones, referred to the influence of the American Invasion: 'Although the exhibitions of the visiting athletes were not successful in the matter of attendances, still the object was attained and the Gaelic Association of America was formed as a result and has grown to large and vigorous proportions.'[21] Such testimony was satisfying to Davin in view of the way some Gaels at home had criticised the Invasion as an abject failure, using it as a means to denigrate Davin and his efforts.

Davin's friend, William Prendergast, who had been secretary of the GAA during 1888, emigrated to America in the early nineties and joined the New York police. He amassed a fortune by dealing in real estate on Long Island and retired from the force in 1907. He was prominent in establishing the GAA in the city. He purchased and equipped Celtic Park which became the home for Gaelic games for many years.[22]

If the GAA was thriving in New York, the situation at home could not be described as vigorous at the dawn of the new century. In fact an atmosphere of lassitude and depression pervaded every sector, both at central and local level. A sharp decline in affiliations occurred even in stronger counties like Dublin, Cork and Tipperary and neglect of the local championships was widespread. No wonder that many of the older generation who had played their part in establishing the Association were becoming disillusioned at the lack of positive direction from the leadership.

Athletics were almost completely neglected by the GAA and the field was left open to the IAAA. The situation had deteriorated to such a degree in 1900 that the national athletics championships were abandoned and even the recently revived all-round championship was allowed to lapse. It is true that it was proposed to inaugurate inter-county athletic contests, but the initiative was passed on to a few enthusiasts to put the idea into practice.[23]

The first contest was held in Dungarvan between Tipperary and Cork; Dan Fraher, Maurice Davin and John Cullinane were in charge of the arrangements and Tipperary's strength in the field events decided the issue in their favour. Following the success of this first venture, Cork scored over the Kerry representatives in a test in Fermoy.[24] Few counties followed this lead and due to the ineptitude of the GAA in promoting athletics, their rivals in the IAAA were gaining ground on them. To meet the challenge, the national athletic championships were revived in 1902 and the Annual Convention of that year decided to discontinue their co-operation with the IAAA regarding the ratification of records and instead appointed their own separate committee for the purpose.[25] The next year a Gaelic Cycling Association was formed and a sports meeting involving athletic and cycling events was held at Jones' Road.

At the Convention of 1905, a motion put forward by F.B.Dinneen was approved calling for the election of a fifteen-member athletic council to control and promote athletics. Dineen was appointed its chairman and the secretary was A.C.Harty. Their first promotion was the successful inauguration of the national cross-country champion-ships in Dublin on St Patrick's Day. A year later a final and definite break was made with the IAAA and any athlete who competed under rules other than the GAA was liable to suspension.[26] A bitter contro-versy ensued which lasted for many years as the two Associations contended for support. On the GAA side it resulted in a dramatic increase in the number of athletic meetings under its rules from year to year.

Many efforts were made, especially by prominent athletes, to resolve the dispute without effect. Olympic Champion, Peter O'Connor, holder of the Long Jump record for twenty years, was hopeful that an amicable settlement could be reached. He approached Maurice Davin in the hope that he might offer his services in an effort to settle the dispute. In a letter to the Irish

Independent in 13 December 1909 he recorded the outcome:

> I made up my mind not to take part again in this regrettable athletic dispute and I only do so now in the hope of effecting an amicable settlement, which I think is possible as a result of a chance interview with my old and esteemed friend, Mr Maurice Davin of Deerpark, Carrick-on-Suir, the Grand Old Man of athletics, whose name, fame and records and those of his athletic brothers, in the seventies and eighties are known to sportsmen in every part of the civilised globe.
>
> Having to go on legal business to Carrick-on-Suir on the 10th inst. I called to see him. I found him in his beautiful home by the silvery Suir, looking hale and hearty and as athletic and robust as he was twenty years ago. Attired in the old Irish style of knee-breeches, erect and manly and with his snow-white hair and beard, he looked as fine and handsome a picture of a typical old Irish gentleman as I ever beheld.
>
> I asked him would he act the 'strong' man referred to in one of your correspondent's letters and offer his services to try and settle the dispute. With sad and dejected look he said he had very strong reasons for not interfering again in the management of the G.A.A and that he wished to live in peace and friendship with all true sportsmen for the rest of his life. He showed me, in his valuable scrap album, dozens of letters which were published in the daily newspapers about the athletic dispute which occurred in the year 1885. It struck me as remarkable that the arguments then used by those anxious to have peace were almost identical with the arguments now used to achieve the same object.

He (Davin) said, 'I cannot see my way to preside at a conference between the representatives of the two Associations; but here', said he, pointing to a letter in his album, 'if that is published I believe it will have the same effect as in 1885 and again settle the unfortunate athletic dispute between brother Irishmen once and for all'.

It was the letter of Most Rev Dr Croke, Archbishop of Cashel, who with Maurice Davin and the late lamented Michael Cusack, founded the GAA.[27] Davin, referring to Dr Croke as the greatest Irishman of his time, said that few knew all that the Archbishop had done for the Association.

Much had changed since 1885. The rising tide of national consciousness which influenced and was influenced by the GAA, created a popular movement which saw in the promotion of the language, games, music and dance the cultural expressions of national identity that would eventually lead to national independence. Those of unionist leanings who controlled the IAAA did not empathise with that movement and the possibility of bringing about a union of minds under those circumstances was remote indeed and had to await a more favourable opportunity.

Varied interests

Maurice Davin welcomed the formation of a camogie club in Carrick-on-Suir and saw it as an extension of the GAA ideal. He gave the club the use of the facilities at the Deerpark ground for training and matches. His account book bears witness to his continuing interest in the welfare of the club; an item of 1 in July 1915 was for the hire of a motor car to take him to Clonmel to see a camogie match between Carrick and Ballinamult. He was in his seventy-fourth year at the time, but he was just as pleased with Carrick's victory as the young people were. His interest in all Gaelic activities never waned and in August of the same year he took a car to Dungarvan for the championship sports in Fraher's field and he was a regular spectator at Munster hurling and football matches, when ever they were played at venues convenient for him.[28]

His account books bear testimony to his efficiency in business management and in addition they constitute a valuable social document about life in a mixed farming economy. They give an insight into the intense activity at milking time when seventeen or more cows were milked by hand and what milk was not required for home use was carted to the creamery. The monthly cheque for the period from May to October averaged over £30, at 5¾d to 6¼d per gallon; and less than half that sum during the winter months when the milk yield was lower.

The sales of farm animals were recorded in detail. In March 1917 a springer, the heifer of 'Dairy Maid', was sold to Hanlon of Bagenalstown for £41.10s 0d and a cow after its second calf was sold to Lucy of Cork for £30. At a fair in 1920, six heifers were sold for £25 each and nine hoggets for £112.

The cornfield presented a colourful and lively scene when the harvesting was done in the old fashion; thirty-two scythes mowed the crop, the sheaves were formed by thirty-two men or women, thirty-two others bound them and twelve people made the stooks.

Davin's close relationship with the river was maintained in the hauling trade, but due to the development of steamboats and road and rail transport, there was less demand for the slower haulage of goods by horses. The last entry of the kind in his account books is dated 14 October 1922, when the number 2 boat and Kehoe's boat hauled 26 tons of coal from Carrick to Clonmel. He was then eighty years old.

When Maurice took over the running of the family business after his father's death in 1859, the workers such as Billy Cahill, Mick Thompson and Jack Quann were well-established employees, each an expert in his own field. As old age or death caught up with them, a new generation filled their positions. Close to Maurice in age and outlook, new employees became life-long supporters who could be relied on to care for the business as if it were their own. Enjoying a relationship of mutual trust and respect, Maurice was their confidant and to him they entrusted their savings rather than going to any of the financial institutions. Whenever a need arose, the savings could be withdrawn immediately with an agreed rate of interest added.

Even in his late years Maurice retained his interest in national and local community affairs. He was a paid-up member of the Carrick branch of the Farmers' Association and attended its meetings; he contributed to the anti-conscription fund in 1919 and to the revival of the Carrick Regatta; in 1920 when a testimonial was organised as a mark of esteem to his colleague of the early GAA, John Cullinane, he gave a subscription of £5, and the same year he handed a contribution of £5 to Dr Murphy of Carrick for the Patriotic Fund. In May 1921 he gave £12 to the cause of national independence.[29]

As an enterprising farmer, Maurice was ready to take on a new challenge and for a number of years he turned to breeding shorthorn bulls for sale. It proved to be a successful undertaking and at one time he had as many as six in the sportsfield. The breed is notorious as being unreliable and one came close to killing one of the workmen and had to be put down, so the project was abandoned.

In another enterprising move he rented the Coolnamuck weir on the Suir from the marquess of Waterford at an annual rent of £32.10s; a licence to take salmon from the river cost £10 per annum and the rates payable to the local authority amounted to £7.4s.6d. He worked the weir for thirty years and it turned out to be a lucrative business. During the salmon fishing season from 1 February to 15 August Davin rowed out to the weir in a cot, a small boat, in the evening and let down the gate; in the morning he returned and using a large net he took whatever fish were caught. These were prepared for the market, packed in sally hampers, taken to the railway station in a hand cart and dispatched to O'Neill's fish merchants in Waterford.

Part of the weir was damaged maliciously during the truce in 1921 and the following March it was blown up by a bomb and wrecked. Not satisfied with that, whoever was responsible broke up the little boat and destroyed the gear and nets. As well as material loss, Maurice suffered the consequential loss of the fishing and portion of the annual fees for the lease, licence and rate, but he received no recompense, although the marquess, as owner of the weir, was awarded £550.

During the 'troubled years' Deerpark House was raided for arms, but nothing was found except a sword. The large barn in the farmyard was sometimes used as a refuge by men 'on the run', and one time the mare and trap were commandeered to be used as an innocent-looking means of transport, that was unlikely to arouse the suspicions of the RIC.

The approach of the second decade of the century witnessed a dramatic upsurge in public support for hurling and football and in the quality of the games, resulting in a big increase in the annual income. Although athletics received more attention following the setting up of the athletic council in 1905, it cannot be said that the GAA in general, devoted much of its resources to developing that branch of its objectives and while some individual performances were outstanding, claims were made that standards were falling.

Olympians

If success in the Olympic Games can be taken as the accepted standard of excellence, Irish athletes earned a very high rating during the period. The list of their achievements is impressive.

> At the Athens Olympics in 1906, Peter O'Connor won the Hop, Step and Jump and was second in the Long Jump; Con Leahy won the High Jump and was second to O'Connor in the Hop, Step and Jump.
>
> Martin Sheridan won the Discus Throw in St Louis in 1904, Athens 1906 and London 1908, and Con Leahy was second in the High Jump in London.
>
> John Flanagan won the Hammer Throw three times, Paris 1900, St Louis 1904 and London 1908.
>
> Matt McGrath was second to Flanagan in 1908 and won the Hammer in Stockholm in 1912; he was second again in 1924.
>
> Denis Horgan was second in the Shot Putt in London to the great Ralph Rose, world record holder.
>
> Paddy Ryan won the Hammer at Antwerp in 1920.

Numerous Irish, British and American championships were won by these and other Irish athletes during these years. Those remarkable achievements on the world scene attracted the attention of commentators on two continents and the Irish were the acknowledged masters in Weight Throwing and in Long, High and Triple Jumping. Interest was focussed on the source of their successes, their training methods and the special skills they had perfected. Maurice rejoiced in their victories and they acknowledged him as their guide and leader. (This writer has a cherished memory of seeing mighty Matt McGrath giving exhibition throws with the old style wooden-handled hammer at a sports in Silvermines in 1936).

A journalist with the *New York Daily News,* William Fletcher, visited Ireland in 1907 and interviewed Maurice Davin in his Deerpark home.[30] He describes their first meeting:

> The old champion walked erect with an easy swinging stride. He

was so broad that his well-set shoulders and massive chest entirely filled the walk. As he came hurriedly to greet me, his head struck slightly against the laurels that flanked the path. He is entering his 65th year. He stands 6 ft 1 in and weighs 225 pounds. He measures 48 inches round the chest and 40 inches round the waist. His eyes are blue, bright and sparkling. His face never knew a razor. Time only frosts his hair and beard. His heart is still on fire. It burns fiercest with love for Ireland and glows warm for any athlete, irrespective of race, who is devoted to the sports at which he excelled. Without expressing it he lets you know that his home is yours when you visit him.

Maurice led his guest to the pavilion in the sports field and having put on his spiked shoes, he gave a demonstration of hammer-throwing in the old style. Grasping the wooden handle in his right hand he twirled the sixteen pound weight round his head as if it weighed only an ounce and after a few turns he let it go. His third throw measured 118 ft which was better than the winning throw at the championships of 1891. He then showed how to throw the 56 pound weight, slinging it from his side in a standing position and as if effortlessly, sending it over 24 ft.

He explained to his guest that the seven foot circle for the Hammer and Shot Putt was based on the size of the grain sieve in an Irish barn. A test of strength for a man was to stand in the sieve and raise a sack of grain over his head without stepping outside the rim. The length of the handle of the hammer was taken from the quarry worker's pick. After dinner they talked about the development of athletics in Ireland, the foundation of the GAA and its growth. When asked about the division between the two athletic bodies he said he preferred not to discuss it. He took down his violin and entertained his visitor to a musical evening, concluding with The Snowy Breasted Pearl and The Coulin (An Chuileann). Fletcher was impressed by the big weight-thrower's delicate touch with the bow and his beautiful playing.

It was customary for American officials on their way home from Olympic Games in Europe to call to Deerpark to honour the old champion. After the Games in Stockholm in 1912, Maurice welcomed to his home the leading quartet of officials with the United States team – Dan Ferris, President of the Amateur Athletic Union of America; James E. Sullivan, Secretary/Treasurer of the AAUA; Charlie Harvey and Matt Halpin. In his account of the visit for a New York paper, Sullivan wrote: 'I never met a finer old man than Mr Davin. He had so much to tell me that I just sat there and listened with rapt attention. He was mighty interesting'. He explained the old training methods, the diet recommended for athletes and how fat could be reduced and muscle fibre built up.

Davin was anxious to hear first-hand accounts from his visitors of the field events at Stockholm and it was a great joy to him that Matt McGrath of Nenagh scored a signal victory in the Hammer Throw, sending the ball 179 ft 7⅛ ins, a new Olympic record. (That was unbeaten until the German, Karl Hein, won in Berlin in 1936).[31]

The example of the Irish-born Olympians failed to create fresh energies on the home scene. The Athletic wing of the GAA was fraught with disputes and even threatened with a breakaway by a section dissatisfied with the administrators. The IAAA was in a moribund state.

The establishment of Saorstat Éireann opened the way for a new beginning. A proposal initiated by the athletic council of the GAA was accepted on all sides and the National Athletic and Cycling Association was born. The GAA ended its involvement in athletics, the IAAA ceased to exist and henceforth the NACA was the controlling body, bringing an end to the dispute that had racked athletics for almost forty years. Of the seven founders who assembled in the billiard room of Hayes' Hotel in November 1884, only T St G McCarthy and Maurice Davin lived to see unity attained. For Davin, who had always believed that the problem would be solved if given time, it was the realisation of a long cherished wish. For the first time Ireland was represented as a separate nation at the Olympic Games in Paris in 1924 and the same year saw the fulfilment of Michael Davitt's dream when the ancient Gaelic festival of Tailtean was successfully revived with the GAA providing full co-operation to the organising committee and Croke Park served as the venue for the outdoor events.

Spotless in the midst of the speckled

Advancing years did not diminish Maurice Davin's zest for life and even in his eighties he went about his routine work on the farm with unflagging energy, being blessed with excellent health. He retained his interest in local affairs and he kept in touch with national events through the newspapers. People recall seeing him pacing up and down on the gravelled walk outside his house or walking in to town to transact some business and meeting the neighbours with a friendly greeting. They remark on his snow-white hair and beard and his healthy rosy complexion. He was a striking figure dressed in a tweed jacket, knee-breeches and long stockings and wearing a miniature gold caman on his watch chain. He spent his evenings reading and playing the violin.

His library of books was selected for improvement of his store of knowledge rather than for relaxation and amusement. Prominent among them were eight volumes each of *Harmsworth Encyclopaedia, The History of the World and Modern Encyclopaedia;* four volumes of *The*

Cabinet of Irish Literature, two volumes of *New Ireland,* eight volumes of *Cassel's New Popular Educator* and a rare book *Thoughts on Sport* by H R Sargent; several books on farming and salmon fishing and many music books and cut-out lectures on Irish Music by Mr B Rogers and Mr Arthur Darley; several branches of sport were represented including boxing; Mr and Mrs Halls' volumes on Ireland in which the account of hurling before the famine had a special interest for him.

Davin was blessed with good health all his life and it was very seldom that he ever complained. One evening, late in January 1927, he felt unwell and went to bed. In spite of the best medical care and attention he declined rapidly and died on 27 January. The last entry in his diary was dated 15 January. The people of Carrick and district mourned the passing of their beloved champion and his sister Bridget and his brother Pat received messages of condolence from many parts of the country, from county committees and public bodies; from the president of the GAA, W.P. Clifford; the President of the NACA, J.J. Keane and from John Cusack, solicitor, son of Michael, who quoted his father's tribute of many years before, 'the spotless amongst the speckled'.

His coffin was borne from the Church of St Nicholas by prominent officials of Tipperary County Board, Johnny Leahy, Wedger Meagher and Joe Maloughney, two of his famous students T F and Larry Kiely, and his life-long friend Dan Fraher of Dungarvan. His last journey was across the Suir to the family burial place in Churchtown where he was laid to rest with past generations of Davins, under the shade of ancient limes with a view across his beloved Suir of a manufacturing plant symbolic of the new industrial Ireland.

The national and provincial papers carried obituaries in tribute to his achievements and his outstanding qualities: 'He was an inspiration to Gaels'; 'He raised the social life of the people'; 'He was the finest type of Irishman'; 'He was an exemplar of the highest ideals of Gaelic athletics'; 'A steadfast supporter of Gaelic principles'. An appreciation in the *Clonmel Nationalist* referred to him as 'the most respected and beloved figure in Irish athletics, ungenerously forgotten'.

The weekly *Sport* published a comprehensive appreciation of Davin by P.J. Devlin who was a regular writer on Gaelic affairs, under the pen name 'Celt'. In it he wrote: 'He was intimately acquainted with the temperament and physical endowments of his countrymen. It was his task to preserve the best characteristics of their sports and at the same time to repress that impulsive spirit which had so frequently marred scenes of recreation by ill will. Such was the ideal he embraced and he infused the essence of that ideal into the laws he drafted and into every action of his life.'[32]

Carbery (P.J. Mehigan) wrote: 'He handled weights as if they were blocks of timber. He came at a period when the national outlook was as bleak as the ace of spades. It was his wonderful weight-throwing that concentrated international attention on the physical capabilities of the Irish race.'

J.J. Healy claimed: 'Leaving no branch of athletics untouched, he was master of all. He had few equals and no superior. He ought not be forgotten by the firesides of Tipperary.'

A group of Carrick-on-Suir businessmen set up The Davin Memorial Park Company Limited and purchased land to be developed for Gaelic Games as a suitable memorial to Maurice. The directors were – Michael Cleary, William Morrissey, Richard Walsh, Thomas F. Kiely, Richard Dalton, Denis O'Driscoll, John J. Higgins, James McCormack and Jeremiah Shelly. Two thousand shares at 1 each were offered to the public; the Munster GAA council invested £600. The field was developed and the official opening took place on the occasion of the Munster Football Final, Kerry v Tipperary in 1932. Declaring the Park open, W.P. Clifford, Chairman of the Munster Council, said that the Park was a fitting memorial to a famous Tipperary athlete whose genius brought the GAA into being. Some years later the directors' interest was purchased by the Carrick-on-Suir clubs, the Tipperary County Board and the Munster Council.

For the best part of fifteen years, before the GAA was founded, Maurice Davin was earning a name as a world-class athlete and a man of honour and integrity. He was an inspirational figure, setting high standards of performance and discipline that had a wide influence on the course of athletics and he was acknowledged as the 'Father of Irish Athletics'.

Because of his status, Michael Cusack consulted him before making his public announcement in 'A Word about Irish Athletics', and in his reply, Davin extended the scope of the revival to include the old Irish games of hurling and football and long distance running, in addition to athletics. While Cusack was a prolific and effective writer, Davin wrote only when he felt a definite reason for doing so, and when he did, it was with clarity, brevity and reasoned argument that was the outcome of long and serious thinking. His letter to the *Freeman* in defence of the GAA in February 1885 effectively refuted charges made by opponents and he repeated his regard for Irish football as a fine manly game, differentiating it from Rugby Union.

He was the Association's law-maker. By unanimous choice, he drafted the first rules for hurling, football and athletics and revised them in 1886. At the Convention in November 1886 he placed before delegates a comprehensive constitution which laid the foundation on which the later development of the GAA was firmly set. He was the architect who conceived the structure built on club and county committees which has endured. The championships based on this arrangement contributed largely to the popularity of the games.

Up to February 1887 he had been willing to co-operate with the IRB majority on the Central Executive. After the open dissent at the 1887 Convention and a leader was needed to guide the Association out of its difficulties a general cry went out for the return of Davin to the presidency. He lost no time in undertaking a re-organisation plan and devising a new constitution to meet the pressing needs.

The All-Ireland hurling final left over from 1887 was staged successfully in Birr, in April. The daunting project of the American Invasion was taken on with courage and purpose but it was branded as a failure by Davin's opponents and it was used as one of the arguments to undermine his position. His plans to solve the recurring financial problems were rejected and he finally resigned. His departure was a grievous loss to the Association as it faced the testing years of the early nineties.

It is doubtful if Davin's contribution to the GAA in its early years has been understood and acknowledged. In his letter to *United Ireland* in October 1884 and again in his inaugural address to the founding meeting on 1 November he expressed his broad vision of the movement that was being launched. He saw it as the instrument to revive and encourage the sports and pastimes characteristic of the Irish people, including athletics, hurling and Irish football.

His knowledge and proficiency in regard to athletics was unrivalled in the country. He was steeped in the hurling tradition popularised in the Carrick area in ballads such as *The Prison of Clonmel (Priosúin Chluain Meala)* and the verses of Mandeville. Alone of the early leaders he joined Irish football with hurling as a traditional game to be revived. Although hurling was acknowledged to be the more traditional game yet as the Association developed and spread into all counties, football gained a wider geographic acceptance and Davin must be accorded the credit of rescuing it from drifting into oblivion. It was a special concern of his that the Association would serve the bulk of the people and more especially 'the humble and hard-working who seem now to be born to no other inheritance than an everlasting round of labour.'

More than most he foresaw the dangers facing the young Association unless the lessons of control were learned and taken to heart and consequently he accepted the responsibility for drafting the rules and devising a well-ordered structure to meet the needs of the movement.

Freely and without stint Maurice Davin devoted his many rich talents to the cause of the Association he loved and he sought no return except its welfare. By his life and example he bequeathed the principle of the primacy of discipline: unless it is based on respect for the laws enacted and acceptance of the authority elected the Association cannot command the esteem and support necessary for its welfare, or even its survival.

References

1. *Cork Examiner*, 25/1/1889.
2. Ibid., 28/1/1889.
3. O'Sullivan, T.F., op. cit., p. 81.
4. As told by Mick and Paddy Callaghan and Hugh Ryan.
5. *Irish Press*, 21/4/1967, article by M. Tierney.
6. O'Sullivan, T.F., op. cit., pp 100-102.
7. Ibid., pp 101-103, 111.
8. Dooley, Wm. *Champions of the Athletic Arena*, Dublin, 1946.
9. Ibid.
10. Fogarty, Canon P., op. cit., Thurles, 1960, pp 50-52.
11. Ibid., p. 53; *Sport*, 15/7/1893.
12. Fogarty, Canon P., op. cit., p. 55.
13. O'Sullivan, T.F., op. cit., pp 111-113.
14. Ibid., p. 116.
15. Ibid., pp 124-5.
16. Ibid.
17. Fogarty, Canon P., op. cit., p. 76.
18. O'Sullivan, T.F., op. cit., p. 136.
19. In Maurice Davin's papers in Deerpark.
20. O'Sullivan, T.F., op. cit., pp 196-8; *The GAA Annual*, 1908-9.
21. Copied by *Sport*, 11/2/1893.
22. *Nenagh News*, 3/8/1907.
23. O'Sullivan, T.F., op. cit., p. 143.
24. Ibid., p. 143; Fogarty, Canon P., op. cit., p. 92.
25. O'Sullivan, T.F., op. cit., p. 156.
26. Ibid., p. 170.
27. *Irish Independent*, 13/12/1909.
28. Maurice Davin's Account Book in Deerpark.
29. Ibid.
30. *The Nationalist Clonmel*, copied from the *Daily News*, New York.
31. From Maurice Davin's papers in Deerpark.
32. *Sport*, 5/2/1927.

Appendix 1

Letters of Dr. Croke, Michael Davitt and Charles Stewart Parnell.

DR. CROKE'S LETTER
At the founding of the Association the following letter was received from the Most Rev. T. W. Croke, Archbishop of Cashel and Emly:-

"The Palace, Thurles,
"December 18th, 1884.

"My Dear Sir — I beg to acknowledge the receipt of your communication inviting me to become a patron of the Gaelic Athletic Association, of which you are, it appears, the Hon. Secretary. I accede to your request with the utmost pleasure.

"One of the most painful, let me assure you, and, at the same time, one of the most frequently recurring, reflections that, as an Irishman, I am compelled to make in connection with the present aspect of things in this country, is derived from the ugly and irritating fact, that we are daily importing from England, not only her manufactured goods, which we cannot help doing, since she has practically strangled our own manufacturing appliances, but, together with her fashions, her accents, her vicious literature, her music, her dances, and her manifold mannerisms, her games also, and her pastimes, to the utter discredit of our own grand national sports, and to the sore humiliation, as I believe, of every genuine son and daughter of the old land.

"Ball-playing, hurling, football-kicking, according to Irish rules, 'casting', leaping in various ways, wrestling, handy-grips, top-pegging, leap-frog, rounders, tip-in-the-hat, and all such favourite exercises and amusements amongst men and boys may now be said to be not only dead and buried, but in several localities to be entirely forgotten and unknown. And what have we got in their stead? We have got such foreign and fantastic field sports as lawn tennis, polo, croquet, cricket, and the like — very excellent, I believe, and health-giving exercises in their way, still not racy of the soil, but rather alien, on the contrary, to it, as are indeed, for the most part, the men and women who first imported, and still continue to patronise them.

"And, unfortunately, it is not our national sports alone that are held in dishonour and are dying out, but even our most suggestive national celebrations are being gradually effaced and extinguished, one after another as well. Who hears now of snap-apple night, pan-cake night, or bon-fire night? They are all things of the past, too vulgar to be spoken of except in ridicule by the degenerate dandies of the day. No doubt, there is something rather pleasing to the eye in the get-up of a modern young man, who arrayed in light attire, with part-coloured cap on and a racquet in hand, is making his way, with or without a companion, to the tennis ground. But, for my part I should vastly prefer to behold, or think of, the youthful athletes whom I used to see in my early days at fair and pattern, bereft of shoes and coat, and thus prepared to play at handball, to fly over any number of horses, to throw the 'sledge', or 'winding-stone', and to test each other's metal and activity by the trying ordeal of 'three leaps', or a 'hop, step and jump'.

"Indeed if we continue travelling for the next score years in the same direction that we have been going in for some time past, condemning the sports that were practised by our forefathers, effacing our national features as though we were ashamed of them, and putting on, with England's stuffs and broadcloths, her masher habits and such other effeminate follies as she may recommend, we had better at once, and publicly, abjure our nationality, clap hands for joy at sight of the Union Jack, and place 'England's bloody red' exultantly above the green.

"Deprecating as I do, any such dire and disgraceful consummation, and seeing in your society of athletes something altogether opposed to it, I shall be happy to do all for it that I can, and authorise you now formally to place my name on the roll of your patrons.

"In conclusion, I earnestly hope that our national journals will not disdain in future to give suitable notices of these Irish sports and pastimes which your Society means to patronise and promote, and that the masters and pupils of our Irish Colleges will not henceforth exclude from their athletic programmes such mainly exercises as I have just referred to and commemorated.

"I remain, my dear Sir,
"Your very faithful servant,
✠ "T. W. CROKE,
"Archbishop of Cashel."

"To Mr. Michael Cusack,
Hon. Sec. of the Gaelic Athletic Association."

CHARLES STEWART PARNELL'S LETTER
Charles Stewart Parnell's letter accepting the invitation to be patron:

Irish Parliamentary Office
Palace Chambers,
9 Bridge St., London S.W.
Dec., 17th., 1884.

Dear Sir,

I have received your letter of the 11th., inst. It gives me great pleasure to learn that a Gaelic Athletic Association has been established for the preservation of National pastimes, with the objects of which I entirely concur.

I feel very much honoured by the resolution adopted at the Thurles meeting, and I accept with appreciation the position of patron of the

Association which has been offered to me. I need not say that I shall do anything I can to render the working of the movement a success,

I am yours very truly,
Charles S. Parnell.

MICHAEL DAVITT'S LETTER
Michael Davitt's letter of acceptance:

The Imperial Hotel,
Dublin.
21st. December, 1884.

Dear Sir,

I accept with great pleasure the position of patron which has been assigned me by the Gaelic Athletic Association, though I am painfully conscious of how little assistance I can render you in your praiseworthy undertaking. Anything however it is in my power to do to further the objects of the Association I will most willingly perform, as I cannot but recognise the urgent necessity which exists for a movement like that which you are organising with such zeal.

I have already explained to you my views on Gaelic sports and hinted at plans by which a nationalist taste for them might be cultivated. I have, therefore, only to express my obligations to yourself and friends, for the honour conferred upon me, and to repeat the assurance of my entire sympathy with the objects of the Gaelic Athletic Association.

I am yours very truly,
Michael Davitt.

Appendix 2

Joseph P. O'Ryan, 1857–1918

Very little was known about Joseph P. O'Ryan until a few years ago. Michael Cusack recorded him as one of the seven at the first meeting in the billiard room of Hayes' Hotel, but he gave the initials as P.J., instead of J.P. It was also known that he was a young solicitor practising in both Callan and Thurles, and it was generally accepted that he took little part in the subsequent affairs of the GAA.

In researching his life a few years ago this writer consulted the *Incorporated Law Society Calendar and Law Directory* which revealed that Joseph P. Ryan qualified as a solicitor in Easter, 1884 and was awarded the Society's silver medal at the final examination. No other solicitor of that name appeared on the list of qualifiers over a thirty year period. He had been apprenticed in the offices of T.H. Menton at 27 Bachelors Walk in Dublin. (John Henry Menton of that firm figures in Joyce's *Ulysses*. A number of law students from Carrick-on-Suir, including Pat Davin, studied in the same office, which suggests that Joseph O'Ryan was also from there.

The Carrick-on-Suir parish register confirmed that Joseph P. Ryan was born in April 1857 the son of James Ryan and his wife, Mary Coughlan of Main Street. With the assistance of Pat Walsh and the courtesy of Quirkes, solicitors, a copy of the minutes of Carrick-on-Suir Amateur Athletic Cricket and Football Club for the years 1879-1883 was located. Maurice Davin was chairman of the club and Joseph P. O'Ryan was joint-treasurer and an active member of the committee. His friendship with the Davins and his interest in athletics probably account for his presence at the foundation meeting of the GAA.

The *Kilkenny Journal* of 1884 confirmed that Joseph P. Ryan was then practising as a solicitor in Callan and that he was an accomplished singer and soloist in the church choir.

In June 1892 the *Nenagh Guardian* reported the marriage of Joseph Ryan, solicitor, Thurles, and Mary Clare Hanly, Castle St., Nenagh at Mount St. Joseph's Abbey, Roscrea. References to Ryan's work as a solicitor in Thurles are found in the *Guardian* up to 1899 when he emigrated to Canada. Alf Mac Lochlainn has established that he settled in Cranbrook in British Columbia, where he practised as a lawyer and was known as Judge Ryan. When he died in 1918 the obituaries testified to his contribution to the legal and business affairs of Cranbrook.

I wish to thank Pat Walsh, C. Quirke, Marcus de Búrca, T.K. O'Dwyer, Alf Mac Lochlainn, Liam Ó Duibhir, and the staff of the National Library for their assistance.

Appendix 3

Presentation to Hon. W.E. Gladstone by Cork G.A.A.

During the height of the campaign for Home Rule in 1887 Parnell's supporters were confident that a measure of self-government was about to be won through the alliance of the Irish Party with the Liberal leader, W.E. Gladstone. Parnell was at the peak of his power and Gladstone enjoyed immense popularity in Ireland even in the most unlikely quarters. This report in *Sport* presents one instance:

> Alderman Horgan and Messrs Lane and O'Riordan, representing the Cork County Executive of the Gaelic Athletic Association travelled to Swansea to make a presentation to W.E. Gladstone in conjunction with the Cork Protestant Home Rule Association. A large number of excursionists travelled with them.
>
> The presentations were:
>
> A shield bearing an inscription: To the Right Honorable W.E. Gladstone, M.P. from Cork County Executive of the G.A.A. 1887. The shield was surmounted by the Arms of Cork and emblems on either side, a wolfhound, harp, round tower, all resting on a spray of shamrock.
>
> A full sized hurley of polished ash with silver plates.
>
> A regular match ball. A copy of the new rules.
>
> A miniature gold hurley for a watch chain with a patent ring.
>
> On the handle of the hurley a series of circles in fine platinum wire and a neat miniature ball of Galway marble mounted on the boss. When Gladstone met them on Sunday morning he was wearing the gold hurley on his watch chain. He removed it and waved it in the air. *The Dublin Weekly News* cartoonist captured the occasion.

Mr. Jack Lynch, former Taoiseach, was informed by a member of the British Government at a reception in London some years ago that such a presentation was made and that it was preserved in some place where memorabilia of Gladstone are kept. Enquiries at the House of Commons Information Office, at St. Deiniol's Residential Library, Hawarden and of Sir William Gladstone at Hawarden Castle failed to establish its present location.

Bibliography

de Búrca, M., *The GAA, a history*, Dublin, 1980.

Idem., *Michael Cusack*, Dublin, 1989.

Burke, Canon W., *History of Clonmel*, Waterford, 1912.

Comerford, R.V., *Charles J. Kickham: a study in Irish nationalism and literature*, Dublin, 1979.

Curtis, L.P., *Coercion and conciliation in Ireland 1880-1892: a study in conservative unionism*, London, 1963.

Davin, P., *Recollections of a veteran Irish athlete. The memoirs of Pat Davin, world's all-round athletic champion*, Dublin, 1939.

Devlin, P.J., *Our native games*, Dublin, 1934.

Dooley, W., *Champions of the athletic arena*, part 1, Dublin, 1946.

Duffy, C.G., *Four years of Irish history 1845-1849: a sequel to 'Young Ireland'*, New York, 1883.

Fogarty, Canon P., *Tipperary's GAA story*, Thurles, 1960.

Gaughan, T.A., *Austin Stack*, Dublin, 1977.

Inglis, H.D., *Ireland in 1834. A journey through Ireland during the spring, summer and autumn of 1834 ... 2 vols (London, 1840)*, London, 1834.

Koester, C.B., *Mr Davin MP - A biography of Nicholas Flood Davin*, Seskatoon, Saskatchewan, 1980.

Larkin, E., *The Roman Catholic Church and the Plan of Campaign in Ireland 1886-1888*, Cork, 1979.

Lawrence, J., *Handbook of cricket in Ireland and record of athletic sports, football etc. seventh number, 1871-72*, Dublin, 1872.

Lee, J., *The modernisation of Irish society 1848-1918*, Dublin, 1973.

Lovesey, J., *Official history of AAA centenary*, London, n.d.

MacDómhnaill, T. agus **Ó Meadhra, P.**, *The spirit of Tipperary*, Nenagh, 1938.

MacDonald, W., *Reminiscences of a Maynooth professor*, London, 1925.

Maher, J., *Chief of the Comeraghs:* a John O'Mahony anthology, Mullinahone, 1957.

Idem., *The valley near Slievenamon: a Kickham anthology*, Kilkenny, 1942.

MacLysaght, E., *Irish life in the seventeenth century after Cromwell*, Dublin, 1939.

Idem., *A guide to Irish surnames*, Dublin, 1939.

Mandle, W.F., *The Gaelic Athletic Association and Irish nationalist politics 1884-1914*, Dublin, 1987.

Marples, M., *A history of football*, London, 1954.

Mehigan, P.D., *Gaelic football*, Dublin, 1941.

Moody, T.W., (ed) *The Fenian movement*, Cork, 1968.

Murphy, N., 'J.K. Bracken' in *Tipperary: History & Society*, Dublin, 1985.

O'Brien, W. and **Ryan, D.**, (ed) Devoy's Postbag 1871-1928, Dublin, 1948-1953.

Ó Caithnia, L.P., *Scéal na hIomána ó thosach ama go 1884*, Baile Átha Cliath, 1980.

Idem., *Michéal Ciosóg*, Baile Átha Cliath, 1982.

Idem., *Bairí Cos in Éirinn*, Baile Átha Cliath, 1984.

Ó Ceallaigh, S., *History of the Limerick GAA from the earliest times to the present day*, Tralee, 1937.

O'C. Bianconi, M. and **Watson, S.J.**, *Bianconi king of the Irish roads*, Dublin, 1962.

O'Donnell, P., *The Irish faction fighters of the nineteenth century*, Dublin, 1975.

Ó hÓgáin, D., *Duanaire Thiobraid Árann, cnuasacht d'fhilíocht na nDaoine ó oirdheisceart an chontae*, Baile Átha Cliath, 1981.

Ó Laoi, P., *Annals of the GAA in Galway 1884-1901*, Vol.1, Galway, 1984.

Ó Maolfabhail, A., *Camán*, 2,000 years of hurling in Ireland, Dundalk, 1973.

Ó Néill, E., *Gleann an Óir*, Baile Átha Cliath, 1988.

O'Neill, P., *Twenty years of the GAA 1910-1930*, Kilkenny, 1931.

O'Sullivan, T.F., *Story of the GAA*, Dublin, 1916.

Power, P.C., *Carrick-on-Suir and its people*, Dublin, 1976.

Puirséal, P., *The GAA in its time*, Dublin, 1982.

Reason, J. and **Carwyn, J.**, *The world of rugby*, London, 1979.

Ryall, T., *Kilkenny: the GAA story*, Kilkenny, 1984.

Tierney, M., *Croke of Cashel: the life of Archbishop Thomas William Croke 1823-1902*, Dublin, 1976.

Van Esbeck, E., *The story of Irish rugby*, Dublin, 1986.

Woodham Smith, C., *The great Hunger*, London, 1962.

Young, A., *A tour in Ireland with general observations on the present State of that kingdom: made in ... 1776, 1777, and 1778, and brought down to the end of 1779*, London, 1780.

Newspapers, Journals etc.

Cashel Sentinel
Celtic Times
Chicago Citizen (in Davin's
   papers)
Cork Daily Herald
Cork Examiner
Daily Telegraph
GAA Annual 1908-9
Gaelic Journal
Irish Athletic and Cycling News
Irish Independent
Irish Independent Golden Jubilee
   Souvenir
Irishman
Irish Press
Irish Press Golden Jubilee
   Souvenir
Irish Sportsman
Irish Times
Irish Weekly Independent

Journal of Kerry Archaeological
   Society 1970
Journal of Waterford
   Archaeological Society 1913
Kilkenny Journal
Leinster Leader
Midland Tribune
Nationalist (Clonmel)
Nenagh Guardian
Nenagh News
Our Games Annual 1964
Shamrock
Sport
The Kerryman
Tipperary Advocate
Tipperary People
Tipperary Star
Tipperary Vindicator
United Irishman
Waterford News

Manuscript Material

Carrick-on-Suir Parish Register.
Constitution and Rules of the GAA 1888. Davin Papers.
Davin papers in Deerpark.
Healy papers in N.L.I.
MS 9515, manuscript room, N.L.I.
Minutes of Carrick-on-Suir Amateur Athletic Football and Cricket Club.
State Paper Office (now National Archives), Crime Branch Special Reports.

Index of Places

Index of Persons

Mandeville, Mrs. Jane, 16
Mandle, W. F., 71
Manning, J. J., 78
Meagher, John, 190
Meagher, Thomas Francis, 8, 44
Mehigan, P. J., 217
Meleady, P., 165, 168, 178
Miller, Reginald, 25
Minogue, P., 165, 168, 179
Mitchell, James S., 50, 77, 78, 132, 159,
    166, 168, 175-178, 191, 203
Molohan, P. J., 165, 168, 179
Molohan, T., 98
Moloney, F. R., 30, 79, 89, 90, 91, 96,
    100, 107, 113, 115, 117, 119, 122-124
Moloney, Rev. John, 140, 146, 148
Mooney, J., 166, 168, 176, 178
Moore, James, 113, 137
Morrissey, William, 217
Moynihan, Maurice, 77, 190
Murphy, Dr., 212
Murphy, J. F., 89
Murphy, John, R.I.C., 134

Nagle, Pierce, 68
Nally, Dr., 137
Nally, P. W., 31-34
Nannetti, J., 119, 120
Neat, Bill, 15
Nolan, James, 165, 168
Nolan, Thomas, 140

O'Brien, Bridget, 3
O'Brien, J., 165, 168
O'Brien, P., 112, 137, 145, 150, 151, 155
O'Brien, Smith, 8
O'Brien, William, M.P., 55, 57, 138, 149,
    152, 153, 154, 202
O'Caithnia, Liam, P., 61, 71
O'Callaghan, M. J., 60
O'Carroll, Captain, 79
O'Connor, Dr., 194
O'Connor, John, 60
O'Connor, M. J., 138
O'Connor, P., 151
O'Connor, Peter, 209, 213
O'Connor, Rev. Fr., 192
O'Connor, T. M., 166, 168, 177
O'Crowley, J. F., 46, 75, 76, 78, 81, 89, 93,
    102, 104, 107, 114, 118, 119, 154, 179

Ó Cuimín, Daithi, 42
Ó Daimhín, 2
O'Donnell, J. R., 18, 19
O'Donnell, P. J., 168, 178
O'Driscoll, Denis, 217
O'Floinn, Seán, 17
O'Gorman, James, 171
O'Grady, Thomas, 63, 98, 113, 114, 165,
    168, 204
O'Hickey, 17
O'Keeffe, P. J., 112, 114, 194
O'Keeffe, W. P., 136
O'Kelly, Major, 135
O'Leary, Con, 17
O'Leary, John, 105, 107, 108, 119, 144,
    145, 148, 155
O'Mahoney, John, 8, 16
O'Mahoney, T. J., 78, 166, 168, 176, 177
O'Meagher, Condon Capt., 171
O'Meagher, Dr. William, 171
O'Neill, Aodh Dubh, 2, 21
O'Neill, Eoghan Rua, 2
O'Neill, Eoin, 42
O'Neill, Padraig, 42
O'Neills, 212
Ó Nualláin, An t-Athair, 42
O'Reilly, J. B., 105, 112, 114, 117, 132,
    134, 135-137, 144, 148, 161, 183, 187,
    197, 200
O'Riordan, Timothy, 105, 107, 113-117,
    119, 128, 135-137, 144, 148, 149, 150-
    152, 154, 161, 162, 179, 183, 186, 187,
    190
O'Ryan, Dr., 8
O'Ryan, Joseph, 35, 36, 40, 55, 56
O'Shea, P., 31, 137
O'Shea, William, 10, 19
O'Sullivan, J. P., 159, 166
O'Sullivan, T. F., 58, 155, 178
Ogilby, J. D., 26
Ormond, Marquess of, 2, 4
Owen, L. P., 37

Page, William, Byrd, 39, 184
Parnell, C. S., 33, 57, 60, 122, 123, 136,
    155, 198, 205
Phibbs, William, 166, 168, 176
Pierce, Mary, 3, 4
Pierce, Parson, 3
Ponsonby, William, 4

ERRATA

p. 119 line 40 for Wyse Power read Hoctor.
p. 120 line 12 for Wyse Power read Hoctor.